Administrative

Reform

Administrative

Reform

GERALD E. CAIDEN
University of California,
Berkeley

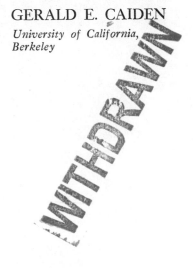

ALDINE PUBLISHING COMPANY / *Chicago*

First published 1969 by
Aldine Publishing Company
529 South Wabash Avenue
Chicago, Illinois 60605

Library of Congress Catalog Card Number 70-75044
Designed by Miller/Schleifer
Printed in the United States of America

TO
Miriam Hannah
AND
Rachel Debra

Contents

Preface

As Guest Lecturer in the Department of Political Science at the Hebrew University, Jerusalem, I was asked in 1966 to give a graduate course in administrative reform as part of an innovating program in public administration directed by Professor Yehezkel Dror. At heart I was a reformer and believed that administrative reform could help solve contemporary problems. I had studied the history of administrative reform in many countries outside the Communist bloc and followed in detail the struggles of individual reforms in Great Britain, Canada, and Australia. I had described and commented on reform proposals and analyzed both successful and unsuccessful reforms. Above all, I was keen to share my knowledge and ideas with a group of young administrators, many of whom would soon be in strategic positions to execute reforms.

Despite the growing volume of literature concerned with administration and organization, I found many references unsatisfactory, unrewarding, and even irrelevant. There was no comprehensive study of administrative reform in any major textbook. If reform was mentioned at all, it was relegated to a small section at the end of a chapter on process or dynamics, or was hurriedly tucked away in the last chapter. Specialized studies, though often using the words "administrative reform" in the title, were usually general administrative histories or case studies in administrative dynamics. The comparatively few writings devoted solely to administrative reform were fragmentary and embryonic, describing and analyzing narrow circumstances.

The students justly complained about terminology, about authors' confusion of description, analysis, prescription and hypothesis, and about the different levels of generalization. We had to work out our own consistent analysis, based on a series of questions: What is administrative reform? How does it compare with other types of social reform? Can we learn anything about strategy and evaluation from past experiences? What administrative reforms do we see taking place, and can we anticipate further reform efforts? Is there a process or series of processes in administrative reform? What factors aid or obstruct administrative reform? What makes a person an administrative reformer? Why is reform needed? What reforms? Who benefits and who suffers? Is it possible to devise a manual of action for potential administrative reformers? Is a theory of administrative reform possible?

Indeed, more time was spent in analyzing the questions than in coming to any satisfactory answers, and certain conclusions were reached that needed further investigation and testing. Much the same happened with various groups of middle management trainees at the Central School of Administration, Ramat Rachel, many of whom had long experience in Israeli administration during turbulent periods and were reform-conscious, though healthily skeptical and critical about the necessity and timing of reforms.

A summary was compiled of what had transpired in all these sessions, in order to pass on the accumulated results. The response by colleagues at the Hebrew University was sufficiently encouraging to induce me to go further and combine the results with a survey of the published research to date. Clearly, the answers to some of the questions are unknown and may always be so, despite further research. At this stage, it is possible to map the territory only in broad outlines, with details in a few places. But an incomplete map is better than no map at all, if it is accurate. One of the purposes of this book is to provide such a preliminary guide as a basis for further exploration.

Such a preliminary survey map of administrative reform is in no way meant to replace the detailed larger scale maps already constructed; there can be no substitute for the existing literature. Here the general history of administrative reform is used only as a source of case studies illustrating specific points of contemporary relevance, and even in these, much of the detail recorded elsewhere is omitted. Further, no attempt is made to expand on the details of specific administrative reforms when these are amply dealt with in the existing literature. Instead, this book is concerned with presenting existing knowledge more systematically, abstracting preliminary generalizations from existing studies, and preparing for the stage when purposeless, superficial, and sporadic research on uncoordinated topics can be avoided.

At the same time, the theories were systematized and consolidated as far as possible without altering the original hypotheses. Once the duplication and overlapping have been eliminated, it is seen that no single individual has preempted this field as Weber has done in bureaucratic theory and Simon in rational decision-making. The field is still young and open. Future approaches can be shaped in socially meaningful ways and with direct relevance to administrative practice. Underlying the theory is the notion that the social sciences should have a positive, even reformative, purpose in improving society as well as building a value-free behavioral science.

Now that the survey is completed, I realize that I have shifted from seeking dramatic and speedy remedies for administrative failings to recognizing the many obstacles in the path of reformers and the virtue of waiting for the opportune time. I still believe that reliance on change alone is insufficient if administration is to keep abreast of current developments. Administrative reform may have to be institutionalized, though not necessarily in a bureaucratic form of organization. But institutionalization will fall below expectations unless administrators become reform-conscious. They need to promote a climate that encourages initiative, combat mediocrity, and avoid wasting potential and talents. Not only should they respond to outside criticism, but they should seek to head it off by developing an awareness of the world beyond their immediate concern.

Acknowledgments

Acknowledgments of help and encouragement are overdue to the staff and students of the Department of Political Science at the Hebrew University, Jerusalem, and of the Central School of Administration, Ramat Rachel, for intellectual stimulation and assistance in preparing preliminary drafts of this book, particularly to Professor Yehezkel Dror, who was responsible for obtaining financial support, and to the hard-pressed staff of the Social Science Library of the Kaplan School who attended to my bibliographic requirements. Final revision was greatly aided by the staff of the Library of the Institute of Governmental Studies at the University of California, Berkeley, and the practical help of Moses Yanes and Walter Oyugi, provided by the Department of Political Science at the Berkeley campus. Enthusiasm for the task in hand was engendered by my colleagues at Berkeley, Todd LaPorte and Robert Biller; and Martin Landau of Brooklyn College, City University of New York, produced that kind of constructive criticism that every author needs but so rarely receives.

Bibliographic Note

No attempt is made in this book to list every reference to man's endeavors to improve the management of his affairs. Such a task would be impracticable, having to include virtually everything ever written about social organization since earliest times. Even limiting it to purely secondary academic sources published in this century would involve listing at least fifty periodicals currently appearing and possibly all 320 journals contained in the 1966 Supplement Guide of *The American Behavioral Scientist*. As everyone's notion of administrative reform differs, most people would disagree with the final result anyway. Instead, the *General Bibliography* contains the principal sources used in this survey to illustrate the complexities of the subject while at the end of each chapter are *Bibliographic Notes* which are confined to more specific sources used therein. Wherever possible, I have cited publication in book form, particularly where the author has duplicated or further expanded his ideas in article form elsewhere. References in the text are confined to books in the *General Bibliography* (shortened to name of author and year of edition consulted). Selection of the source material was governed largely by its originality, accessibility, brevity, and clarity. There are no published bibliographies, the closest being the *International Bibliography of Public Administration* (1957) produced by the United Nations Technical Assistance Program and D. V. Hart and P. Meadows, *Annotated Bibliography of Directed Social Change* (Syracuse University Press, 1961).

ONE

Introduction and Perspective

Administrative reform—the artificial inducement of administrative transformation against resistance—has existed ever since men conceived better ways of organizing their social activities. Yet it has not received any systematic analysis and is barely mentioned in the growing literature on social arrangements. More interest has been shown in stability, but now, in possibly the most turbulent period in human history, increasing attention is being paid to the causes and consequences of continuous social change. The time is opportune to summarize concisely the state of current thinking about administrative reform.

THEORY FOR WHAT?

The discipline of administrative theory is relatively new, and is beset by controversial philosophical and methodological issues. It is still at a pre-paradigmatic stage "marked by a plethora of competing schools, a polyglot of languages, and, accordingly, a confusion of logics. There is neither a common research tradition nor the necessary consensus for a common field of inquiry. Each of the competing schools questions the others, adventurism is rampant, and commonly accepted standards of control do not exist" (Landau 1966, p. 39). Consequently, work in administrative reform is patchy in appearance and variable in quality. Few new ideas are intellectually and scien-

1

tifically satisfying, and virtually none have been tested by further
empirical research or incorporated into administrative practice.

Practitioners and theorists must share the blame. The practitioners
have suppressed unpalatable truths, doctored evidence, and denied
outsiders access to crucial areas. When information banks have been
opened, the theorists have not always taken advantage or followed
the dictates of scholarship. Much theorizing has seemed unreal and
the theorists have fallen back on methodological short-cuts and pure
intellection. The most lifelike and appreciated theory has come from
practitioners-turned-philosophers and theorists with experience in practice during national emergencies or access to the facts as advisers and
consultants to practitioners in difficulties.

The practitioners have demonstrated that they can be successful
without the theorists, while the theorists have preferred one another's
company and have not tried to influence a wider audience. The latter
have sheltered behind logical positivism and scientism, divorcing themselves from real world situations and political advocacy, and defending
the position by arguing that immediate and spectacular practical implications are less important than a solid intellectual base for further
theorizing. Although theorists concede that there are irrelevant theory,
unintelligible jargon, and pointless generalities in the growing output of
propositions and schema, they argue that this is the price of creativity.

The theorists have rather overdone things. First, they spend too
much time fighting against each other and for their pet ideas, paying
only lip service to mutuality. They ignore the results of theorists in
other disciplines which disprove their basic assumptions and make
meaningless their fine academic constructs.

> Overspecialization narrows the scope of scientific analysis; it dis-
> perses the factors which must be assembled before the actions of the
> agents can be explained. . . . In cases where correction or reform
> are required, it leads specialists to propose or agree to the transfer
> of institutions to an environment ill-fitted to receive them. Those
> who are in control end by forgetting that no system for organizing
> or regulating one branch or aspect of human relations has any value
> in itself; the essential question is whether it will function properly
> and produce the desired results.

It is true that the parts and the whole are constantly inter-acting and that a change made at one point may have general repercussions and help to alter the context in the desired way. However, it equally often happens that the effect of the innovations thus introduced is cancelled out or completely distorted by variables whose existence, or at least strength, had not been revealed by an analysis which was incomplete (Meynaud, 1963, pp. 17-18).

Not only are scarce resources frittered away on internecine warfare but the battles destroy the practical worth of theory.

Second, independence creates a random approach to common problems, with a resulting reluctance to follow somebody else's definitions and usages. The semantic confusion produces a mass of terminologies that pass as new theories.

Third, the value of many genuine theories is questionable. The overabundance of bad theory threatens the recognition of good theory; as Landau points out, few theories are ever discarded. He warns that metaphorical schemes "can neither be justified nor invalidated and they remain outside the scientific domain quite impregnable to the tests of experience. Such transfers not only clutter our vocabularies but they are pregnant sources of myth" (Landau 1965, pp. 7-8). He further warns against "the mixing of models which not only obscures imagery and confuses meaning but . . . frequently leads to contradictory results" and "may lead to nonsense results as well as erroneous conclusions."

Fourth, too much theory is produced for theory's sake. It serves only to feed the egos of a privileged few.

These shortcomings are by no means confined to administrative reform theorists; they apply equally to administrative theory in general (Simon 1946, Waldo 1948, Biller 1968, LaPorte 1968). However, the influx of theorists from other disciplines, along with the younger generation of theorists, can be expected to make their impact on the general level of theory. Improvement accompanied by a general shift toward socially relevant theory will not end the variable quality of theory, but it could infuse a new spirit of incentive and help to integrate theory more with the practitioners' world.

The crucial role of administrative reform in contemporary society reflects the general importance of administration in a complex civilization, where increased specialization, diversification, and fragmentation depend on complicated mechanisms of integration and coordination controlled largely by professional administrators. Modern society has for some time been one in which social actions take place mainly through organizations, either bureaucratic or cooperative. As everyone is on the end of someone else's administration, no one is immune from administrative deficiencies and shortcomings, and no one can fail to benefit from administrative improvements. Administrative reform is part of societal reform, and, logically, the wider reform movement should be studied first. As no such study is available, it is necessary to fill the gap by outlining the major components of a theory of societal reform, emphasizing those aspects most relevant to administrative reform theory.

Societies cannot help changing. There is always movement arising from (a) changing relationships with the environment, (b) new ideas and innovations, (c) powerful drives to progress by eradicating observable social ills, and (d) natural inclinations to compare and evaluate social activities. There can be little doubt that the pace of change has increased considerably and that vast changes in every aspect of life can no longer be considered incidental anomalies. They place tremendous strain on existing social arrangements and demand wholesale revaluations of traditional activities and attitudes.

Response always lags behind social needs, aspirations, and expectations so that some measure of dissatisfaction, frustration, and tension, the harbingers of reform, is always present. The aims of change may be ambiguous; the necessary mechanisms for making the appropriate decisions may be absent or inadequate for the task. Inadequate response to change needs is further exaggerated by deliberate resistance to change and stubborn support for the traditional. Resistance may stem from overcommitment and overinvestment in existing or traditional institutions, reluctance to expend the energy and resources in adopting new patterns, fear of the unknown, or sheer inability to create and conceive new forms to tackle the new conditions presented by change.

The confrontation between change and resistance is resolved in different ways, none of which are conclusive. A common cycle commences with institutional elites varying institutionalized values in accordance with changed conditions, while keeping the established framework intact. Not all constituent members accept the institutionalized values or are satisfied by the decisions of the institutional elites or the established framework. As deviants, they challenge the institutionalized values and seek support from other constituent members. To prevent threats to the established framework and to retain support from the majority of constituents, the elites make concessions to the deviants. If they persist in resisting innovation, popular support swings to the deviants, and the elites lose control of the situation. In the ensuing crisis, they may be replaced by leading deviants who now become the institutional elites with authority to alter the established framework and institutionalized values.

Those amenable to change fall into three main categories. *(a) Societal changers* accept those changes recognized by most to be inevitable. The institutional elites administer the changes within the established framework but resist innovations that they believe do not have substantial support or that threaten the established framework and their positions within it. *(b) Societal revolutionaries* want to become the new institutional elites, so that with a monopoly of social power they can impose their ideas of change on the remainder of society. They seek substantial and speedy changes in the established framework and institutionalized values and will not compromise on this objective. They object to haphazard, divisive, piecemeal approaches to change which, in their view, will not achieve substantial and speedy changes because concessions reconcile deviants to the established framework and set deviants against one another. *(c) Societal reformers* work within the established framework while aiming to replace it eventually. Ready to compromise for the sake of greater unity, they seek to educate, persuade, and pressurize others—elites and constituents—to their way of thinking so as to avoid crisis. These three types differ in the extent to which they envisage the nature and speed of change, tolerate resistance to their ideas, and accept crisis and imposition as means to change, but each claims that his approach is the only true way.

Societal reform involves changes in communal attitudes, for which good communications are essential. Existing knowledge and opinions also have to be altered to recognize, accept, assimilate, and integrate innovation. How quickly a reform is integrated depends on *(a)* the manner and means of presentation, *(b)* the number of contacts between the informed and the uninformed, *(c)* whether it promises solutions to felt needs, *(d)* how sharply it contrasts with existing beliefs, *(e)* the prestige and charisma of the propagators, and *(f)* the intensity of resistance. Timing is crucial; receptivity to reforms is never the same, and choosing the opportune moment takes judgment, skill, and luck. The use of social power (the capacity to produce intended effects) by reformers is also important, particularly the possibility of pushing changes beyond people's understanding and beyond the ability of the established framework to accommodate them.

Once a course of action for solving a problem has been decided on, it may preclude the adoption of any of the alternatives and so alter conditions that it is impossible to determine afterward whether it was the best possible course available at the time. In evaluating societal reforms, speculation as to what might have happened seems pointless. Possibly the only way to evaluate a societal reform is in terms of expectations and results, noting unforeseen factors that intervened and the unpremeditated side effects. Did the reform achieve what was expected of it? If not, why not? Is the reform integrated with the culture? If not, why has it been rejected or dropped? Is the society proud that it adopted the reform? If not, why is there disappointment? Has the reform become part of a larger program? If not, why has it been isolated and not followed by other reform programs? Does the society endeavor to export the reform? If not, why not? What permanent effects have resulted from the reform experience? Was anything learned at all?

This brief outline of societal reform provides a backdrop to an enquiry into administrative reform. Many questions immediately spring to mind:

1. *Administrative Reform and Societal Reform.*   What is the relationship between administrative reform and societal reform? Is administrative reform a dependent or independent variable? What exactly is administrative reform? What distinguishes it from other

kinds of societal reform? Who are administrative reformers? What common characteristics do they share?

2. *Administrative Reform and Social Change.* How is administrative reform related to social change? What do social change theories say about administrative reform? How does awareness of administrative reform needs arise? Can reforms be anticipated? How is awareness crystallized around specific grievances? Who formulates the problem and devises reform proposals? How do administrative reformers gain general acceptance for their proposals? How do those affected by reform react? At what point can a reform be considered assimilated into the culture?

3. *Administrative Reformers and Resistance.* Why do people oppose administrative reforms? In what ways do they express their resistance? How do administrative reformers react to resistance? What determines the tactics to be employed in overcoming resistance? How do administrative reformers employ social power? How are reform opponents eventually reconciled? What are the root causes of failure to overcome resistance?

4. *Administrative Reformers and Administrative Performance.* What are the aims of administrative reformers? To what extent are they realizable? How can administrative reforms be evaluated? What constitutes administrative effectiveness? What are the prospects for intercultural transfers of reform successes?

5. *Administrative Reform and Administrative Theory.* What do administrative theorists say about administrative reform? How does administrative reform fit into the general body of theory? Is there a theory of administrative reform? Is administrative reform predictable?

6. *Administrative Reform and Administrative Practice.* Do case studies of past reforms say anything of value? Can practitioners learn from the successes and failures of administrative reformers? What check list of factors should a practitioner use before embarking on a reform program? How can practitioners assist theory? Does theory in turn assist them?

7. *The Study of Administrative Reform.* What is known about administrative reform? What needs to be known further about it? What about reform concerns theorists and practitioners most? What

questions do they want answered? What are or should be the priorities in research? What are the next steps in the study of administrative reform? Can the full truth ever be known?

These are all important questions that deserve an answer. Unfortunately so little has been thought or written about societal reform or administrative reform as such (unlike the pros and cons of concrete reform proposals), that few answers can be conclusive at this time. The questions were constantly in mind while surveying the available literature, and they have influenced the arrangement of the results of that survey, as the chapter headings and subheadings reveal. Those that did not lend themselves to separate treatment or would have involved considerable repetition were integrated or consolidated with other questions. Nevertheless, there still remain some unresolved basic issues that demand separate treatment.

WHAT IS ADMINISTRATIVE REFORM?

The matter of definition arises repeatedly in this survey. Both "administration" and "reform" convey different things to different people, and it is desirable to settle on a definition to cover both lexical usage and the meanings implied by the theorists. To some modern advocates, administrative reform is synonymous with the rationalizing process that commenced with the bureaucratic revolution in the absolutist European monarchies during the Thirty Years War. Though reference is made here to the principal meanings in the theoretical literature, the analysis is based on the author's own definition—*the artificial inducement of administrative transformation against resistance*. A different definition would produce a different analysis and hence different yields. Is the author's definition more useful than other definitions? Does it produce higher yields? If it is too restrictive, then it should be replaced by a more inclusive definition. No definition should be so original and novel that it obscures the theory and alienates the wider audience, or so generalized and simple that it becomes a deceiving catch phrase or half-truth slogan.

If the social sciences are to make an impact on policy-makers, then their findings and conclusions should be clear to all. Jargon is justifiable when it improves upon the brief expression of frequently used ideas that need clarification and precision (Levy 1966, pp. 6-7). It may be unavoidable when conventional meanings are used inconsistently, when they conjure up different images from that intended, or when they are insufficient for specialized communication. But new terminology limits the audience, involves difficulties in translation and comprehension, and may be just as ambiguous. Rarely in the study of administrative reform should it be necessary to depart from conventionality to convey meaning. Every man is his own reformer and needs to exchange his ideas with like-minded souls. "Men, considering the world, see things that are bad, situations that are wrong, conditions that affront and feel compelled to reflect upon the source of anomalies which distress their natural desire to inhabit a world that yields their own high standards of desirability" (Cowling 1963, p. 138). Jargon would impede, not assist, contact and action.

Whatever definition is adopted, there remains the question of delineating administrative reforms from other kinds of societal reform. Where does administration stop and politics or economics or sociology or psychology begin? Take, for instance, the links between administrative reform and political science. Administrative reform is power politics in action; it contains ideological rationalizations, fights for control of areas, services, and people, political participants and institutions, power drives, campaign strategies and obstructive tactics, compromises and concessions. Montgomery (1967, p. 1) goes so far as to define administrative reform as "a political process designed to adjust the relationships between a bureaucracy and other elements in a society, or within the bureaucracy itself . . . both the purposes of reforms and the evils addressed vary with their political circumstances." Similarly one could describe administrative reform as an economic process (redistribution of resources and the alteration of end products) or a psychological process (the alteration of behavior patterns, beliefs, attitudes, and individual actions). But what is there *administrative* about it? What kinds of reforms are *administrative* reforms?

Before World War II, administration or the administrative aspects of social activities were identified functionally—administration was what administrators did that could not be identified under the rubric of any other discipline. After World War II, Simon added rational decision-making to the POSDCORB formula, and then the strict dichotomy between "policy" and "administration" collapsed. Attention turned from what administrators did to how they did it (processes), where they did it (institutions), and finally within what circumstances they did it (ecology). What constitutes administration is still under debate. In the meantime, its scope has so widened "that any definition . . . would be either so encompassing as to call forth the wrath or ridicule of others, or so limiting as to stultify its own disciples. Perhaps it is best that it not be defined" (Mosher 1956, p. 177). Short of opening afresh the whole issue, conventional meanings are preferred in this instance.

Since much of the literature on administrative reform has been devoted to public administration, most examples and illustrations are drawn from the public sector. In contrast to many other areas of administrative theory where analysis is based almost exclusively on business practices, the general analysis of administrative reform is more applicable to public administration. Nowhere in private administration exist such institutions so intimately involved in administrative reform as the public inquiry (e.g., Royal Commission, Special Committee), the central personnel agency (e.g., Civil Service Commission, Public Service Board), the post-audit (e.g., Comptroller-General, Auditor-General, State Comptroller), or the political overseers (e.g., Ministry of Reform, Select Committee on Nationalized Industries, Cabinet Sub-committee on Administrative Matters, President's Advisory Committee on Management). However, sufficient similarity seems to exist in administrative reform so that different types of administration can be considered together.

Further research may find that this lumping together of all administrations is highly misleading or sufficiently distorting to nullify any hypotheses or generalizations arrived at. One would expect that reforming the administrations of the United Nations Organization or the Roman Catholic Church would be somewhat different from reforming the administrations of neighborhood supermarkets or small voluntary associations. If the analysis stands up to empirical testing in diverse situations, then it may point the way to a unified discipline of administration and a general theory of administration. If not, then a new survey based on the opposite assumption—that the differences are of greater importance—would have to be constructed and the subject of administrative reform split into its varied components and specialties. In either case, much more order and meaning would be brought to a mass of what at present remains largely disconnected and unintelligible.

ADMINISTRATIVE TECHNICIANS OR SOCIETAL REFORMERS?

Administrative reform can be a dependent variable, an independent variable, or both at the same time in circular fashion. Administrative reforms do not just happen. They are not Acts of God. They are deliberate social actions premeditated by administrative reformers and implemented through an established administrative system which is thereby transformed in some way. The originators of a reform need not be part of the administrative system, but their proposals must appear to fulfill a felt need of the system. Its successful implementation and assimilation is a function of the system. Successful reform in the administrative system may set in motion a whole series of chain events that lead to other kinds of reform, and those reforms in turn may indicate the need for further administrative reforms. The variations are endless.

Administration is a cultural product, a social subsystem reflecting the values of the wider society. The common culture and values tend to reinforce one another and block reform innovations. Successful reforms need to be preceded or accompanied by changes in the common culture and values that permit the accommodation and assimilation of reform. To this extent, administrative reform is a dependent variable. Where the common culture and values are changing very slowly and dependence on administrative performance is quite low, as is the case in backward countries, it may be possible that "administrative reform is successful only when associated with major social, political or economic reform. It is doomed to failure when undertaken for its own sake, for the traditional rationale of efficiency or economy" (Birkhead 1966, p. 186). But even in these countries, professional administrators (who may also be political leaders, tribal chieftains, clergymen, entrepreneurs, and landowners) are strategically placed to be able to change the common culture and values through administrative reforms. They may respond quickest to outside pressures and internal needs. They may place their social power and institutional resources behind social reform. They may institutionalize societal and administrative reform as is done in the most advanced countries, where bureaucracies routinize change and filter reforms, where administration and administrative reform are independent variables, and where they function so as to avoid the wholesale displacement of existing arrangements and provide alternatives whenever an existing arrangement is abandoned.

Societal reforms have to be administered. What administrative arrangements best promote the flow of human knowledge and enable decision makers to assimilate new knowledge as soon as it becomes available? What is the most effective method of organizing political propaganda to induce transformation of human values? How can institutional deficiencies be discovered and rectified with the minimum dislocation? How does administrative behavior detract from societal ends, and to what extent can administration be minimized in the conduct of human affairs? These are the sorts of questions that societal reformers consider, further complicating the distinction between societal and administrative reform. Should administrative reformers concentrate their attention on perfecting administrative performance or should they use administrative reform as a means for achieving wider societal reforms?

The traditional answer in administrative theory is that the specialist should concentrate on those areas where he is best qualified to offer an opinion. The administrative reformer's task is to improve the administrative performance of individuals, groups, and institutions and to advise them how they can achieve their operating goals more effectively, more economically, and more quickly. The factors that he examines are listed as follows:

INDIVIDUALS

skills and aptitude, practical ability, health, output, competence; knowledge and information, range of experience, articulation;

judgment, wisdom, values, ethics, responsibility;
attitudes, beliefs, opinions, will, aims and ambitions;
personality, character, morality;
enthusiasm, incentive, drive, expectations;
job satisfaction, mobility, security;
creativity, originality.

GROUPS

permanence;
unity, cohesion, cooperation, compatibility, common interests,
   interdependence, conformity, congruence, conflict;
morale, loyalty, identification;
sense of justice, fairness, reliability, equality, power distribution;
norms, self-control, standards, targets, productivity;
rank order, status, prestige;
autonomy, dependence;
composition, openness;
discipline.

INSTITUTIONS

legitimacy, relations with other institutions;
structure, centralization, concentration, size;
functions, range and type;
goals, nature and compatibility, ideology;
communications—frequency, direction, flow, intimacy,
   creditability;
sanctions, controls, rules;
specialization, division of labor, departmentalization, factor mix;
coordination;
planning, waste;
adaptiveness, flexibility, competitiveness, survivability;
capitalization, mechanization, information retrieval;
continuity of work flow, continuous system, interlocking processes;
leadership, participation, representation;
record-keeping, financial accounting, staffing procedures, contract
   conditions, property management;
decision-making style, problem-solving, conflict resolution;

distribution of power, authority;
public relations, image;
monopoly, restrictive practices, autonomy, independence;
constituency, clientele relations;
labor relations;
capacity, productivity, economy, efficiency;
spatial mobility;
resources, reserves, stores, supplies.

None of these overlap significantly with the central concerns of other disciplines or other types of societal reform. Like other specialists, the administrative reformer would stop short of the wider societal implications of his actions.

Should there be another category—societal effectiveness—to take into account the combined ramifications of the others? Administrations have always been heavily involved in societal reform, especially in highly sophisticated civilizations.

1. Administrations, backed by technical competence, command of resources, and wide public contacts, are power centers in their own right and influence the fate of people outside their reach.
2. Administrations are strategically placed to prevent or assist societal reforms. They institutionalize social change.
3. The performance of administrations and the amount of resources they absorb in themselves profoundly affect the level of end products and services available to society.
4. In many instances, administrations are expected to perform the role of societal reformer by remedying social evils and by anticipating social needs in advance of social recognition.

The administrator is a social entrepreneur, an advocate for his clientele and a humanizer of institutions. Administrative reformers cannot ignore such obvious facts by refusing to cross self-imposed artificial disciplinary boundaries. The factors making for societal effectiveness should also be the concern of administrative reformers:

SOCIETIES

capacity to deal with crisis, new problems and new conditions;
reduction of suffering, humanitarianism;

enhancement of life opportunities and the quality of life;

social justice, equalization of rewards and privilege;

civil liberties, recognition of talent and effort;

reduction of unused productive capacity, unemployment, waste, conspicuous consumption;

awareness of social costs—pollution, preventable deaths, civil disorders, overcrowding;

preservation of nonreplaceable natural resources and unique cultural amenities;

prevention of wars, physical violence, needless destruction;

elimination of artificial barriers between men.

Once this category is added, the administrative reformer becomes a societal reformer without objective guidelines. He has only his own conscience and view of progress to aid him. At least the administrative technician avoids this dilemma.

SO WHAT?

Irrespective of the direction from which administrative reform is approached, there is some doubt whether the whole truth can ever be revealed in the social sciences. As Morgenthau states, "One of the main purposes of society is to conceal the truth about man and society from its members. That concealment, that elaborate and subtle and purposeful misunderstanding of the nature of man and of society, is one of the cornerstones upon which all societies are founded" (Young 1958, p. 73). The truth is unpopular. To vested interests, it is a subversive and revolutionary force. Those who dedicate themselves to the truth in matters political are rewarded, like reformers in unfavorable circumstances, with unpopularity, social ostracism, and criminal penalties for such offences as putting the truth above convenience and ambition, penetrating the ideological veil with which society conceals the nature of political relations, disturbing the complacency of the powers that be, and stirring up the conscience of society. Cowling pursues the same point when he says that those who govern do not reveal publicly the factors, trivial and important, which determine the decisions they take (Cowling 1963, p. 21).

Reform, like politics, depends on a certain measure of calculated deception. The self-respect of reformers, like that of politicians, involves pretending that the consequences of their actions were really meant, even if at the time they lacked any comprehensive views of the probable consequences of any particular action. The observer must therefore be aware that he should not take reformers at their face-value, that what actually happened was not necessarily intended or foreseen, that material from which judgments (as opposed to description) about reform ought to be made will not be readily available, and that the facts as presented may be far from the truth.

But a start must be made somewhere, recalling Toynbee's statement that "no collection of facts is ever complete, because the universe is without bonds. And no synthesis or interpretation is ever final, because there are always fresh facts to be bound after the first collection has been provisionally arranged." Let us begin with what the administrative theorists have had to say about the phenomenon of administrative reform.

TWO

Administrative Theory
and Administrative Reform

The advancement of knowledge proves how little we know about nature and man. Less than a hundred years ago, we knew nothing about the internal composition of the atom, psychoanalysis, or the Impressionist movement, and a hundred years hence others will wonder how we failed to see things that will be obvious to them. On the other hand, we also stumble across old discoveries then neglected because they were too far ahead of their time and could be appreciated only when knowledge had advanced on a wider front. In administrative theory, the phenomenon of administrative reform is being rediscovered, although it has been explored ever since *homo sapiens* found that he was a born reformer.

> As long as humanity lasts, men will be reformers . . . endeavouring to change others in order to maintain or create desired situations for themselves, or to change themselves in order to accommodate to unyielding circumstances or to realize a new dream. . . . When our own interests are at stake, be they material or emotional, we become reformers ourselves, rationalizing our actions as in enlightened self-interest, as for the good of others, as demanded by moral principle, or as in the interest of a transcendent value such as Progress or the Glory of God. Whatever else he may be, Man is also a reformer. . . . As reformers, too often we are inept. We defeat our goals or achieve them at unnecessarily great human cost. Better understanding of the reforming process and of human limitations within it may enable us to reduce our ineptitude. . . . Our concern, then, is not with whether people should or should not try to change their own or their fellows'

17

ways. We take it for granted that they will (Goodenough, 1963, p. 15).

Unaided by supernatural forces, man could improve himself, and every improvement could be further improved on, providing human resistance to novelty could be overcome. Machiavelli remarked in *The Prince:*

> There is nothing more difficult to carry out, nor more doubtful of success, nor more dangerous to handle than to initiate a new order of things. For the reformer has enemies in all who profit by the old order, and only lukewarm defenders in all those who would profit by the new order. This lukewarmness arises partly from fear of their adversaries, who have the law in their favor; and partly from the incredulity of mankind, who do not truly believe in anything new until they have had actual experience of it.

Machiavelli was not the first to philosophize on the nature of reform, but not until the present century has there been a concerted effort to approach the subject systematically. Hardly an educated person is not involved in administrative reform or reminded of it through modern mass media. One day it takes the form of proposals for improving welfare services; the next it is the extension of automation; and on the day after that it becomes a campaign to eliminate corruption and extravagance in high places. The need for reform strengthens rather than diminishes in time. We need only to refer to such contemporary problems as the control of nuclear weapons and the threat of overpopulation, where the solutions entail reshaping existing institutions, or devising new ones and transforming existing habits and attitudes against considerable resistance. Huge sums are spent on administrative reform programs based on untested premises. Much of the aid given to backward countries for technical assistance is wasted, and modernization is actually impeded. Reform failures attract increasing attention, especially from the Comparative Administration Group of the American Society of Public Administration, in the belief that a clearer understanding of what is involved in the reform process should influence practice by reshaping future strategy and replacing wishful thinking with rational analysis.

Exaggerated ideas about the potential contribution of administrative reform stem largely from the indiscriminate use of the term for any improvement or change in administrative or government effectiveness. This lack of precision is attributable in part to the past preoccupation of administrative theorists, like other social scientists, with order and stability (though of course the exceptions are numerous, such as Marx, Bagehot, Dewey, and Maritain). Scientific method was first applied to administrative phenomena in pursuit of universal principles that would make more intelligible the complex interrelationships that characterize human cooperation for collective purposes. Naturally, the most promising results came from analyses of fairly orderly institutions, such as bureaucratic organizations, and from relatively permanent working arrangements, such as formal codes of administrative conduct.

Though no less important, the more elusive informal relationships and adaptive processes tended to be neglected. More recent studies of administrative dynamics, through case study methods and analyses of decision-making, have not yet quite redressed the imbalance. Consequently, while we know a great deal about structures and relationships, movement and innovation are only now beginning to receive the attention demanded by the quickening pace of change in the twentieth century. Administrative reform has shared the general fate of administrative dynamics, eluding concerted probes based on agreed terminology. Despite this neglect, it remains an important factor in every administrative situation.

An administrative situation can be approached in two ways. One approach seeks the essence of administration, the unchanging element present in all administrative situations. Administrative dynamics are the changing elements that take the essence from one state to the next in time. Accordingly, changes take place in well-organized (i.e., controlled) steps (see Fig. 1), leaving the essence of the administrative situation unaltered. Presumably change could be reversed so that the progress or regress of an administration could take any step-like pattern (see Fig. 2). This essentially structural approach is mechanical, formal, planned, and rational. Change is anticipated, coordinated, and assimilated in an organized manner. Many elaborate bureaucracies picture change taking place in this fashion; it is their image of the way they operate, regardless of the source and direction of change.

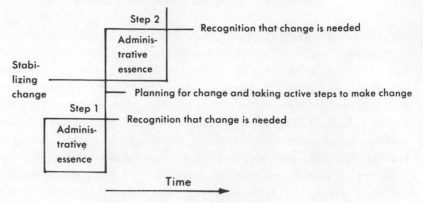

Fig. 1—STRUCTURED CHANGE.

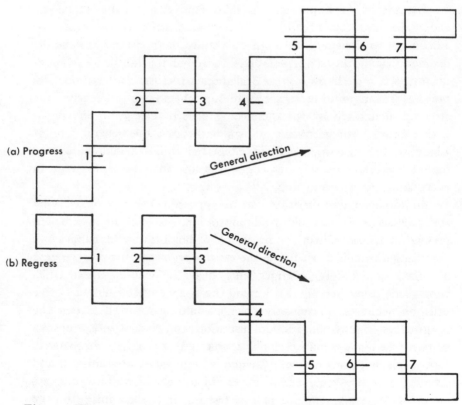

Fig. 2—EXAMPLES OF FOUR STEP PROGRESS OR REGRESS OVER SEVEN
TIME STAGES.

The structural approach to change tends to obscure the significance of ubiquitous reform pressures in administrative dynamics, which cannot be revealed by any sequence of administrative statics. Administrative snapshots show only an uninterrupted procession of results. Administration appears more harmonious and smooth-working than it really is, and administrators appear to follow predetermined courses that adjust automatically to changing circumstances. Little can be learned about the processes leading to the observed results, the estimation of possible alternative outcomes, or the interaction of the perceived phenomena with the wider context—how things are made to happen, how men are commanded and why they obey, and what the agents anticipate when activities are consciously undertaken. Missing altogether, then, is the interplay of tensions that produces the pressure of administrative reform, sufficient to keep every administrative situation fluid in the absence of even more compelling factors, such as insecurity, adjustment and innovation. Successful reforms appear, but they are undifferentiated from natural changes that do not involve resistance. They are shorn of the nuances and subtleties of the reform process. Unsuccessful reforms do not appear, and so reform pressures that influence decisions can almost escape notice.

The other approach views administration as a ceaselessly changing entity wherein the apparent static factors result from homeostasis in administrative relationships or a temporary balance (or equilibrium or even mutual cancelation) between opposed moving forces. Change is continuous as long as the administration survives. Its shape and pattern are determined by the variable relationships (see Fig. 3). Administrative leadership does not react to events, as in the structural approach, by anticipating, guiding, and assessing them as a rational calculator. It is a political sounding board that sorts out competing pressures and somehow succeeds in getting them to work together for the time being. It pushes in favor of innovation, inspiration, encouragement, and experimentation. It is composed of change agents with vision, will, and power, who understand common objectives, forecast the ramifications of change, and recognize the values at stake. They possess the ability to break through artificial barriers and stubborn resistance.

In this unstructured approach to change, omnipresent reform pressure cannot be ignored. In any administrative situation, the status quo

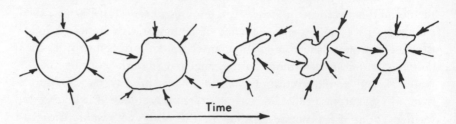

Fig. 3—Continuous Change.

may be preferred to any conceivable alternative. The results of change may not be worth the effort of overcoming initial inertia. A persistent tug-of-war exists between the conservatives who stick by the status quo and the reformers who are willing to take a risk to improve on it. Only reactionaries resist when the risks are small, but when they are great only dogmatic revolutionaries are willing to press on. Otherwise, the two camps are locked in battle, with the participants frequently changing sides according to the specific issue and their personal convictions or self-interests. The tension generated by reform pressures can be ascertained by (a) the extent to which cooperation between administrators is withdrawn, either permanently (between confirmed rivals) or temporarily (between colleagues who agree to differ over a particular matter); and by (b) the diversion of effort from the collective purposes to internecine warfare, thereby reducing administrative performance. Thus resistance to reform, by reducing overall efficacy, may be self-defeating if the reformers' case is based on the improvement in general performance. Continued resistance will strengthen the reformers' case. On the other hand, reforms may prove impractical, overambitious, or misconceived. Studies of reform processes that reveal something about the way administrators adjust to changing conditions, the nature of administrative resistance, the effect of controversy on administrative performance, and the balance between order and stability and innovation and movement might have as great an impact on administrative theory as on practice. These are virtually uncharted areas awaiting the adventurous academic wayfarer.

THE UBIQUITY OF ADMINISTRATIVE REFORM

Administrative reform rests on the assumption (or belief) that there is always a better alternative to the status quo. This idea of improvement is now widely accepted, though it is less than two centuries since the optimistic notion that human affairs move forward to greater good was elaborated by Turgot (1717-1781). Before then, men believed that the golden age had passed, or that it came in recurring cycles, or that it was to come in the future as determined by divine will. Bacon (1561-1626) and Descartes (1596-1650) had emphasized the power of man over his own destiny, but it took centuries for people to overcome their instinctive fear of change and to challenge religious determinism. The growing acceptance of the idea of progress or irreversible meliorative change means that more people are actively seeking and are being encouraged to seek better ways of doing things. Reforms and reformers are no longer treated with the same degree of contempt and hostility that once greeted any challenge to the established order. Indeed the balance may have swung in the opposite direction—the future may belong to those societies that can absorb reforms quickly and with minimum dislocation. Today reform may be not only respectable but also desirable for the sake of the future. The great powers have already discovered this in technology and possibly in defense administration, and it may not be long before the idea spreads to other facets of social life.

Perhaps there has never been a period in recorded history when men fired by achievement were not somewhere experimenting with reforms. Even isolation and a hostile physical environment have rarely combined to produce complete cultural stagnation. Anthropologists are constantly readjusting their ideas about seemingly unprogressive peoples (Arensberg and Niehoff 1964, Barnett 1956, Goodenough 1963). Reforms have been stimulated by natural disasters that reduced populations or wiped out elites. They have followed military defeats, civil disturbances, and economic crises. They have been urged by visionaries and by the great men of the time. In all cases, they have been resisted by those who had something to lose by the new situation or who preferred the status quo to the unknown and the

unfamiliar. Reformers have to contend with *(a)* loyalty to the established order; *(b)* the inertia of habit, social conditioning, apathy, and
indifference; *(c)* lack of imagination and appreciation for the untried;
and *(d)* suspicion of possible ulterior motives of the reformers. Yet no
sooner does one set of reformers disappear than another set appears.
Despite the obstacles, there has been no shortage of people willing to
try their hand at reform. Conformity eventually succumbs to
innovation.

As all reforms entail changes in mental and moral attitudes, it is
necessary to distinguish administrative reforms from reform achieved
through administration. Many administrative theorists have attempted
to describe those human activities to which the term "administrative"
can be applied. They broadly agree that administration as such is
intangible and invisible—a process involving mental activity directed
toward achieving cooperation among people for collective purposes
and blending resources, human and nonhuman, to produce tangible
goods and services; a means involving power, skill, leadership, and
communication directed toward ultimate ends. It includes subprocesses, identified as planning, organizing, staffing, financing, supplying, directing, coordinating, controlling, informing, and evaluating,
and seeks to fulfill intermediate goals, such as satisfaction of clientele,
harmonious working relationships, intelligent and economic utilization
of resources, and the adoption of good management/administrative
practices. Apart from this, they have not been able to discern precisely
where administration shades off into nonadministrative activities or
how much administrative content is present in a particular job. The
same activity may be used for many different purposes, and administrative devices may promote reforms unrelated to administration. For
example, the creation of a research and development organization by
combining previously scattered scientific research units may constitute
an administrative reform although the ultimate purpose may be the
stimulation of other reforms. Even if agreement were reached as to
which activities and reforms are specifically administrative, there
would still be considerable overlapping with other kinds of activity
and reform.

One way of distinguishing administrative reforms is to confine
the use of the term to those reforms for the implementation of other

kinds of reform. They would include proposals to *(a)* change collective purposes and goals, *(b)* alter the mix of resources, *(c)* transform attitudes and methods, *(d)* improve relationships and standards, *(e)* speed decisions, *(f)* rearrange patterns of authority and communication, and *(g)* achieve a higher level of efficiency, wherever human cooperation is involved and resistance is expected. This wide interpretation incorporates most uses of the term "administrative reform" currently employed. More importantly, it explains the persistence of administrative reform, the need for which will disappear only when perfection is achieved.

It would be foolhardy for anyone to predict that such perfection is near. Only utopians have attempted to picture the perfect world where presumably there would be lasting peace, permanent security, ideal cooperation, endless bounty, absence of waste, automatic adjustment, and painless existence. Administrative imperfections are likely to exist while *(a)* man is incapable of predicting the future accurately, *(b)* solutions to administrative problems are mutually incompatible, *(c)* administration is subordinated to irrational considerations, *(d)* ideal administrative arrangements are wrongly used to implement bad policies and plans, *(e)* provision is not made for the unexpected, and *(f)* no profound changes take place in man's physical environment, biological make-up, and cultural values. Administrative perfection is beyond man's present capabilities. Hence, administrative reform continues to be a natural pursuit unless man is prepared to reconcile himself to administrative deficiencies of his own making.

THE CONCEPT OF ADMINISTRATIVE HEALTH

What constitutes administrative deficiency depends on one's idea of administrative health. Presumably any departure from that standard calls for remedial action. Normally an administration is considered healthy if it meets all demands put on it and if it gives no cause for alarm. Its performance is measured by different standards of satisfaction, but once an administration falls below a certain point (wherever that may be), it is deemed to require attention. This satisficing criterion (March and Simon 1958, pp. 40-1) fails to meet the perfectionist element in administrative reform, which considers an administration unhealthy if it falls below its optimum performance capability. But some reformers have an even higher ideal of administrative health, that of a vaguely conceived ideal which has yet to be transcribed on paper. There are, then, three different concepts of administrative health, (1) the ideal optimum—attaining administrative perfection; (2) the practical optimum—attaining the highest level of performance within given conditions, and (3) the satisficing optimum—attaining a satisfactory level of performance within given conditions. As the ideal optimum is unobtainable, it can be ignored here. The other two concepts, however, require further elaboration.

The practical optimum is perhaps that at which, according to most textbook writers and consultants, all administrators *should* aim. It is the value premise of much administrative theory. It is more realistic than the ideal optimum and can accommodate changing conditions if the criteria used include dynamic measures (flexibility, freedom to respond to stimuli, innovative capacity, institutionalization of change) as well as static ones (performance, efficiency, satisfaction, morale, teamwork, loyalty, stability, continuity, minimization of conflict). On the other hand, the satisficing optimum is that which administrators *seem* to aim at as it requires less demanding abilities—namely, the skills of keeping out of trouble. It is geared to clientele expectations and it is largely self-adjusting through feedback. It secures a reserve capacity that can be used at peak demand or during emergencies. But keeping just above complaint level is a risky business. Society, if not the administration loses at a cumulative rate from unused excess capacity, and performance tends to be lower than could be achieved with only slightly more effort. From the viewpoint of administrative reform, the satisficing optimum is much less demanding than the practical optimum. In the one case, reforms are adopted whenever defects are revealed by the clientele. In the other, reform pressures are self-generated whenever performance falls below the level that administrators and outside perfectionists believe it can attain. One administration will keep a piece of machinery running as long as it performs satisfactorily; the other will replace it as soon as something better comes on the market.

Their approaches to administrative ill health likewise differ. The satisficing optimizers wait for a crisis to develop before they institute reforms. The clientele must have already complained and the damage has been done. Demands have not been met. Changes in taste have not been recognized. Staff have left. The plaint has failed. In short, the symptoms of impending failure have been ignored too long and failure has taken place. This was the norm before scientific methods were applied to administration and it persists wherever scientific methods are ignored. In contrast, the practical optimizers head off crises and seek to diminish the possibility of failure. They promote innovation and experimentation to improve on existing performance. In their wake have developed the management sciences, still heavily dependent on mathematics and models borrowed from the physical sciences and confined to administrations that can afford computers and lengthy scientific training. Scientific techniques reduce dependence on innate ability and personal inclination. Reforms are warranted whenever the implementation of something new would improve administrative performance, allowing for temporary dislocation and errors in initial assumptions and calculations.

One of the principal differences between the two approaches is the extent to which they take internal satisfaction into account. The practical optimizers concentrate more on satisfying collective purposes by maximizing the output available to the community for the minimum expenditure of resources. The satisficing optimizers are more concerned with the internal quest for a quiet life, even at somebody else's expense through loss of output or waste of resources that could be put to better use. Both approaches could be combined if the practical optimizers concentrated more on internal satisfaction as one of the collective purposes of human cooperation. Other measurements of administrative health may also be needed. For example, much more stress may have to be placed on the efficacy of administrative dynamics in coping with rapid change and the need to plan change and to train administrators to be their own change agents. These, too, should be added to the growing list of indices of administrative health (e.g., Price 1968).

Indices of administrative health must be used cautiously. At best, they are only rough indicators of trends. They tend to ignore non-measurable factors. They can be contradictory and cancel one another. They cannot replace values when administrative deficiencies have to be translated into practical reform proposals. The central problem remains that of relating collective purposes to available resources. As these two factors vary and move independently, administrative health differs from one moment to the next and from one place to another. Continuous structural differentiation in modernizing societies further complicates the problem, though administrative competence has been strengthened by the growth of central institutions and by a greater capacity to generate and absorb persistent transformation. Demands on administration have grown, especially in recent decades; in response, the means of satisfying demand have also grown, sometimes quite dramatically through new discoveries (telecommunications) or through the exceptional talents of one individual (philosopher king, messianic law-giver). In general, response has lagged. Administrators have waited for events to justify further action; they have not anticipated future demand. In particular, bureaucracies are thought to be less responsive than nonbureaucratic organizations (though bureaucracy can institutionalize change agents and transform change into a routine). Administrations in advanced countries are believed to be more responsive than those in under-developed states (see *Bibliographic Notes*). Which of these is in greater need of reform? Until the nature of demand and available resources are closely examined, one cannot tell. A rich country like Australia or Canada may be doing far worse in meeting its demands than a poor country like Israel or Cambodia, but the consequences of failing to meet demands in a poor country may be far more serious in terms of loss of life, poverty, starvation, political upheaval, and economic stagnation. Much depends on what concept of administrative health is adopted, what indices are used to measure it, and what value judgments are made about factors that cannot be reduced to statistics and about conflicting trends in measurable factors.

At this point it is useful to refer to "the six blind men and the elephant" dilemma. The Second Annual Conference (1965) on the Role of Management Analysis in Government, which devoted itself to the possibilities and potentialities of measuring the health of government organization, concluded that "everyone who defines organizational health tends to operate from his own frame of reference in initiating such a definition" (University of Connecticut 1965, p.96). The management auditor measures economy and efficiency, *i.e.*, "the operation of the engine itself, and does not take into account the driver, the passengers, nor the direction of the vehicle" (p. 97); the program evaluator concentrates on measuring the effective achievement of program objectives and goals. The behavioralist is concerned with the achievement satisfaction of the individuals who participate in the program, while the political scientist examines adaptability, survival and growth, and democratization. In contrast, the bureaupathologist investigates diseases and factors detracting from cooperation. The Conference proposed that all different views and all factors should be combined into an integrated mathematical model. Even if it were, the measurement would be disregarded by the idealists and the satisficers, while the practical optimizers would be handed a diagnosis but no prescription.

SUBJECTIVITY IN ADMINISTRATIVE REFORM

According to the different concepts of administrative health, there are three main approaches to administrative reform. Satisficing optimizers justify reforms when feedback reveals an administration failing to satisfy its clientele. Practical optimizers support reforms whenever an administration fails to attain the potential performance indicated by scientific measurement. Idealistic optimizers persist with reforms until their visions of administrative perfection are fulfilled. Exactly why and how individuals come to their different views or at what point they decide remedial action is required is not known. It is likely that the majority of mankind is indifferent to administrative reform until they learn what is involved. However, those entrusted with administrative decisions invariably take sides, and feelings run high. Whether individuals are naturally inclined to pessimism or optimism, to conservatism or radicalism, they can usually be placed along a reactionary-revolutionary continuum on specific reform issues. It is virtually impossible for anyone personally affected by reform to be indifferent and objective.

The subjective factor goes much deeper. Reformers assume that their proposals, if implemented, will improve on the status quo and that the anticipated results are worth overcoming resistance. Neither assumption can be supported by conclusive evidence. What exactly constitutes an administrative improvement? Indices of administrative health are not entirely satisfactory and can be quite misleading if badly constructed. Because of the scarcity of resources and the multiplicity of collective purposes, no change is without its repercussions. "Every cause is the effect of a prior cause and every effect is the cause of a posterior effect" (MacIver 1942, p. 30). Improvement in one area may be more than offset by deterioration elsewhere. There is no certainty that what happened in conditions ABC can be repeated in conditions DEF or CDE or BCD. Further, a causal relationship is assumed: if Y is done, then Z will follow. But in human affairs infallible predictability is unknown. It may be that every known cause indicates the existence of a causal relationship, but this is no comfort if things do not happen as expected in the next case. MacIver warned:

> When a social phenomenon is defined by law, convention or any institutional procedure, we should not assume that it can be referred to any one set of causes lying outside the institutional system itself.

> We should beware of identifying, for purposes of causal derivation, the phenomena we are seeking to explain with any category narrower or broader than that constituted by the phenomena themselves.

> In our search for causes we should never rest content with the establishment of a positive correlation, no matter how high or how continuous, between the social phenomena to be explained and any other phenomena.

> We should not assume that when a number of conditions are together operative in the production or emergence of any phenomenon each of these conditions can be assigned a specific weight or influence, a percentage of contribution towards the resultant phenomenon (MacIver 1942, pp. 88-94).

The chances of causal success diminish with elaboration and complexity in interrelationships.

Even assuming that administrative reform will indeed produce the anticipated improvement, not everyone will be convinced that such improvement is desirable if other values are compromised in the process. For the sake of military effectiveness, for instance, individual freedoms are subordinated to discipline. In civil bureaucracies, there is a continuous conflict between administrative requirements and professional values. The mere suggestion of reforms is enough to offend some people; it connotes that they are not good enough for their jobs. Implementation of reforms against their resistance may be costly in terms of withdrawn cooperation, permanently embittered relations, and persistent suspicion. It is difficult for reformers to know when to withdraw with grace and when to continue in spite of consequences known and unknown. The expected results may bear no relation to the final results and, far from being an improvement, may prove to be a disaster.

As the underlying value judgment behind reform, it is becoming increasingly difficult to reject the idea of progress and continuous improvement. Once something better is known, there is no doubt what people prefer. The search for improvement can be highly rewarding. In the more advanced countries, it has become a moral imperative impressed on younger generations by socializing agents; this preconditioning impedes the development of a value-free social science. As Myrdal has pointed out, "the social sciences have all received their impetus much more from the urge to improve society than from simple curiosity about its working" (Myrdal 1953, p. 210). Their bedrock is the ultraradical idea that social ills stem not from "human nature" but from social organization. Thus men and society could be improved by reforms in the social institutions that condition them. Myrdal, acknowledging the debt of the social sciences to reform movements, emphasizes the essential function of independent social scientists in democratic states in keeping alive the discussion of general issues "above opportunist party lines, taking the larger and broader views," which "has assured a disposition and momentum for change in people's thinking about society" (pp. 217-8). They should assume "the long-range intellectual leadership thrusting society forward to overcome primitive impulses and prejudices and to move in the direction of rationality and progress" (p. 221). Myrdal does not claim for the social scientist the detachment of the physical scientist. He is proud of his moral commitment to improving man's lot. This may well account for the attraction of the social sciences for potential reformers. Certainly, the reform tradition continues, playing an important part in shaping the minds of younger generations who will later fill positions of power.

Administrative theorists have never hidden their reformist intentions. If modern administration is dated from the eighteenth-century revolutions, it appears that much administrative theory has been developed by empirical reformers seeking rational and ideological foundations for their practical remedies for administrative deficiencies. The first administration textbooks were used to train civil and military officials in the absolutist Prussian monarchy to strengthen loyalty and to improve public services. The Federalists, particularly Hamilton, reflected on the nature of public administration, partly to justify the new constitutional arrangements adopted after the Declaration of Independence. Burke's plea for economy and efficiency in administration arose out of British defeats at war. The first manual of ideal administrative practices, Bentham's *Constitutional Code* (1832), was based on the twin principles—"the greatest happiness of the greatest number" and "official aptitude maximized, expense minimized." Jacksonian democracy aimed at wider participation in public office. Charles Babbage sought higher productivity.

When Woodrow Wilson urged his fellow political scientists to turn away from making constitutions to running them, he was following a well-beaten path. His ideas about the nature of administrative studies were heavily reform-oriented:

> It is the object of administrative study to discover, first, what government can properly and successfully do, and, secondly, how it can do these proper things with the utmost possible efficiency and the least possible cost either of money or of energy. . . . There should be a science of administration which shall seek to straighten the paths of government, to make its business less unbusinesslike, to strengthen and purify its organization. . . . The principles on which to base a science of administration for America must be principles which have democratic policy very much at heart . . . (Wilson 1887, pp. 481, 485, 504).

The purpose of studying administration was to improve administrative practices, more particularly to rid America of its "poisonous atmosphere of city government, the crooked secrets of state administration, the confusion, sinecurism and corruption ever and again discovered in the bureaus of Washington" (pp. 485-486). Similarly, most of the founding fathers of modern administrative theory could be quoted to show their commitment to administrative reform. When questioned as to why he wanted to substitute exact scientific management for personal judgment, F. W. Taylor replied that greater efficiency would lead to cheaper production, lower prices, and wider distribution, and ultimately to a more uniformly happy society. Follett saw administration as a means of bringing the ideal into everyday affairs. She believed "in the individual not trusting to fate or chance or inheritance or environment, but learning to control his own life" and nowhere did she see such complete acceptance of control as in business (Follett 1941, p. 18). Even the Hawthorne investigations by Mayo and Roesthlisberger were not without their moral motives, though they further demonstrated that values could be separated from scientific methods.

Gulick admitted that the social scientist may "be led on his quest for truth by his individual value-interests" but "the results of his work, if scientifically done, may be used by others with different values" (Gulick and Urwick 1937, p. 192). He can have reform at heart yet analyse human phenomena with scientific detachment, and his results may or may not be significant for reform. Values and ends can be considered as constants except for efficiency, which Gulick believed to be the basic "good" in administrative science, whose fundamental objective was "the accomplishment of the work in hand with the least expenditure of manpower and materials." At the time, administrative theorists were committed to the search for efficiency. Since then the behavioralists have cast aside even that, but they have by no means usurped the field. The reform tradition in administrative theory is bravely continued by other disciples who are committed reform advocates. Students of administrative theory cannot avoid contact with the subjective element and may unconsciously embrace the values of efficiency, rationality, reform, and practical optimization projected by their teachers and much of the literature.

The subjectivity of administrative reform makes it prey to fashion, fad, and fancy. One particular type of reform inexplicably catches on and spreads rapidly through administrative teaching and practice. For a time, it is considered a universal panacea, until, wrongly applied, it fails expectations and quickly falls from grace as something else replaces it. When the situation is desperate, even cranks gain a wide hearing; even after they have been utterly discredited, some cultist is always willing to stand by his pet remedy, attributing coincidences to it. Occasionally, overcommitment to a particular reform safeguards its reputation long after disillusionment has set in, simply because of the loss of face involved in admitting a mistake. Reforms seem to go through a peculiar cycle, starting out with a revolutionary reputation, succumbing to respectability, and finishing as reactionary, a process that closely parallels the gradual institutionalization and routinization of deviant behavior and elimination of sanctions. Administrative history is littered with reform discards and every so often a few are rediscovered and reshaped for different circumstances. Some have rightly been deserted but others have fallen unjustly victim to an unwarranted assumption of good faith. On the one hand, it was assumed that the reformers were genuinely interested in seeking remedial action, and that they knew exactly what they wanted to reform and why their specific proposals would bring improvement. On the other, it was assumed that administrators were genuinely open to proposals. In fact, the reformers were more interested in improving their own social standing than in remedying administrative ills, or the administrators were deaf to pleas or incapable of recognizing valuable proposals. Further, the assumption of good faith was abused by cranks and unscrupulous administrators.

THE PERVASIVENESS OF ADMINISTRATIVE REFORM

The prevalence of reform-mindedness is a consequence of the transformation of human values since the eighteenth century, particularly the general acceptance of the concept of social welfare. Man is responsible for his own predicament; he has nobody else to blame for social ills. His problems might be fewer if he were not always aspiring to new heights of achievement without completing existing tasks and if the spread of knowledge did not awaken new aspirations. Normative administrative theorists believe that one of the major keys to a permanent solution of man's predicament is efficient administration, which is variously defined. Their reforms, which seek to maximize both individual and organizational performance can be classified as follows:

REFORMS CONCERNING INDIVIDUALS AND GROUPS

1. Ideological: promoting the will to develop and to succeed, the acceptance of progress, the habit of working, the capitalist ethic, the urge to self-improvement, the subordination of self to the common good, incentives, participation.
2. Moral: insisting on high integrity, compassion, truth, respect for law and authority, loyalty.
3. Educational: encouraging personal aptitudes and skills, latent abilities, correct social attitudes, acceptance of change and innovation, group participation, self-expression, new ideas, rationality, scientific attitudes, leadership, self-evaluation, delegation, democratization.

REFORMS CONCERNING INSTITUTIONS

1. Decision-making: adopting devices to improve policymaking, forecasting, programming, budgeting, planning, information processing, performance evaluation, coordination, control, resource allocation, deployment.
2. Structural arrangements: designing new organizations and institutions, formal working codes, laws, physical layout, communications, authority patterns.
3. Procedures: changing methods, processes, techniques, routes, functions, roles, contacts, controls, factor mix.
4. Communications: reappraising images, decisions, information, standards, results, events, norms, leadership, values, motivation, behavior, policies, power relationships.
5. Adaptability: providing for environmental changes, research, innovation, accidents, breakdowns, delays, failures, crises, abnormalities, transformations.

Many of these go beyond administration into politics, psychology, teaching, industrial design, public law, and other areas; reforms in these other areas are likely to have repercussions on administration. There is no firm boundary line; demarcation has more theoretical convenience than practical significance. Even if self-professed administrative reformers were suddenly to disappear, there would still be administrative reforms.

Unlike other kinds of reform, administrative reform is not and can never be a final goal in itself. Even efficiency, the only likely final goal of reform, is a catalyst in attaining other goals. Administration is only a function of ultimate ends. Different ends require different means. Efficiency in exterminating peoples or suppressing civil liberties requires different methods from efficiency in ensuring equal consideration and treatment of all citizens. Woodrow Wilson was well aware that ends and means are interrelated. He recognized that the values incorporated in certain administrative practices prevent the attainment of other values. The Nazi bureaucracy illustrated what happens when perverted values introduced by psychopaths drive out other values. Much maladministration occurs because people fail to live up to their cherished values when these are abused in their sight. For example, nothing is done when a customer is tricked or an inspector fails to do his job properly. Through negligence, a different set of values becomes enthroned, and ultimate goals (the good society) are compromised. Basic to administrative reform, or to any reform, is a sense of responsibility; people must really care. When they do, only problems that need solution exist, not artificial boundaries between disciplines. Administrative reform directs attention to neglected problems at the uncertain frontier between disciplines, particularly where the links are weakest. If the administrative reformer is to make an impact, he has to be aware of the total cultural configuration. It is not enough for him to convince an elite or to rely on coercion alone. Reform requires voluntary response at all levels. The extent of reform-mindedness among a representative sample of a society could well be a measure of social dynamics.

Administrative reform permeates all administration. No aspect of administration is incapable of reform or has not been reformed at some time. This does not necessarily mean that reform *per se* is good, desirable, preferable, successful, workable, or necessary. Whether it is any or all of these things depends on the nature of the reform, its context, and evaluation of events both before and after its implementation.

Judgment must be suspended until the term is properly defined, not used as a catchall for movements that do not seem to fit elsewhere, and until other methodological difficulties are overcome. Private bodies have been reluctant to reveal internal matters, especially of a detrimental nature, that concern administrative reform; public bodies have closed vital areas altogether or limited access in the interests of public welfare and individual protection. Even when one has taken part in administrative reform controversies, it is difficult to reconstruct the scene after the event. Sometimes what has been recorded is not the most important part, and occasionally it is irrelevant, being concocted afterwards to rationalize a sordid affair or to enhance contemporary mythology or to support currently fashionable theories. Taboos surround much of the power play, manipulation, and hypocrisy involved in administrative reform processes. Successful reforms obviously receive the most attention; no one parades unsuccessful reforms, although these may reveal much more than distorted successes. Fortunately, the subject has been stimulated since World War II by a number of events that have added considerably to source materials, including *(a)* political revolutions committed to social transformation; *(b)* technological innovations affecting administration; *(c)* full employment policies and the spread of the human relations approach; *(d)* technical assistance programs attempting to modernize traditional societies and overhaul outmoded administrations; *(e)* national planning geared to generating and absorbing changes; *(f)* comparative studies provoking emulation; and *(g)* the general expansion of knowledge which throws new light on continuity, stability, stimulus, innovation, resistance, motivation, and flexibility. It is time for administrative theorists to recognize that administrative reform has taken on a new significance.

CONCLUSION

Although as old as civilization itself, administrative reform has not been studied in any systematic way. Yet it is an important factor in administrative dynamics, being present in every administrative situation as the hidden hand directing attention to maladministration. Whenever men's thoughts have turned to betterment, they have rearranged their affairs to accommodate progress; while opposition has always come from those who stood to lose by change or who doubted that the anticipated benefits justified the risks. This perpetual struggle between conservatives and radicals, which is the essence of administrative reform, keeps administration fluid. Although the study of these fluctuations should prove fruitful for administrative theorists, it has proved barren so far, despite accumulating source material, the pervasiveness of administrative reform, a climate favoring progress in general and reform in particular, concern with administrative malfunctioning, and a reformist tradition in administrative theory. The fault lies partly in the preoccupation with administrative statics and partly in methodological difficulties concerning the nature of the source material, the delimitation of the subject, and the imprecise use of the term "administrative reform." Until these preliminaries are settled satisfactorily, the potential contribution to administrative theory of the study of administrative reform will remain unrealized.

BIBLIOGRAPHIC NOTES

Though the literature on administrative theory is rapidly expanding, the number of truly outstanding works is small. The main schools disagree over the nature and boundaries of administrative activities, and so the discipline is very open. Little is lost if study is confined to the major classics, the principal schools, and the independent forays into new territory. Many of the early classics were grounded in reform, and their authors were notable reform advocates (Wilson 1887, Taylor 1947, Weber 1947, Fayol 1959, White 1955, Follett 1941, Gulick and Urwick 1937, Barnard 1938, 1948, Roesthlisberger and Dickson 1941) but they barely mention administrative reform. The later classics, those written since World War II, reflect the changing times and intellectual movements and do not overlook the topic but again their attention is focused elsewhere (Simon 1946, Waldo 1948, Lewin 1948, Simon, Smithburg, and Thompson 1950, Merton 1952, Gouldner 1954,

Blau 1955, Argyris 1957, March and Simon 1958, McGregor 1960, Likert 1961, Gross 1964, March 1965).

The major textbooks in administrative theory are little better (Blau and Scott 1962, Cyert and March 1963, Davis 1956, Etzioni 1961, 1964, 1968, Forrester 1961, Haire 1959, Koontz and O'Donnell 1959, 1964, Lepawsky 1949, Litterer 1963, Marx 1957, 1961, Mee 1963, Millett 1959, Newman 1963, Pfiffner and Presthus 1953, Pfiffner and Sherwood 1960, Rubenstein and Haberstroh 1966, Tead 1951, Terry 1958, Waldo 1953). A discernible trend is a shift from static analysis to the dynamics of the administrative process and from there into considerations of administrative change and reform. On the verge of reform territory are the behavioralists (Argyris 1953, 1960, 1962, 1964, 1965; Bradford, Gibbs, and Benne 1964; Cartwright and Zander 1960; Cooper, Leavitt, and Shelly 1964; Katz and Kahn 1966; Mailick and Van Ness 1962; Presthus 1962, 1965; Sayles and Strauss 1966; Selznick 1957; J. D. Thompson 1966; V. A. Thompson, 1961) but they never quite enter it in the way that organizational process analysts do (Banfield 1961; Banfield and Meyerson 1955; Braybrooke and Lindblom 1963; Buchanan and Tullock 1962; Dahl and Lindblom 1953; Deutsch 1963; Dror 1968; Downs 1967; Golembiewski 1962; Selznick 1949; Tullock 1965).

Much closer than these are *(a)* those who are concerned with change processes (Bennis 1966; Bennis, Benne, and Chin 1961; Blake and Mouton 1962; Blake, Shepard, and Mouton 1964; Gouldner 1965; Grove and Dyons 1964; Guest 1962; Leighton 1945, 1949; Liddell-Hart 1954; Lippett, Watson, and Westley 1958; Mann and Neff 1961; March 1965; Mills 1951, 1956, 1959; Rogers 1962; Thelan 1954); *(b)* case studies of administration in operation (Bock 1963, Bock and Campbell 1962, Mosher 1967, Stein 1952); and *(c)* empirical studies of administrative problems from which generalizations are made (Appleby 1957, Chapman 1959, Clark 1964, Durham 1958, Hanson 1959, 1966, Robson 1960, Smallwood 1965, Stanley 1965). It is necessary also to draw heavily on social change and reform literature from other disciplines, particularly sociology and anthropology (Adams 1960, Allen 1963, Arensberg and Niehoff 1964, Barnett 1953, 1956, Burns and Saul 1967, Fayerweather 1959, Friedmann 1955, 1961, Goodenough 1963, Hagen 1962, Hodgkinson 1967, Horowitz 1964, Hoselitz 1952,

Kornhauser 1959, LaPiere 1954, Leavitt 1959, Leighton 1945, Martindale 1962, Nordskog 1960, Ponsioen 1962, Sims 1939, Smelser 1959, Sorokin 1947, Toynbee 1966, Wagner 1959, Znaniecki 1952, Zollschan and Hirsch 1964).

In recent years the situation has been improved considerably by the emergence of the subdiscipline *development administration*, fostered by *(a)* international bodies, such as the United Nations and the International Labor Organization, with a practical responsibility for aiding the poorer countries; *(b)* newly independent states confronted with administrative problems beyond their capacity to solve; *(c)* richer countries with moral and political obligations toward less fortunate allies; and *(d)* universities and training institutes involved in technical assistance and comparative studies. Between them they have contributed most to the study of administrative reform. They have maintained journals devoted to administrative problems and related areas (e.g., *Chinese Journal of Public Administration, Community Development, Economic Development and Cultural Change, Indian Journal of Public Administration, International Development Review, International Review of Administrative Sciences, International Social Science Journal, Journal of African Administration, Philippine Journal of Public Administration, Public Administration, Public Administration Review, Comparative Political Studies* and *Journal of Comparative Administration*). They have initiated studies of international technical assistance in administration (Alexander 1966, Glick 1957, Montgomery 1962, Sharp 1961, Weidner 1964) and the administrative problems of poor countries. The most concerted attack has been conducted by the Comparative Administration Group of the American Society for Public Administration, which has encouraged advanced research and the publication and distribution of the results to depositories throughout the world (Braibanti 1966, Braibanti and Spengler 1961, 1963, Diamant 1964, Eisenstadt 1963, Groves and Levy 1965, Heaphey 1966, Heaphey and Kronenberg 1966, Landau 1968, LaPalombara 1963, Montgomery 1967, Montgomery and Siffin 1966, Riggs 1963, 1967). Foundation and institutional support has enabled members of the Group to produce a growing list of country studies (see *Bibliographic Notes* to Chapter 3).

Administrative reform is tied to the notion of progress, examined in detail by philosophers. The most helpful studies from the viewpoint of administrative reform are J. B. Bury, *The Idea of Progress* (New York: Dover, 1955); L. W. Doub, *Becoming More Civilized* (New Haven: Yale University Press, 1960); M. Ginsberg, *The Idea of Progress: A Re-evaluation* (London: Methuen, 1953); Moore 1963; Myrdal 1960; Sorokin 1947; and F. J. Teggart, *The Idea of Progress* (Berkeley: University of California Press, 1949). None of these is referred to by any administrative theorist concerned with the problems of measuring administrative and organizational effectiveness, productivity, efficiency, betterment. The value aspects have tended to be eclipsed by practical measurement of performance in terms of output cost ratios. A greater awareness of the full meaning of performance is achieved by Argyris 1960, 1962, 1964, Bennis 1966, Likert 1961, McGregor 1960, Price 1968, Rakowski 1966, Robson 1960, University of Connecticut 1965, and Wasserman 1959. The value aspects behind administrative reform are part of the wider debate between value-free social scientists and social science moralists (Appleby 1952; Arrow 1951; Becker and Boskoff 1957; Eulau 1963; Gross 1959; Haire 1959; Lawrence 1966; McEwen 1963; MacIver 1942; Merton, Lerner, and Lasswell 1957; Myrdal 1953, 1960; Parsons 1951, 1961; Schubert 1960; Vickers 1965, 1967; and Wadia 1966).

THREE

Social Change and
Administrative Reform

The study of administrative reform is handicapped by the absence of a universally accepted definition. The indiscriminate use of the term has led to confusion and to difficulties in setting parameters for research and theorizing. Although no one would want to shackle the subject with restrictive chains merely for academic neatness, the present position is too liberal. The term has been applied, for instance, to all improvements in administration (Finan and Dean 1957, Rosholt 1966); to general administrative overhauls in difficult circumstances (Braibanti 1966, Siegel 1966); to specific remedies for maladministration (Raj 1967, Singh 1963, Martin 1965); to any suggestion for better government (Elton 1953, Kiernan 1966); and to the intentions of self-styled administrative reformers (Chen 1960, Van Riper 1958). It has also been interpreted in specific ways. For instance,

> la réforme administrative doit tendre à doter le Pays d'une administration qui, tout en garantissant à son personnel le bénéfice des lois sociales, agira avec le maximum d'efficacité et de célérité, aux moindres frais pour le contribuable, en imposant au public le minimum de gêne et de formalités (Mariani, 1958, p. 8).[1]

Not only do students in the same field have difficulty in communicating with each other, but laymen cannot understand the reservations academics have about each other's work and they are puzzled by the

[1] Administrative reform should aim to endow a country with an administration that, while guaranteeing to its staff the benefits of public law, will act with maximum efficacy and speed, at the least cost to the taxpayer, while imposing minimum inconvenience and formality on the public.

43

different uses of the same term in referring to vaguely related phenomena. The lack of a universally shared and standardized vocabulary is common to all social science, with the same consequence—namely, that semantic confusion leads to errors of a theoretical and explanatory nature.

One of the most difficult semantic problems is the careless use of the words "reform" and "change." Administrative reform is a relatively minor factor in the totality of social change compared with acculturation, technological innovation, modernization, and migration. Social change is only part of the ceaseless flow that characterizes the universe. Even seemingly stable elements, such as the relationships between galaxies in space, the physical face of the earth, and man's biological and cultural make-up, are changing all the time. Nothing stays the same for long; nothing repeats itself identically. There is tension within all things and in the relationships between things, which causes them to become different, to vary, to alter, to deviate, to convert, to transform themselves. This endemic tension arises from competition, scarcity, maladjustment, creativity, incompatibility, originality and other factors as yet undiscovered by man. It keeps all things in persistent flux. But man cannot contemplate uncaused change; he looks for sequential chains that simplify, explain, and order universal chaos. Consequently he has proposed many theories to explain the phenomenon of change and to predict its future course as it affects man himself.

Theories of social change reflect the ebb and flow of human optimism. At the peak of optimism, the theories place man at the center of the universe and attribute to him sole power over his own destiny. At the trough, they are deterministic, denying him any influence at all and attributing all events to supernatural entities or uncontrollable forces. Between them lies every kind of permutation and combination. The trend has been away from determinism to a greater acknowledgment of man's ability to alter history deliberately. The possibility of reform is increasingly admitted; that is, man can choose among different changes according to a scale of values and priorities and select a particular path even if the chosen values must be imposed on dissenters. In response, those who agree that things should not be left to chance, but are perturbed by the idea of one set of values being imposed, seek a measure of compromise, involving a search for compatibility between different sets of values, with more emphasis on the carrot than on the stick. Thus the province of reform is clouded by the subtleties with which power is exercised to overcome resistance. Instead of the law, there is social engineering. Instead of bureaucratic authority, there is mass persuasion, joint consultation, and human relations. Instead of indoctrination, there is socialization, education, and planned change. Instead of sanctions, there are incentives. Somewhere in this confusion is administrative reform. To find out exactly where it is located, it is necessary to take some of the more prominent contemporary theories as landmarks. How does reform differ from change? Is there anything distinctive about administrative reform?

THE IDEA OF SYSTEM

On closer scrutiny, universal chaos turns out to be a highly sophisticated order in which everything is interrelated. The latest analogy, succeeding the machine and the organism, is the *system*, a coherent, purposeful collection of entities. The existence of this complex, probablistic, and self-regulating arrangement can be assumed without proof, and its boundaries (if any) need no universal agreement. It is a set of relationships perceived by intelligence, not something given in nature. The idea of system can be employed without defining the relevant relationships or the coherence, pattern, and purpose of the system. It is a valuable theoretical tool which is being used to integrate human knowledge by discovering basic common principles that will lead to interdisciplinary hypotheses and formal identities between various systems, both physical and social (Boulding 1956). The application of the idea of system to social phenomena has important bearings on theories of social change and of administrative reform.

Systems are merely sets of related variables, the boundaries being set by their overall purposes. The relationships between the variables are different; they change as the variables interact with variables outside the system. Isolating the system keeps external relations constant except for those affecting the system in operation (inputs) and those affected by the system (outputs). The system itself evidences continuous tension due to the different relationships of the variables, the changes in the variables through external relationships, the imperfections of integration, and the impact of disturbances from within and without (*e.g.*, accidents, innovations, Acts of God). The tension, while providing the system's internal dynamics, may erupt into conflicts and trigger changes. But such changes may not affect the overall purpose although changes in purpose invariably do change the system and its internal relationships and variables. Given an unchanging purpose, the system tends to preserve itself within a reasonable range of normal operating conditions by maintaining its internal relationships in a steady balance (around an equilibrium oscillating between the limits set by homeostasis) and by adjusting to the changing environment (according to natural laws discovered by cybernetics) revealed by feedback from multiple external contacts. The system learns to be what it is from a self-organizing activity so that it is able to respond to unanticipated stimuli, to learn the optimal response from repeated experience, and to grow and renew itself. It can cope with crisis, heal its own wounds, and deal with uncertainty. As long as the system has greater capacity than any specific part to generate and absorb proliferating variety, it can adjust to disturbances and survive.

The idea of system can be used to analyze social behavior or motivated relations existing, developing, and changing between the system and its environment, between systems, and between components of a system. Action theory attempts to discover why relations between component parts in a closed system (one isolated from its environment for theoretical purposes) tend to remain stable or static and why they follow an orderly pattern of development. Such investigations should also reveal why systems disintegrate and disappear. The search is for systems that do maintain their boundaries—their overall goals and functions, their component parts and structures, the relationships between the parts through which the overall goals are attained, and, in a closed system, the transformation of inputs into outputs that can be analyzed to reveal the stable elements, *e.g.*, adaptation, goal attainment, tension management, and pattern maintenance (motivation to conformity, institutionalization of norms and values, control mechanisms to ensure consistency) and integration (Parsons 1951, Parsons and Shils 1951).

The analysis of boundary-maintaining systems that are components of higher order systems should also reveal much about internal tensions and the way they are managed, and about integration. In time, it should be possible to distinguish between *(a)* changes that can be absorbed by the social system and those that transform the system; *(b)* changes that are peacefully absorbed or to which the system is self-adjusting and those that upset the system without transforming it; and *(c)* changes that are conforming or whose conformity is predictable (*e.g.*, built-in continuity, perpetuation of existing relationships) and those that are unpredictable and unaccommodable, and potentially explosive.

Several conclusions important for reform can be drawn from the idea of system. First, as all systems perform some purpose, uncertainty about that purpose creates instability; anything (such as reform) that clarifies the purpose aids stability. Second, as the purposes can be met in different ways under different circumstances, there is no ideal isolated system. Third, natural laws guarantee the survival of the system but not of particular relationships or their institutionalized forms. Disturbances beyond absorption capacity will cause the system to collapse, but other disturbances will produce violent, perhaps incessant, oscillations if natural controls are blocked. Remedies may be self-defeating if they further block or hinder the natural controls. Fourth, the natural laws of self-maintenance may require the malfunctioning or nonfunctioning of a component while the system adjusts to altered conditions. Fifth, reform measures should avoid wholesale displacement of existing arrangements and interests without providing adequate substitutes or alternative structures. Finally, if systems learn for themselves, generate and absorb changes under reasonable operating conditions, and deal with uncertainty, the prospect for reform appears quite limited. But caution is advised. The analogy of system, attractive as it is, remains one of questionable significance and applicability. It does not prove anything; on the contrary, any suggestions arising from the use of the analogy have to be empirically tested. The suggestions may prove to be purely coincidental and hardly relevant to the way human beings behave individually and collectively. For example, social systems may well be self-regulating, but how they adjust themselves is more important. Even if cybernetics reveal the processes, human problems will be no less pressing and the solutions no less value-free. Parsons and Smelser admit that the four stable elements cannot be maximized at the same time and that in reality it is doubtful whether any one of them achieves its specific purposes simply because no social system is perfect (Parsons and Smelser 1956). None can eliminate "inconsistencies among values, norms, beliefs and interests" which are "sources of potential complaint, deviance and therefore change" (Mitchell 1967, p. 149).

With these warnings in mind, it is possible to conceive of administration as a set of relationships between variables, absorbing changes yet capable of being transformed. The administrative system comprises the four fundamental and interrelated processes (adaptation, goal-attainment, tension management, and pattern maintenance and integration), and much analysis of administration fits very easily into this framework. Changes occur within the system, and in time the system itself also changes. Innovations arise within the system or are introduced through one of its variables or component parts that has external relations. The system may absorb or resist the innovations but somewhere within it they are recognized and evaluated. The process of absorption without resistance is considered administrative change; the process of absorption with resistance is considered administrative reform. Outright rejection of innovations cannot be considered administrative reform, but attempts that fail may be considered reform failures. Administrative reform cannot take place by default—that is, through "ineffectiveness in controlling the cumulation of variations and the strains of inconsistencies derived from such variations" (Zollschan and Hirsch 1964, p. 225)—but only by deliberate institutional facilitation.

Boskoff (Zollschan and Hirsch, pp. 226-39) has advanced several relevant hypotheses concerning this theoretical system of social change:

1. The greater the functional differentiation in social systems, the greater the opportunity for variation and innovation.
2. "Adaptive and goal-attainment functions provide more opportunity for variation than pattern-maintenance and integrative functions" (p. 226).
3. "The opportunity for adaptive and goal-attainment variations

is directly related to complexity of societal types" (p. 227).

4. "The opportunity for variation is directly associated with significant shifts in the proportional effort . . . devoted by the social system to the four functional problems" (p. 227).

5. "Opportunity and motivation for innovation are directly related to the amount of interpersonal and intergroup conflict within each of the four functional areas . . ." (p. 228).

6. "The opportunity and motivation for innovation within one or more functional areas are directly related to the amount of intergroup competition for dominance on the institutional level" (p. 228).

7. "The opportunity and motivation for innovation are inversely related to *perceived* levels of efficiency in meeting specific functional needs" (p. 228). They are also related to perceptions of failure in existing practices, overemphasis in otherwise legitimate objectives, and threats to traditional operation that stem from changes introduced by other sub-systems or by external systems.

8. "Control or containment of innovation—within any functional area—or within the system as a whole—is directly associated with success in pattern-maintenance and tension-management" (p. 231).

9. "Control or support of innovations by institutional groups is . . . related to characteristic patterns of interaction with subordinate levels" (p. 231). The more diffuse and flexible they are, the greater the opportunity for diffusion of innovations and the greater the likelihood the innovations will be ignored at the institutional level. Similarly, the more extensive the communications system, the greater the perception of innovations by institutional groups.

10. When recruitment into institutional elites is based on achievement criteria, receptivity to innovation is greater than when recruitment is ascriptively based. Similarly, elites with varied social composition are more disposed to innovation than restrictive elites.

11. After innovation has been implemented, the relative efforts given to the four functional problems are altered.

12. Innovation in one activity affects other functionally significant activities.
13. Derivative change is uneven; lags occur. During the transition period, attempts are made "to provide integration by direct mechanisms (force, fear, hysteria, witch-hunting, tightened controls and the like)" (p. 237) and social movements arise seeking administrative innovations to consolidate and effectively operate previously sanctioned innovations.
14. Some change in the stratification of systems occurs.
15. Derivative cultural changes also take place to justify or oppose the innovations.

The significance of these hypotheses will become clearer as this survey of administrative reform proceeds.

Boskoff's main concern was to link social change with order and stability through "*the variable capacity of social systems for generating and channeling innovative processes*" (p. 239). A different approach to the means by which systems change in time is contained in development models. Systems have their own life cycles: they grow and decline, live and die, divide and unite. But the only direction is forward in time until the system serves no useful purpose and disappears. The life cycle is characterized by different stages and by dull and lively periods sprinkled with sudden changes in direction and traumatic events. There is an irresistible temptation to perceive systems in human terms and to ascribe to them human values, such as steady growth toward a predestined end, or a preference for rationality, security, and assured repetition. Many development models assume that the predestined course of a system is growth, that environmental stimuli and internal tension make for growth, and that each system has latent capabilities for growth awaiting the right circumstances. They hope that their explanation of change will reveal ways of speeding the process, obtaining the benefits without suffering unduly from artificial stimulation, and undergoing change while preserving stability and continuity.

Chin suggests that the confusion might be avoided if three different models were separated (Bennis, Benne, Chin 1961, pp. 201-14). The *system* model concentrates on stability. Changes spring from conflicts in the system, internally created or externally induced; the process of change is the process of tension reduction. The *development* model reviews the life cycle of a system. The direction of change is toward purpose fulfillment, and difficulties result from impediments to growth forces. The model for *changing* concentrates on induced forces producing change, studying stability "in order to unfreeze and move parts of the system."

The first of these models emphasizes adaptation and the reduction of structural tension. The second recommends the removal of blockages hampering progress. The third stresses control and choice, deliberate improvement based on perceived need. The last is far removed from laissez-faire and social atomism, which replaced deliberate social control with automatic adjustment on the grounds that "tampering and social tinkering with man's natural and social universe interferes with the homeostatic forces, which if left unfettered, will bring about the perfectly maximized 'good life'" (Bennis, Benne, Chin 1961, p. 2).

This turn of the circle is important. There is a danger that general systems analysis and supporting studies such as cybernetics might fall back on the laissez-faire doctrine revised in a new form. The analogy of the system may be enthroned. Systems are found everywhere, and everything is reduced to a system. Man may be told to forget his ideas of deliberate reform, if it is not in the nature of the system to promote human values. Presumably if it is inherent in the social system that mankind should eventually exterminate itself, then the value-free systems worshippers would do nothing to prevent its happening. Fortunately, nothing seems further from the truth. The idea of system is used by administrative scientists at least to safeguard human values and to retain the benefits of order and stability without sacrificing the advantages of progress. It has long been recognized that while every social system tends to maintain itself, there is no self-maintaining order, no closed system, no doctrine of permanence (MacIver 1942). Accidents do happen. People do strive to change the natural order of things. No better example exists today than the process of induced modernization which assumes a desirable end, seeks to remove obstacles in traditional societies, and deliberately interferes with natural processes in order to speed the development of modern characteristics. Reform, then, is not only possible but welcome. Indeed, it is impossible to avoid its repercussions, if for no other reason than that modernization is now universal.

MODERNIZATION

There is general agreement concerning the most significant features of modern societies, especially their capacity to generate and absorb continuous change. By maintaining uninterrupted growth, they permit the continuous expansion of human endeavors. Their social systems absorb changes in demand and accommodate different institutional forms. Traditional behavior patterns are eroded and replaced by new patterns. Old institutions acquire new functions or are replaced by new institutions better able to perform traditional and new functions. Everything is in flux. Capacity for social mobilization is increased; structural differentiation and specialization are extended; integrative organization is strengthened; the power base is broadened; and an institutional framework capable of self-sustained growth is widened. The social system develops ability to respond to new problems, new facts, and temporary solutions; its greater flexibility makes it more stable. Total eradication of the traditional or pre-modern (that is, conditions at take-off) is not essential; old and new may coexist for lengthy periods. As social systems do not have equal capacity for dealing with problems, the requirements of modernization conflict differently with traditional patterns of social action. Structural changes are uneven; while modernization is occurring in some areas, traditionalism is strengthened in others.

Discontinuities between modernization and traditionalism may produce conflict. Protest movements by those facing displacement and upheaval may obstruct further growth, depending on (a) the intensity of social dislocation, (b) the structural complexity of the society at take-off, (c) access to policy-makers, (d) overlapping interests between protest groups, and (e) outside support for the protesters (Eisenstadt 1966). Under certain conditions (e.g., undifferentiated institutional structures, inadequate integrative mechanisms, inertia inherent in overpopulation, lack of skilled persons to run new organizations, mass disillusionment with growth, rigid social stratification) obstruction becomes institutionalized, and breakdowns in modernization occur. The system is disrupted or demands are restricted to the level the system can handle. Only when the obstacles are removed can modernization proceed further. Possible remedies are to incorporate traditional symbols in the new order, prevent the alienation of unprogressive groups, minimize social cleavages, widen the base of recruitment to elites, improve effectiveness of integrative mechanisms, transform values and ideology, and institutionalize the continuing capacity to absorb change.

Modernity consists of things that advanced (modernized) societies have to which backward (modernizing) societies aspire. They include, for example, literacy, rising income per capita, industrialization, mass media, consumer durables, and adequate public services. More important are the processes and structures that bring these end products into being. Four processes are identified by Smelser (Hoselitz and Moore 1966, p. 33)—(1) technological change toward the application of scientific knowledge, (2) agrarian change from subsistence farming toward commercial production, (3) industrial change from muscle power to machine power, and (4) ecological change from rural settlement toward urbanization. These changes involve the establishment of more specialized and autonomous institutions and the decline of multi-functional role structures in the economic, political, social, and cultural systems. Increased functional differentiation is accompanied by increased integration through new social organizations, nationalistic ideology, bureaucratization, and an enlarged political system (Eisenstadt 1963, LaPalombara 1963). Where integration falls behind differentiation, social disturbances may block further progress.

The simplest way of discerning the indispensable factors for modernization is to compare models of traditional or modernizing societies with modernized societies. Riggs has attempted this in his Industria-Agraria model (Siffin 1957, pp. 23-116) as has Sutton in his comparison of agricultural society and modern industrial society (Finkle and Gable 1966, pp. 19-27), but both have been criticized indirectly by Eisenstadt, who queries whether there is a direct relationship between, on the one hand, indices of social mobilization and specific forms of structural differentiation and, on the other, the capacity to absorb continuous growth and change (Eisenstadt 1963, pp. 14-23). Apter also points to the variety of structural forms through which modernization can be accomplished (Apter 1955, 1961, 1965). More important than structural forms are the nature of premodern societies at take-off, the ideology and composition of modernizing elites, the pressures and forces behind modernization, the resources available, the areas where modernization is first manifested, the response of different social strata to social problems, and the ability of the political system to absorb innovation. In modern societies, change is institutionalized. It appears natural and automatic. The main effort is devoted to preventing obstruction. While the threat to institutionalize change in modernizing societies produces protest movements, the threat to institutionalize obstruction in modern societies produces reform movements. The two types of movement exist side by side in all societies experiencing rapid change.

Analysts of modernization do not pretend to offer an operating guide to which institutions and processes aid or impede modernization in general though they may adopt a normative approach for particular societies. There are certain general principles such as an innovative ideology or an open elite or an expanding political system, but much depends on what purposes institutions serve, when, for whom, and under what conditions. In guiding development, modernizing societies are thrown back on value judgments, prejudices, unconfirmed hypotheses, and sheer instinct. In his review of the concept of political development, Pye illustrates the shortcomings of academic analysis by comparing the various definitions and the choice that has to be made between conflicting demands (Finkle and Gable 1966, pp. 83-90). More serious charges can be leveled against modernization analysis. It does not adequately explain how change is generated. It uses an inclusive term "change" for all social movement, failing to distinguish between different types of social change and to indicate the intensity and direction of change. Change, in fact, takes place at different rates and in different directions (Moore 1963, Moore and Cooke 1967). Changes affect each other and the quantity of change may not affect the quality of change. Several important questions are not answered. When is a premodern system judged to be modern? How does a society tell that change has been institutionalized? If change leads to self-destruction, should obstruction be institutionalized or should a society reverse the process? Is determinism implied in modernization?

Parsons denies that a general theory of the processes of change of social systems, as attempted by modernization analysts, is possible; it must be a theory of particular subprocesses of change *within* the system (Parsons 1951, p. 486). He is challenged by LaPiere, who believes that changes are neither a product of society nor a consequence of some universal law of social life. Changes are more like violations of normal organic processes, abnormalities that disturb the established structures and processes of life. "Society in all its various aspects," he argues, "operates constantly and consistently toward self-maintenance; that all social organization . . . is . . . inherently resistant to change, and that social change is the work of socially deviant individuals acting in asocial ways" (LaPiere 1965, p. 39). He rejects the idea that change is a "socially normal process that arises, inevitably and effortlessly, out of the conditions that are thereby modified" (p. vii). Change is effected by individuals freed of "conventionalizing effects of social ideology and of organizational membership" (p. vii). He attempts an explanation of social change by concentrating on social innovators, advocates, and adopters, and on the social circumstances favorable to the emergence of such individuals. Conformist actions do not change systems; only innovative actions do that.

Though no general theory of social change emerges from the analysis of modernization, Boskoff's hypotheses are strengthened and extended. Modernization involves ceaseless change. Both specialization and integration of functions are increased. New organizations are introduced and bureaucratization is extended. Efficient uses of energy, enlarged capacity, and improved performance are emphasized. Administration becomes increasingly complex in form, specialized in role, integrative in function, and professional in outlook. Much more is expected of it in maintaining harmonious relationships, accommodating proliferating variety, responding to change, ensuring the acceptability of decisions, and absorbing innovation while preserving stability and continuity. It may aid or impede modernization and may itself become subject to protest and reform movements. Without blueprints for the future, it becomes harder to decide which path to follow, what pressures to acknowledge, and what concessions to make. Expediency and compromise rather than detachment or commitment to abstract ideas tend to govern decisions. More reliance is placed on feedback but the information may be distorted en route; progressively subjective interpretations may produce inadequate solutions, increasing tension and social dissatisfaction. The inability of administrators to anticipate and handle social conflict is a symptom of ill-health that encourages self-appointed doctors to push their pet remedies, either adjusting existing relationships within the administrative system (change), permanently upsetting existing relationships (reform), or permanently changing the system itself (revolution).

THE ASSUMPTION OF ADMINISTRATIVE CHANGE

The ability of modernized systems to deal with continuous systematic transformation distinguishes them from all previous historical transformations, which only created closed systems. Modernization is a revolution that transforms an order unaccustomed to systematic change to an order based on ceaseless change. The best of traditionalism cannot be combined with the best in modern society. In the modern society, nothing is static and sooner or later everything comes to an end. Barnard first pointed this out when he drew attention to the failure of organizations. "Most cooperation fails in the attempt, or dies in infancy or is short-lived. . . . Failure to cooperate, failure of cooperation, failure of organization, disorganization, destruction of organization—and reorganization—are characteristic facts of human history" (Barnard 1938, p. 5). Administrative theorists who ignore the obvious facts of change and temporariness should be reminded of Heraclitus's warning that one cannot step into the same river twice. Mann and Neff noted that the most conspicuous values in American culture had produced

> a highly dynamic society—a society in which the predominant characteristic is *change*. Consumer demand for more and better products and management's concern with efficiency, profits, and growth combine with a sharply rising curve of scientific discovery and technological innovation to thrust our society squarely against the problems of managing change. Small businesses, large industrial organizations,

and whole governments find they must devote an increasing proportion of their organizational resources to introducing, engineering, and handling change (Mann and Neff 1961, p. 1).

The realm of administration is one of flux and becoming. . . . It consists not of separate actions as disparate entities, but of interlocking activities. One activity blends into another. It is hard to find a beginning and still harder to find the end. Every achievement creates difficulties. Every solution creates new problems. Neither people nor purposes ever remain immobile. Organizations are born and they die. Their members enter and leave; of those who remain, some grow wise and all get older. If the process of change is not evident from outside or is not formally legitimized, it takes place beneath the surface (Gross 1964, p. 249).

In this wonderland of change, decisions are made, values judged, facts weighed, matters arranged, and conflicts resolved. Ceaseless change in administration can be taken for granted. It takes place whether or not people recognize its inevitability, have the ability to prepare for and cope with it, understand how it operates, anticipate its consequences, and accept it.

Complex theoretical frameworks are not necessary to show that administration is largely self-adjusting to ceaseless change. Most changes are absorbed imperceptibly in the natural course of things. People adjust and adapt instinctively. Cooperation is continuously created and recreated. Without it, man cannot survive for long. People are trained from birth to accept its requirements and much cooperation is institutionalized. Relatively few issues arise to make people question their cooperation. As it is difficult to break habits and to resist pressure, and much more comforting to conform and to accept others' expectations, most people answer the question by doing what everyone else seems to have decided. This is best seen in voluntary associations and informal groups where sanctions against non-cooperation are less coercive than in formal organizations. Probably few people are inner-directed or independent enough to question their response to change.

When it comes to formal structures such as bureaucratic organizations, self-adjustment is no less automatic although the processes may be slower and more elaborate. They must fulfill some social purpose (not necessarily that professed by the organizations themselves) and their output must be wanted by someone. The world cannot afford obsolete organizations. In a situation of extreme scarcity, whatever is provided can be used by somebody if only in exchange for something else. Above bare subsistence level, choice has to be reckoned with even if the organizations can manipulate their clientele into demanding what they are prepared to supply. They must respond to changing moods, tastes, and attitudes if they are to continue to serve any useful purpose. This is where feedback is crucial. Besides responding to clientele pressures, organizations must adjust to changing community mores and laws. The choice of location is governed by population movements and the availability of labor (unless labor can be attracted away from existing settlements). Once physical plant exists, depreciation must be considered; the replacement of capital and enlargement of plant depend on changes in demand, savings, and taxation. Within the organization, there is continuous turnover in staff. The newcomers are not identical replacements; they differ in age, background, personality, and so forth, and previous patterns of cooperation have to be altered accordingly. Promotion may reveal in individuals hitherto hidden traits, and changes at the very top may have profound repercussions throughout the organization, as no two sets of work styles, values, friendships and connections are identical. Procedures are altered and with them group norms and informal arrangements.

Such organizational response to fluctuating conditions through administrative changes is so familiar that it is no longer recognized for what it is. Only the unusual attracts attention such as quarrels within royal families or ideological disputes between revolutionaries, which have the potentiality of destroying whole systems. Violent upheavals may overshadow more important "deliberate, rational, peaceful types of change" (Mitchell 1967, p. 149).

Cooperation is a delicate thing that requires constant attention. As long as it is forthcoming, the requirements of change are accepted without protest, and the necessary concessions are automatically made. Once it is threatened, the natural accommodation of change is obstructed; and it is threatened whenever people do not like being together, a condition common to a variety of situations from incompatible personalities to class warfare, from territorial aggrandizement to differences in race, color, sex, and age. When reconciliation fails, change is obstructed, as, for instance, in the following circumstances:

1. Feedback is interpreted differently or no agreement can be reached about the consequences of a decision or the direction of change and what to do about it.
2. Delays, bottlenecks, gaps, and other signs appear indicating that change is taking place at different rates and that unless immediate remedial action is taken the progressive will be held back.
3. Methods for reconciling differences are too elaborate, too rigid. If too autocratic, they may not allow adequate representation of diverse views. If too democratic, they may involve the search for every divergent view and complete consensus in all decisions.
4. Decision-makers prefer the familiar; they will not alter the status quo if there is any dispute over what is to be done or if those who are likely to suffer are not to be compensated in other ways.
5. Nobody is prepared to move from a declared position, or to compromise. People refuse to conceive of anything different or to alter norms.
6. Communications break down and information is not passed on, deliberately in the case of insecure supervisors whose power rests on commanding information denied to their charges.
7. Staff are unable to recognize change or the need for change and suspect new ideas as heresy; they are caught by their own mediocrity but are still competent enough to ensnarl innovators in tradition, established rules, routine details, diversions from more important work, and reasonable-sounding excuses why action cannot be taken in the desired direction.

In these and other ways resistance to administrative change is generated. Change must be accepted voluntarily; it is a process of self-realization assisted by harmonious interaction. Once resistance is generated, change gives way to reform. The resistance has to be overcome and the dissenters have to be forced into cooperation; the end result is not always that intended. "Resistance is a sign that there are unresolved problems in the change situation. . . . Coercion is likely to magnify these problems, although it may result in the temporary accomplishment of some purely technical objective" (Goodenough 1963, p. 43). Resistance has many diverse origins and may appear at the most unexpected times but always it is preceded by a breakdown in cooperation.

> Because we don't like having our own lives arranged according to someone else's blueprint for us, we have ethical scruples against attempting to impose blueprints on others. As a practical matter, other people are likely to have similar objections to being reformed or subjected to somebody's plan. Development that is undertaken in the spirit of imposing our will on others or getting them to see the folly of their ways and the wisdom of our counsel inevitably meets with resistance. After all his efforts on behalf of others, the agent of reform is repaid with what he interprets as ingratitude. The truth is that to accomplish purposive change in another usually requires the other's cooperation (Goodenough 1963, pp. 16-17).

Resistance to change is indispensable for stability. Were people able and willing to change whenever an alternative presented itself, there would be chaos. They are more selective, accepting only those changes that appear to be beneficial to themselves (and in this proof and imagery are equally important). They are not inherently conservative or naturally resistant to change. When they do resist, they do so for good emotional, moral, aesthetic, rational, and self-protective reasons (LaPiere 1965, pp. 174-198). To some extent they are creatures of habit and routine, but these do not entirely exclude change. Even ritual does not embody the principle of the dangerous precedent— that "every action which is not customary is wrong or if it is right, a dangerous precedent," so that "nothing should ever be done for the first time" (Beer 1964, p. 33). They prefer to live a comfortable, cozy, settled existence, concerned with their own personal problems, but they can also be stirred deeply by outside influences. When they want to, they can adopt changes quickly. On the other hand, the fear of the unknown is ever-present, and it may well be that people who derive security from familiar institutions and relationships fear the threat of change (Esman 1963).

When resistance occurs, it is not necessary to exert coercion to overcome it. The coercive approach implies that unless a man is personally threatened, he will not change his ways. Perhaps this may be true of penal and other institutions where people are held against their will or are compelled to lose their individual identity in the common cause, but it certainly does not apply in voluntary associations where the exercise of authority and power is avoided as much as possible to save members' feelings. Otherwise, the extensive practice of human relations would be so much wasted effort except merely to sweeten the bitter pill of power. Many other approaches are tried before coercion. For instance, there is the combination of reason and persuasion in the appeal to friendship, goodwill, established relationships, and past results, backed by kindly instruction, explanation, and information with the idea of letting resisters see for themselves that their fears are groundless and their resistance useless. Lasting change can be achieved only through individuals' being permitted to work out their problems for themselves. This idea is the basis of the human relations approach, which is less personal though still designed to persuade and convince. The techniques employed range from the open-door approach to mass persuasion with strong emphasis on individual dignity, creative freedom, and self-development through participation in decision-making and delegation of authority. The inculcation of new ideas and attitudes merges into the more formal methods of training and education to teach new skills in a receptive environment. Nobody as yet is required to do anything against his better judgment. Sanctions are not contemplated though disappointment may be shown and interpreted as a mark of disapproval.

The question arises whether these techniques for overcoming resistance work only because the resisters realize that sanctions will be employed if they do not appear to be persuaded. This knowledge alone may be sufficient to make them conform, at least outwardly. In practice, more emphasis is placed on impersonal authority and the habitual acknowledgment of status within the organization, which usually ensure deference to decisions made at higher levels. Changes embodied in instructions are carried out merely because they are issued from above. Resisters appeal upwards, thereby acknowledging that the final decision is not theirs. Only if the resisters persist do set rules dealing with insubordination come into operation, though the very threat of their application or the withholding of an expected action may be sufficient to overcome resistance. Sanctions, based on power, are rarely used but usually succeed. Should organizational sanctions be insufficient to deal with resistance, appeal to political and legal processes, and further still to communal sanctions and physical coercion, usually enables those in power to crush resistance. Jones (1966), in analyzing planned organizational change, classified the various strategies and tactics as follows:

A. *Coercive* strategy, characterized by one-sided goal setting and unbalanced power relationship, rests "upon the application or the threat of application of physical sanctions and/or generation of frustration through restriction of movement or controlling through force the satisfaction of human needs. . . ."
  1. Hierarchy—superior/subordinate authority relationship.
  2. Elite involvement—participation of organizational or community elites.
  3. Pressure—use or show of force by physical sanctions or deprivation of privileges.
  4. Stress induction—deliberate heightening of tension prepatory to change.

B. *Normative* strategy relies on proper and legitimate directions and the manipulation of symbols.
  5. Participation—free and spontaneous contribution.
  6. Involvement/commitment—obligations understood.
  7. Cybernetics—collection and use of information.
  8. Value displacement—new values made to appear to conform with existing values.
  9. External relations—change of clientele attitudes through public relations and improved image.
  10. Social awareness—staff treated as human beings not manipulable things.
  11. Education/training—institutionalized transfer of knowledge.
  12. Exposition and propagation—publication of explanatory material.
  13. Voluntary association—cooperative endeavor.

14. Role definition.
15. Legitimization—appropriate blessing and support.
16. Emulation—imitation of superiors.

C. *Utilitarian* strategy makes use of rewards.
   17. Placement—secure in strategic areas.
   18. Empiricism—proof of value.
   19. Conditional assistance—bargaining.
   20. Goal setting—careful planning.

D. *Neutral-like* tactics include those with no individual quality or distinctiveness.
   21. Action research—researchers and consultants as observers and manipulators.
   22. Training-Counseling Syndrome—self-appraisal and development.
   23. Timing.
   24. Technical modification.
   25. Manipulation of charisma.
   26. Communication.
   27. Marginality—go-betweens.
   28. Catharsis.

This classification includes methods for inducing change as well as for overcoming resistance to change. However, it is based on a bureaucratic change mechanism that is by no means universal, though it is the predominant working model in modern industrialized societies.

The bureaucratic change mechanism assumes that only the leaders (the power-holders) are capable of deciding on change and that they can enforce their decision throughout the organization. In a rigid social structure where education and wealth are confined to a top layer in society that controls all bureaucracies and can rely on governmental authority to enforce its decisions, deference from the ranks is no doubt a reasonable expectation. But the modernizing society is not amenable in this way. Change itself is institutionalized. The leaders cannot control it nor can they contain social conflict, pluralism, democratization, innovation, and governmental authority. Hierarchical discipline is weakened by countervailing power, extra-bureaucratic rewards, and full employment. The bureaucratic change mechanism has to rely less on imposed change and much more on feedback. The lower echelons have greater freedom to decide on change, and greater trust is placed in their choice. Reimposing autocratic procedures delays change because an overburdened leadership works sluggishly and the lower echelons fail to exercise discretion. The inability of Weber's ideal-type bureaucracy to adopt and assimilate change in contemporary conditions is dealt with extensively in administrative theory. The real issue is not the formal authority structure but the actual power structure, which takes into account informal relationships, decentralization, key points, professionalization, and isolation, power being the ability to prevent effective action.

A good illustration is the way public administration operates in democratic societies, where resistance is expected. If everyone were to comply with all political decisions there would be less need for political and administrative manipulation of rewards and punishments. As in autocratic societies, officials have sufficient ultimate power to enforce compliance, but their clientele are sufficiently well organized to form power centers of their own and to prevent, through political processes, the officials' exercise of ultimate powers. Mutual dependence gives rise to a complicated system of interaction whereby both parties acknowledge and accommodate the power of the other. There are informal rules as to the boundaries of evasion and the extent to which penalties will apply to rule-breakers who cannot exploit built-in loopholes. Each system is different but in every case strong informal links bind the parties, and roles and even personnel are exchanged. If anyone insists that the formal rules be followed, he is quickly told of the informal rules, and if he still persists, means are employed to remove him from the scene. If he challenges the "system" from the outside, he may be treated as a harmless embarrassment, silenced by forces whose operation he does not understand, or martyred for his cause if the justice of his stand is acknowledged later. Individual resistance may be as ineffectual as it is in nondemocratic regimes, but the potentiality for group effectiveness is much higher.

THE MEANING OF ADMINISTRATIVE REFORM

The need for administrative reform arises from the malfunctioning of the natural processes of administrative change. Reform movements begin with the intention of removing obstacles to change or of improving on the results of change where it is being accommodated. The distinction is somewhat artificial—the removal of resistance is seen as an improvement on the status quo, while the artificial inducement of improvements on the status quo entails the removal of resistance. From this, a clearer definition of administrative reform emerges. *Administrative reform is the artificial inducement of administrative transformation, against resistance.* It is artificial because it is man-made, deliberate, planned; it is not natural, accidental or automatic. It is induced because it involves persuasion, argument, and the ultimate threat of sanctions; it is not universally accepted as the obvious or true course. It is an irreversible process. It has moral connotations; it is undertaken in the belief that the end results will always be better than the status quo and so worth the effort to overcome resistance. These three distinguishing features—moral purpose, artificial transformation, and administrative resistance—give administrative reform its distinctiveness.

Moral Purpose. The object of administrative reform is to improve on the status quo by removing alleged defects, ending evil or wrong ways, and curing administrative faults. It is subjective and evaluative, hopefully based on probability rather than demonstration. Seeking to attain higher performance standards, it is progressive, not, like change, just any movement in any direction. Its ulterior objective is grounded in moral values in accord with existing morality, in contrast to the revolutionary who sets himself up against existing morality. The moral conscience of reformers does not permit them to stand idly by when their moral imperatives are being compromised. They must act or react to challenge with a crusading zeal. But they may be wrong. Their diagnosis may be mistaken, their moral imperatives unacceptable, their reasoning faulty, their calculations of probability grossly misleading. Moreover they may project selfish ambition as the general good. Their crusading zeal may blind them to goodness found elsewhere and to the worse abuses they leave in their wake. Until they clarify their intentions and prove their worth, they remain suspect.

Artificial Transformation. Reform is a calculated contravention of the principle of the dangerous precedent. It is innovating. Things can never be the same again even if the attempt fails. It is more than a series of incremental changes or marginal adjustments, though it may result from the "cumulation of small changes which periodically creates the requirement for comprehensive and systematic efforts" (Martin 1965, p. 133).

Reform is altogether a more radical process, carrying a higher degree of risk and uncertainty and correspondingly higher stakes. It contravenes agreed policies based on past experience (Dror 1964, p. 154), and departs radically from existing arrangements and policies. It is a form of creative destruction in that an old order is broken down to pave the way for a new order.

Merely incremental changes fail to respond adequately to shifting problems and needs, changes in the role and character of government and administrative structures, development of new knowledge, changing qualifications of personnel, and increased tensions generated by jarring elements. In time, however, incremental changes must lead to episodic changes or to more comprehensive reorganizations (reforms) resulting from internal maladjustments. Reform would seem inevitable either way according to Mosher's argument.

Administrative Resistance. Resistance distinguishes reform from change (though it should be noted in passing that Parsons believes that it distinguishes change from alteration [Parsons 1951, p. 491]). Because of opposition, reform needs to be backed by power either through existing channels or by usurpation of authority. It is a political process. Reformers are politicians with a mission. They may seek leadership as a reforming elite, using (and thereby enforcing) traditional or normal patterns of authority. They may content themselves by influencing, converting, and advising leaders as experts, idea men, spiritual guides, and gray eminences. They may, as publicists, propagandists, ideologists, and philosophers, attempt to appeal more widely and indirectly convince the leaders of reform. They may prefer to keep out of active politics by criticizing from the outside and, as intellectuals, mystics, dreamers, and romantics, direct their appeals to no one in particular. But in contrast to revolutionaries, they are not thoroughgoing. As dissatisfied conformists, they may support reform less for its intrinsic value than as an emblem of challenge to authority and complacency, and an opportunity for self-advancement. They may be prepared, too, to compromise on makeshift arrangements that incorporate some of their proposals. Reform movements are open to internal dissension between rival factions at both extremes, to opportunism, confusion, and accusations of hypocrisy and lip service to ideals when compromises are made.

Reform and change are similar in many respects, and it is not surprising that the words are used synonymously, as for instance in this definition: " 'Administrative reform' means any change of principles, organization, structure, methods or procedures which is aimed at improving the administrative process. . . . [It] is a continued, sometimes hardly perceptible, change, a process of evolution and not a revolution" (*Progress in Public Administration*, No. 19, p. 2). Both result from tension. Both depend on mobility but rely on some semblance of security, order, and stability. Both can be premeditated, planned, expected, and uneven. They merge imperceptibly whenever resistance appears or disappears. The differences between them are not clear-cut either. (1) Reform tends to be purposive, willed, manipulated, artificial; change tends to be automatic, self-adjusting, autonomous, and unforeseen. (2) Reform tends to be avoidable, episodic, particularistic, identifiable; change tends to be ceaseless, universal, anonymous, imperceptible. (3) Reform tends to stress conflict and difference; change tends to stress consensus, conformity and acceptance. (4) Reform tends to arise out of crisis, threats to treasured values, loss of vitality, and inflexibility; change tends to be multicausal, normal, and unavoidable. These, though, are secondary criteria, subordinate to moral purpose, artificial transformation, and administrative resistance.

Reforms need not be implemented by reformers or advocated by reform movements. The most spectacular (qualitative) reforms usually are spearheaded by reformers and reform movements, but the great bulk (quantitative) arise in the normal course of administration, rarely extend beyond the specific situation, and are quickly incorporated and forgotten. Reforms take the form of solutions to problems disputed between rival claimants. After a certain amount of initial discomfiture, resistance is overcome, and the administration continues without interruption and probably without battle scars. Those who brought about the agreed solution would not describe themselves as reformers unless pressed, and even then would prefer the title of decision-maker or expert adviser or confidential consultant. In contrast, the professional reformer is fully aware of his role as critic, diagnostician, and advocate. He is also aware of the personal risks he runs, such as ridicule for ideas deemed impractical and visionary, misunderstanding and distortion of what he says, or lack of appreciation for what he is doing. His mental health is severely tried by frequent frustration of his plans, constant plotting and conniving by vested interests, and treachery by deserters. He must guard continually against overstating his case, raising false expectations, fighting an opposition that has already conceded, failing to provide for defeat, concentrating on surface ills while ignoring root causes, and curing administrative ills at the cost of worsening other ills. Biographies of successful reformers attest to their own qualities—moral strength, abundant energy, tenacity, creativity, organizing ability, and mastery of political arts—but also some reluctance to accept other people's innovations.

Reforms cannot be measured by the qualities of their advocates. Only results matter. Intentions, plans, diagnoses, strategies, and even attempted implementation do not constitute reform. Progress reports are only a prelude to real achievements. Naturally enough, reformers exaggerate the expected outcome, minimize dislocation effects, and ignore unforeseen consequences and lesser alternatives. The reforms themselves may be the wrong answers to the right questions or the right answers to the wrong questions. The reformers may wreck their own schemes, good or bad, by personal failings. The situation in which reform is taking place may change so fast that the reforms may quickly be outdated or superfluous. In short, the eventual outcome may be quite disappointing. "Successful reform is not so readily accomplished by attempts to reform others as by helping others to reform themselves" (Goodenough 1963, p. 17).

REFORM AND REVOLUTION

Reformers are persistent; when they fail, they try again. They are reluctant to leave the field to conservatives who will restore a previous state of affairs (renovation) or maintain the status quo and permit only those changes that have universal support. If the resistance of a closed privileged elite proves too strong, reformers may be tempted to create a revitalization movement (Wallace 1956, Goodenough 1963), a grass roots organization aimed at preparing the community for a new social order. If the elite persists in ignoring the need for social change or for a greater degree of change, or if it refuses to make concessions to the revitalization movement and pressures continue to build, a revolutionary situation is created. Changes in the elite that do not bring the new social order any nearer cannot be considered revolutions, not if the newcomers do nothing. Revolution usually refers to the violence of means used to bring about radical change. Neither violence of means alone nor radical change alone constitutes revolution. When they coincide, as when a conservative elite is deposed violently or when reformers are forcibly replaced by others who want to go much further and faster, there is a sharp break in continuity, accompanied by physical force and visible signs of relief at the departure of the previous elite or elated expectations for what the new elite will accomplish.

"Revolution" in these terms can hardly be applied to administration. The term might be used only if reform were imposed through the political system without regard for the internal situation, or if internally those who advocated radical change captured authority and eliminated all resistance. The first possibility assumes that the administrators (or anyone connected with the administration) are unable to influence the politicians and must obey political decisions to which they are fundamentally opposed. Such circumstances cannot be envisaged even in a totalitarian one-party state or in war. The second possibility is a little more likely where administrators resist both reform and change and their administration is inflexible, immobile, and probably incompetent and repressive. Their very incompetence would encourage radical reformers to attempt a takeover, providing they felt sure of support from lower echelons. Their takeover—a palace revolution that would appear to outsiders as somewhat theatrical—would release suppressed enthusiasm and energy that would be beneficial while they were establishing a more effective administration. For instance, charismatic authority might be replaced by legal-rational authority or a bureaucracy might be transformed into an egalitarian cooperative. From this point, flights of fancy take over. Comparison with political revolution is not really tenable. In administration the crucial line is between change and reform, not reform and revolution.

More valid is differentiation according to personal disposition. Reactionaries are reluctant to interfere with the natural order of things, fearing any departure from the status quo that challenges their own position. Conservatives, while not so stubborn, prefer to rely on change and view any artificially induced acceleration of change as illegal, unjust and undeserved expropriation of power by the incapable and jealous. In contrast revolutionaries are convinced that social ideals can only be achieved by root and branch transformations and consider concessional incremental reforms as delusions which leave fundamentals intact. Sandwiched between them are the reformers, split into many factions like the others, but sharing the belief that change can be controlled and improved upon without incurring the trauma and dislocation of revolution. They are convinced that they could win over the uncommitted providing they have the same opportunity of presenting their case, more particularly demonstrating the inadequacy of self-adjusting mechanisms, the deficiencies of alternatives and the expected gains from reform.

CONCLUSION

A working definition of administrative reform should meet certain requirements. It needs to be more precise than the one in common usage, yet understandable to the layman. It should embrace the most frequently employed usages of the term without becoming too ambiguous. Above all, it should distinguish reform from social change and administrative change, while acknowledging that in the future it may become a component of a general theory of administrative dynamics and a general theory of social change. The definition arrived at in this chapter can be abbreviated for working purposes to "induced permanent improvement in administration," denoting its artificial, transformatory, and moral aspects while acknowledging the prospect of resistance. It is these characteristics that separate administrative reform from other types of social change. The practicality of the definition can be judged in the next chapter, where different perspectives on administrative reform are abstracted from a variety of case studies, past, present and future.

BIBLIOGRAPHIC NOTES

The term "administrative reform" is used to cover a wide variety of vaguely related phenomena concerning administrative improvement. Much can be learned about it from the study of overall social change and the various models used to explain the patterns of human activity observed. At the present time the systems model is overshadowing the mechanical, organic and process models. Several systems analysts have applied their models to the administrative system in ways helpful to the study of administrative reform quite different from its use as a management science tool. Among those with the wider view are Ashby 1956; Barish 1951; Beer, 1959, 1964; C. P. Bonini, R. K. Jaedicke, and H. M. Wagner (Eds.), *Management Controls: New Direction in Basic Research* (New York: McGraw-Hill, 1964); Boulding 1956; R. Carzo and J. N. Yanouzas, *Formal Organizations: A Systems Approach* (Homewood: Irwin-Dorsey, 1967); S. M. Katz, *A Systems Approach to Development Administration* (Washington, D.C.: American Society for Public Administration, 1965); O. Ramsoy, *Social Groups as System and Sub-System* (New York: Free Press of Glencoe, 1963); N. Wiener, *The Human Use of Human Beings: Cybernetics* (New York: Doubleday, 1954); S. Young, *Management—A Systems Analysis* (Glenview, Ill.: Scott, Foresman, 1966).

The idea of social system is employed by those who conceive modernization as a social process that transforms a social system unaccustomed to systematic change to one based on ceaseless change.

This theme is propounded by Eisenstadt 1963, 1965, 1966, and is echoed in Apter 1965, Finkle and Gable 1966, Levy 1966, and Weiner 1966. Less reliant on the idea of social system are other attempts at evolving a general theory of social or cultural change without referring to modernization as such: Barnett 1953; Barringer, Blanksten, and Mack, 1965; Childe 1951; D. Easton, *The Political System* (New York: Knopf, 1953); Hagen 1962; Hoselitz and Moore 1963; LaPiere 1965; D. C. McClelland, *The Achieving Society* (New York: Van Nostrand, 1961); Moore 1963; Neal 1965; Nordskog 1960; Ogburn 1950; Parsons 1951, 1961; Parsons and Shils 1951; Parsons and Smelser 1956; Sims 1939; Smelser 1959; A. J. Toynbee, *A Study of History*, ed. by Somervell (New York: Oxford University Press, 1947); L. A. O. Van Nieuwenhijzo, *Social Process* (The Hague: Mouton, 1962); Zollschan and Hirsch 1964.

Increased interest in the general processes of social change is reflected in studies of administrative dynamics and administration in rapid change. The assimilation of change is discussed in Blau 1955, 1956, Blau and Scott 1962, Crozier 1964, Dubin 1958, Gouldner 1954, Guest 1962, Johns 1963, Lawrence 1958, and Tead 1951, while some methods for overcoming resistance to change are also dealt with in Argyris 1964, Cartwright and Zander 1960, and Mosher 1967 (see also *Bibliographic Notes* to Chapter 5 and Chapter 6). The hardening of bureaucratic arteries is mentioned in most books dealing with bureaucratic organization (*e.g.*, Bennis 1966, Blau 1956, Dimock 1959, Mises 1946) and the participation method for overcoming bureaupathology receives extensive treatment, particularly by the human relations school (Argyris 1957, 1960, 1962, 1964, 1965; Bales 1950; Bernays 1955; Boulding and Kahn 1964; Costello and Zalkind 1963; Golembiewski 1962; Herzberg, Mausner, and Synderman 1959; Katz and Kahn 1966; Likert 1961, McGregor 1960) with some caveats by Mosher 1967. Other methods for improving the adaptability of bureaucracies are considered by Appleby 1953, 1956; Braibanti and Spengler 1961; Emmerich 1950; Hsueh 1962; Langrod 1965; and Stanley 1965.

In proposing solutions to administrative and organization problems, students become reform advocates. Despite the ubiquity of administrative reform, there are few descriptions of administrative reformers compared with the number of texts on revolutionaries. Not that reformers are less colorful, as some studies show: A. Briggs, *William Morris* (Middlesex: Penguin Books, 1962); Caiden 1965; S. C. Chu, *Reformers in Modern China: Chang Chien 1853-1926* (Columbia University Press, 1965); A. L. Husny, *Three Reformers* (Beirut: American University, 1966); Karl 1963; Liu 1959; A. Mann, *Yankee Reformers in the Urban Age* (Cambridge, Harvard University Press, 1950); J. W. Smith, *Florence Nightingale* (London: Constable, 1950); Van Riper 1958; Wagner 1959; R. Zeitlin, *Henrietta Szold* (New York: Dial Press, 1952). The distinction between reformers and revolutionaries is best drawn by Friedrich 1966 and Johnson 1966.

FOUR

Perspectives of Administrative Reform

Of the different ways in which administrative reform can be approached, the case method, at this stage in the study of the subject, still seems to have some advantages. It assumes nothing, least of all exact rules with scientific precision. It is problem-oriented and seeks answers in descriptions of actual situations, that is, what really happens and what people do at the time. It is the most interesting approach, illustrating the richness and complexity of the subject. It is also a flexible tool, permitting selective treatment and different forms of presentation. General principles drawn from series of cases can be further tested and mishandling of facts soon discovered. Each case is unique but may have universal features that can be combined into a general theory of administrative reform. Few cases are needed, for instance, to show that reform is controversial. Its moral and political overtones alone highlight differences between reformers and their critics.

Such controversy is beneficial to society though it may not be comforting to the reformers. It encourages debate, competition between proposals, and perhaps agreement where differences are narrow. The major issues are sharply defined, expectations are more realistic, and fallacies are exposed. When the balance of opinion is about even, the advantage lies with the conservatives. The reformers have to tip the scales their way, and the extent to which they can do this at the outset depends on the cultural, technological, and geographical context. Administrative reform takes place in different environments at every level of human cooperation and at all times for a great variety of objectives and motives under diverse pressures. To draw meaningful conclusions from selected cases, the related background must be known. The best illustrations occur in the public bureaucracy because more comprehensive records have been maintained for longer periods than in private enterprise and, as public property, they are more accessible than those of private bodies. Most cases used in this chapter are drawn from the realm of the public bureaucracy but they are treated in such a way that the generalizations could be compared and contrasted with generalizations from other types. More importantly, public bureaucracies have always been among the largest organizations in any society. Reforms have not only affected more employees, but they have affected all citizens who have come into contact with them and have attracted wide public attention through the political system and the debate over underlying values. As the importance of administrative reform depends on the number of people who participate directly and indirectly in the process and whose conduct is altered by reform, the public sector generally attracts the greater attention.

Though administrative reform can take place wherever people cooperate for a collective purpose, it has little meaning at the lower levels of administration. In partnerships between two more or less equals, disagreements are likely to be settled amicably through compromise, yielding by one side, or acceptance of the decision of a non-involved third party. Deadlocks usually end the partnership. Reform becomes more meaningful in a group where the members know one another well, determine their continuous participation, and perform each other's roles when necessary. Administrative reform is still not significant, since administrative activity is comparatively low, resistance can be overcome informally, and deadlocks can be resolved by recomposing the group. Small organizations composed of large groups are significantly different. The members no longer know one another. Ensuring their continuous cooperation is a full-time activity that requires specialized knowledge; administrative direction is conducted either through intermediaries or through uniform set procedures. The individual's ability to choose with whom he will cooperate is limited by his place within an authority structure. Here the reform process is more formal and involves power play. It is more difficult to contract out even though the individual as such is more dispensable, for it is not easy to find another organization that better suits him or places fewer restrictions on his freedom of action. Even so, administrative reform is still not significant. The members are still expected to be flexible and interchange roles when necessary. Knowledge is well-diffused and communications are good. The consequences of reform affect few outsiders. Such is the situation in most small private organizations and a number of small public authorities, particularly single-purpose public enterprises and local government organs with restricted territorial jurisdiction. If administrative reform arises at all, it is likely to be recognized only as the outside imposition by a higher level authority such as a parent company or central government or international association.

Administrative reform only becomes significant in markedly bureaucratic middle-size organizations. There, roles are strictly differentiated, and members are not expected to perform other roles unless formally qualified and trained. The leaders cannot know everything they should about the organization's activities or about its relationships with the wider environment. Whatever large-scale organizations do, society is directly affected. They are power centers in their own right; they are able to shape as well as be shaped by social forces. They are newsworthy, and it is difficult to hide their administrative reforms when contending parties within seek external support. Size alone may preclude some approaches to administrative reform that are employed at lower levels of administration; to this extent generalizations based on middle- and large-scale bureaucracies may not be strictly relevant beyond them. Similarly, tactics that succeed at lower levels may fail miserably when employed in larger scale administrations. But size is more a matter of relativity than of absolutes such as number of members, total capital assets, or distribution outlets. The organization needed to build the Great Wall of China was large in its time but has since been dwarfed by contemporary war machines. The crucial distinction is relative size within the same environment.

The criterion of relative size covers a wide range of organizational typologies that functionally have little in common. By concentrating largely on public bureaucracies, problems of boundary definition and voluntary membership are avoided, but at some sacrifice of generality. The range of reform strategies employable in nonpublic bodies may be limited. On the other hand, a survey of administrative reform in public bureaucracies over the past three thousand years reveals that it is timeless—the same sorts of motives stirred reform advocates in ancient China as in Czarist Russia and modern Brazil, and the same tactics were employed by reform activists for the same mixed reasons. Administrative behavior does not appear to have changed so radically or to be so different in public and private bodies, as the following cases indicate.

DIFFERENCES IN ATTITUDE—
THE PREMODERN BUREAUCRATIC EMPIRES

Modernization tends to obscure one of the most obvious features of administrative reform in public bureaucracies, namely, the continuing class basis of different attitudes toward reform. Because it is so familiar, it is overlooked altogether or taken too much for granted. One has to go back to premodern societies to observe the operation of these class differences in the raw. Eisenstadt (1963) has done this for the historic bureaucratic empires that preceded the modern bureaucratic state. His analysis constitutes a model of class conflict within the bureaucratic empires, which can be extended and applied to administrative reform. First, however, it is necessary to sketch the political background of these empires founded in crisis by rulers intent on restoring order. The rulers' aim was to monopolize office unfettered by traditional ties, in a centrally unified governmental system embracing the whole empire. In this, they were opposed largely by the aristocracy and other traditional elites who had benefited from the former regimes and felt menaced by the new regime. To overcome such resistance, the rulers sought allies from anti-aristocratic classes and strengthened their own power through transforming existing political and administrative organs by reallocating functions and resources, restaffing the bureaucracy with loyal technocrats, and permitting greater autonomy. Their administrative reforms were intended to improve administrative execution of their decisions, to ensure the dependence of officialdom on them, and to break any hold the traditional elites might have retained over public finances and offices.

Governmental functions were used to strengthen the rulers' position, to unify the empire (and perhaps extend its boundaries), and to develop a distinctive bureaucracy. The rulers and their dependent (nonautonomous) bureaucracies, for instance, owned land and controlled water supplies; they regulated the money supply and controlled trade; they held monopolies and owned workshops and warehouses; they were associated with religious values and institutions; they influenced the growth and variety of new social classes. As long as they held the empire together, they determined administrative reform.

The key to differences in attitude toward administrative reform lay in the power conflict between the rulers and the major social classes. The prime object of the *rulers* was to stay in power, which they did by consolidating their position, reducing the possibility of challenge, preventing internal collapse and external defeat, and subordinating their bureaucracy. Administratively, the results were a centralized bureaucracy staffed by professionals, uniform rules and procedures throughout the empire, the reorganization of public services, new forms of public management (public enterprise, taxation, planning, and budgeting), and changes in official ethics. It was in the rulers' interest to maintain the highest administrative standards and to support all reforms that promised to improve administrative performance, providing, of course, they were compatible with the rulers' political aims. The reforms would be expected to (a) strengthen the centralized polity, (b) promote official loyalty, (c) preserve internal stability, (d) increase dependence on the rulers, and (e) strengthen the rulers' control over the polity and the bureaucracy, sometimes by employing dependent outsiders as officials, or by frequently reshuffling official positions, or by using spies, inspectors, and inner councils. The rulers wanted an efficient bureaucracy to bolster their own image and to prevent weaknesses that could be exploited by rivals.

What the rulers gained, the *aristocracy* lost. The aristocrats were opposed to the premises of a centralized bureaucratic empire and never ceased their opposition to it. But in time they learned how to accommodate themselves and extract the maximum benefits from it. They endeavored to retain what traditional status they could, to perpetuate their political rights, and to make the ruler dependent on their resources, loyalty, and values. They sought to replace the ruler and to limit the bureaucracy. While attempting to infiltrate the ruler's inner councils and to monopolize strategic bureaucratic positions, they also tried to evade bureaucratic decisions and to entice leading officials to join them. Their overall strategy was to disorganize the polity and to weaken the ruler's hold over the polity and bureaucracy from within. In general, they did not favor administrative reforms that would strengthen the ruler and his bureaucracy. Inefficient administration enabled them to evade bureaucratic controls, to determine major decisions, and to corrupt officialdom. They supported reforms that benefited themselves and would also support general reforms when invasion or internal collapse threatened to sweep them away with the ruler and the polity. Today, the general broadening of the power base makes it difficult to distinguish the aristocracy (of capital or labor or intellect?), and contemporary aristocrats must clothe their narrow interests in a more universal ideology. They resemble past aristocrats in resisting government interference with their autonomy while seeking exceptional privileges and favors for themselves. They favor reforms that promise to diminish bureaucratic powers and activities, to reduce governmental expenditure, and to strengthen their position within the bureaucracy. They oppose reforms that would increase bureaucratic power and efficiency at their expense.

In contrast to the aristocracy, the *gentry* was one of the mainstays of the bureaucratic empire. It had much to gain over traditional elites as a favored middle-status group, and employment opportunities in the bureaucracy were opened to it. Being a self-centered conservative group, it tended to be impartial in administrative reform, except when its own specific interests were directly affected. Today, the rural middle class continues to provide loyal officials and professionals and remains one of the most patriotic groups, backing the rulers in most things but highly militant in its own cause.

The *peasantry*, the largest but politically least powerful class, carried the heaviest financial and military burdens of the empire. It expressed its frustration in rebellions and passive resistance though it was usually acquiescent. When stirred it could align itself alongside or against the ruler, depending on who promised it greater relief. Maladministration was to its advantage as taxes and military service could be avoided. Administrative reform spelled retribution rather than less victimization and abuse of power. Today the peasant in many parts of the world is no better off. Although he may desire uniform just treatment, he still must conform to traditional practices that expect a fee for every bureaucratic service rendered.

The *urban classes* were more favored than the peasantry because of their close association with the elites and their general support of the ruler and bureaucracy. They thrived for much the same reasons as the gentry, only more so. At first they supported the polity until they were sufficiently strong to safeguard their own interests. Their attitudes to reform depended again on the direct effects on their interests, whether, for instance, business would be generated, taxes reduced, or urban employment expanded. Since then, the bureaucracy and the town have grown together. While urban classes may resent bureaucratic intrusion, they also demand more intrusion to cope with urban problems. Their attitudes to reform tend to be ambivalent.

The *cultural and religious elites* could clothe the ruler with traditional legitimacy and present him as a transmitter of the cultural heritage while he protected them and permitted them to extend their hegemony. But they were not bound to him or any other group and could change allegiance as self-interest directed. They could be ultra-conservative in defense of the bureaucratic polity or they could switch to the opposition in protest against the ruler's policies or in support of rival groups that promised them a better deal. Their creativity was an asset in reform but it could be used equally in defense of the status quo, a situation little different from today except that while religion tends to conservatism, science pushes the other way. The *professional elites* are now in a much stronger position to influence rulers than they were in the bureaucratic polity. Over the years, their aim of greater autonomy has been fulfilled, though the pendulum is swinging back as increasing numbers can find employment only in the bureaucracy or under bureaucratic patronage. Their adherence to their own universalistic values prevents their total subservience to the regime. They can be found on both sides in the reform issue but while they may support reform for everybody else, they are notoriously conservative toward reform in their own specialties. The *military* can also be classed with these other groups for present purposes, as it shows the same kind of mixture. In some countries, the military has

reforms thrust on it; in others it is the spearhead not only of administrative reform but also of sweeping social changes. Such was also
the case in the bureaucratic empires. The military, like other classes
outside the bureaucracy, could be found paying lip service to the
general principle of administrative reform without going much further
in the way of practical support.

The *bureaucracy* itself was hardly a homogeneous class, being
composed of people drawn from all other classes and internally divided
by region, function, level, career pattern, and technical ability. The
bureaucracy was viewed as a means of political influence or upward
social mobility. Initially its members aligned themselves with the ruler.
Once their positions were secure, they evolved their own traditions,
attained some degree of autonomy, and developed an ideology emphasizing their autonomy and the bureaucracy's "direct ethical, professional
(and, sometimes, even legal) responsibility for implementing the
society's chief values and goals, in contrast to the vicissitudes of political experiences or of the arbitrary policies of the rulers" (Eisenstadt
1963, p. 159). Strategically they were in a good position to become
their own masters, bus the ruler could, if so minded, completely
subjugate them. Administrative reform movements aimed at something
between the two, namely, "at increasing the bureaucracy's efficiency
and at securing its impartial execution of its duties and its devotion to
the monarch's interests rather than to those of any other group."

> It is significant that, in many of the cases in which the bureaucracy
> became both independent and corrupt, movements of reform and
> change were initiated within the bureaucracy itself—at times in con-
> junction with the monarch and at times in opposition to him. Reform
> movements were more or less oriented to the prevention of the
> bureaucracy's being completely subjugated by any strong group
> within the society, to the establishment of a more equitable pattern
> of service provision, and to more efficient patterns of mobilizing
> resources by the bureaucracy (Eisenstadt 1963, p. 169).

To this day, the motives of loyalty to the polity, open access to
official employment, just and impartial administration, and efficiency
in the use of scarce resources can be found behind every reform of
the public bureaucracy, whether imposed from above (ruler), within

(bureaucracy), or outside (classes and interest groups). Officials are still tempted to divert their services to their own personal benefit or to the classes with which they are identified (usually urban middle classes) and away from governmental goals and the general interest. To prevent possible usurpation or abuse of power, governments subjugate their bureaucracies (even copying old methods such as recruitment of officials from weak and alien classes, staff rotation, strong arbitrary discipline, and social isolation). In this they can go too far and in the long run diminish efficiency, quash official initiative, produce overformalistic attitudes and activities, and encourage officials in subterfuge to avoid controls, without preventing bureaucratic "rapacity and self assertion" (Eisenstadt 1963, p. 279). But if they do not go far enough, the bureaucracy may close in on itself and confine positions to bureaucratic families as hereditary possessions.

Several conclusions of more general applicability can be drawn from the bureaucratic empires. Administrative reform was more likely to be accepted where (a) the bureaucracy maintained its service orientation either to the ruler or to the polity but not to their own classes or to self-aggrandizement; (b) the bureaucracy was permitted some degree of autonomy; (c) the bureaucracy maintained links with other classes and was not drawn exclusively from any particular class; (d) the bureaucracy developed a professional outlook with concern for recruitment standards, official conduct, and effective performance; (e) the bureaucracy implemented consistent policies.

Reform was likely to be rejected where (a) creativity and authority were limited to the rulers or bureaucracy; (b) officials used their positions solely as a means of enhancing their economic, political, and social standing; (c) the bureaucracy placed self-aggrandizement above other goals, or had too little or too much autonomy; (d) the rulers' goals and the aims of the major classes were incompatible, permitting the bureaucracy to become more autonomous and powerful as a regulative mechanism; (e) the middle social strata were small and weak; (f) the rulers became too dependent on conservative aristocratic forces; (g) the bureaucracy performed predominantly regulative activities. In time, the bureaucracy tended to become less subservient and more service-oriented to both rulers and major groups and, later still, more self-interested. At each juncture, reform movements were instituted to restore the previous position. Significantly successful reforms were the joint effort of the rulers and different classes, particularly the rising middle classes (Eisenstadt 1963, p. 292). Where reforms failed, the bureaucracy declined into a self-centered aristocratic body that could not accommodate different classes and so undermined the continuity of the political system.

Differences in class attitudes to administrative reform depended on whether the reforms were considered as strengthening or weakening the rulers and/or the bureaucracy; whether the anticipated benefits were expected to apply generally or to be confined to a select group; whether motivation was disinterested, professional, ulterior, selfish or corrupt; whether the methods conformed to tradition or broke new ground; and whether specific class interests were adversely affected without corresponding benefits. The need for reform was not self-evident nor were reform objectives obvious. Reforms involved a choice between alternative ends. They may have prevented maladministration but they also reduced civil liberties, suppressed creativity, brought fear and ill will, and strengthened bureaucratic power. They had important unforeseen consequences. For instance, the education system was distorted to meet bureaucratic entry requirements. The reformers had different aims in mind, mixed motives, conflicting methods, and separate areas of support. Finally their success depended on the extent of transformation advocated, the variety and intensity of support they could muster, their own strategic position within the political system, and the compatibility of their proposals with the rulers' political aims. These generalizations are no less applicable today.

DIFFERENCES IN APPROACH— THE PRECONTEMPORARY BUREAUCRATIC STATE

Modern European bureaucratic states descended from the bureaucratic empire or from the transformation of an intermediary form of polity that followed the disintegration of the bureaucratic empire. The penultimate stage in the evolution of the modern bureaucratic state in France, Britain, Russia, and the United States of America illustrates different approaches to bureaucratic reform. Each had a definite landmark that separated the contemporary bureaucratic state from the precontemporary—France experienced the Revolution and the Napoleonic Code in the same generation, Britain took a generation to accept the Northcote-Trevelyan proposals, the United States witnessed the assassination of a President which set in motion the first legal checks on the spoils system, and Russia had two revolutions in the same year—but no definite take-off point can be established to distinguish the precontemporary bureaucratic state from its administrative predecessor. The evolution of the bureaucratic state was lengthy and complicated, dating back to the decline of feudalism. In France and Russia the emergence of the absolute monarchy is as good a beginning as any, but in Britain it could be any one of numerous events before the Glorious Revolution. Only for the United States is there a precise date, namely, the Declaration of Independence. The details of administrative history are less important than the general processes at work. For this reason, the analysis abstracts a model of evolutionary processes in the continental European states until the Napoleonic wars, but thereafter differences in approach to bureaucratic reform are illustrated by details of administrative history.

To appreciate the process of bureaucratic evolution, one must keep certain background features in mind. (1) Population growth followed longer life expectancy with a decline in post-infant mortality. (2) More people found employment away from the land, in the towns, in trade, commerce and extractive industries, and in communications. (3) Wealth tended to replace land as the basis of power. (4) Religion lost ground and the church relinquished nontheological functions. (5) Living became more complex. (6) Administration advanced to meet problems presented by these trends, such as equipping armies for colonial conquest, registering land titles, and constructing large-scale public works. Changing patterns of trade, wealth, population, and administration enabled the monarch to outstrip his nearest rivals by exploiting his privileges, more particularly his ability to reward and punish, to raise and billet armies, to secure taxes, and to assume emergency powers. To assist him, his household staff was expanded by drawing on loyal supporters, educated people, and elevated bondsmen who were permitted to retain the perquisites of office where they had not already developed proprietary claims to their positions. His personal officials had much to gain in establishing him as the undisputed ruler over a defined area; and more and more people came to recognize the advantages of a stable central authority capable of maintaining order and warding off invaders.

Once the church, aristocracy, and burghers acknowledged the monarch's rule in temporal matters, his personal symbols became symbols of unity (and later, with modifications, national emblems) reinforced by "the idea of the reasonable will of a single Supreme Person, who, as God's vice-regent, connects and constitutes a community under a scheme of order which he creates, and for the realization of which he appoints a government and an administration" (Barker 1944, p. 6). New responsibilities entailed a larger staff, recruited through loyal contacts and self-perpetuating family dynasties willing to serve the monarch in return for the rewards to be gained. Nevertheless the monarch still worked largely through intermediaries such as local nobles, burgher contractors, chartered boroughs, and royal companies. Even allowing for low-level technology, bad communications, and widespread illiteracy, public administration was inefficient. Everything centered on the monarch's will, which in turn was subject to the whims and fancies of his court. The quality of his staff varied widely but their methods were primitive, and the whole system was so corrupt and wasteful that the monarch was perpetually short of funds. He devalued the currency, borrowed from moneylenders, imposed higher taxes, and sold more offices. The administration continued to expand at great cost. Eventually, he took steps to improve matters. Different items of public business he delegated to trusted advisers who began to specialize and consolidate the administration into broad general areas they could each supervise. The influence of the central administration was extended by giving an administrative role to local inspectors, competing with local autonomous bodies in providing governmental services, and by opening low-level positions to rising social classes.

After the French Revolution, monarchs could no longer claim divine selection. When they were deposed, it was nobility and bourgeoisie who restored them. Monarchs became increasingly dependent until they lost all pretense of absolute power and declined into mere figureheads of the bureaucratic state. Power passed to the major social classes which dominated the representative assemblies and the upper echelons of the bureaucracy. But while the representative assemblies later became responsible to a widening electorate, the senior official positions remained in the hands of the upper classes even after open entry and universal education broadened the basis of selection. State affairs were separated from the monarch's personal affairs and taken over by career professionals. Local affairs were placed under the control of locally elected bodies or agencies of the central administration. The functions of the state increased steadily; it replaced the church, nobility, and burghers in providing communal services. Public administration became more noticeable as the state demanded more of the citizen in return for its fast-growing services. Clear chains of command and accountability were established; regional units were created to link the center with the localities. The state bureaucracy was subjected to the law, and as public law developed, special bodies were created to adjudicate between the aggrieved citizen and the public official representing the impersonal power of the state. To counteract a return to absolutism, strict separation of powers was maintained (though it was still relatively easy to circumvent).

Accompanying functional and structural changes were financial reforms. Before they were instituted, no one had any idea what was collected, where the money went, or who spent it. Sums collected were not placed into a central fund but were designated for special purposes; before being used they could accumulate interest in the officials' private accounts. Substantial frauds and embezzlements were committed. Taxes, mainly indirect, fell on those least able to pay, while those who could pay were exempted or found it cheaper to pay bribes. Once the state assumed direct responsibility for functions previously contracted or farmed out, a more accurate picture of income and expenditure was possible. The separation of the monarch's personal finances from state finances encouraged the creation of a central fund into which all public monies could be placed. Officials who handled public monies were held accountable for missing sums. Accounting practices were improved and a strict check kept in annual statements of accounts preparatory to the imposition of taxes. Postaudit was introduced later, but already the finance minister could coordinate overall policy through financial controls.

These processes took up to two hundred years to complete. Some countries have not completed them yet, while others skipped a stage or two and leaped into the present with a revolution. No model, certainly not one so simplified as this, can do justice to the richness of European administrative history between feudalism and Napoleon. Each country went through its own cycle of development. What seems consistent is the underevaluation of administration although administrative performance was often a key factor in the power struggle. Strong administration could compensate for deficiencies in other directions. The monarch's rise to absolutism was often handicapped by his inattention to administrative performance; certainly in many cases maladministration was a contributory factor in his downfall. Similarly the monarch's rivals—church, nobles, burghers—could block the monarch's progress by their administrative ability and the image that could be derived from it. For instance, a province reputed to be ill-organized, divided, corrupt, and incapable of prompt action was more likely to attract the monarch's attention than one that had demonstrated sharp reaction to threat in the past. Naturally other factors predominated in the end. Where administration was undervalued, reform followed crisis. As long as administration performed according to low expectations without producing crisis, reforms were treated as harmless novelties adopted more to pacify their advocates rather than for their intrinsic value.

France. In any administrative history the French Revolution and the Napoleonic wars must receive special attention, as together they speeded the development of the modern bureaucratic state, the one giving it an ideological base while the other paraded its administrative superiority across Europe. French administrative reforms seemingly had transformed the shaky administrative apparatus of the *ancien régime* into Napoleon's efficient instrument. The advantage of victory from the viewpoint of historiography is that the victors can rewrite history to their advantage. It is likely, therefore, that administratively the *ancien régime* was probably better than it was made out to be and the post-revolutionary administration was not so different, certainly not so good as it was supposed to be. Both were faced with the same problem of how to fight a long succession of wars without exhausting the country. But the *ancien régime* was badly led toward the end and suffered from an inflation of sinecures and proprietary positions. The administration was concentrated in and about Paris; local administration was closely tied to the center through the *intendants*. Once the revolutionaries captured Paris, they controlled the state apparatus and could impose their reforms by using the existing system if they had no ready-made alternative of their own. Their original intention was to decentralize the state apparatus, but where they found that the centralized system was effective for implementing their policies, they postponed their plans for a new hierarchy of regional, district and communal bodies. Apart from local purges, abolition of sinecures and proprietary positions, and some reshaping of existing arrangements, the public bureaucracy survived the revolution relatively intact.

The crucial difference was the revolutionaries' stand that government was an instrument for effecting the general will of the people, not the particular will of the monarch. As the public bureaucracy was the collective property of the nation, it should be open to all citizens, not confined to a privileged elite around the monarch. These ideas were reflected in Napoleon's administrative reforms from 1799 to 1804. Napoleon himself maintained that he was merely the representative of the general will directing a state apparatus established for public service. His direction would be checked by the *Conseil d'État*, an expert body of professionals drawn from public life, which would design administrative ordinances and settle administrative disputes. It would also codify the law which would be binding on all, officials and citizens alike. Henceforth officials would be servants (not masters or interpreters) of the public interest. Beyond this, he personally insisted on efficiency. Officials were appointed according to loyalty, ability, rectitude and devotion to duty. The central administration was severely overhauled. Local administration was reorganized and central control continued through the prefecture system. The *prefects* were to be aided by local deliberative bodies and nominated *conseils de préfecture*, local versions of the Conseil d'État. Authority was depersonalized and made general, anonymous, and impartial through legal codes and administrative committees.

The Napoleonic administrative state was a strong, coherent, closely articulated affair. It closely resembled the administrative system first elaborated by the Romans. It too had many military features. A clear chain of command, duties clearly and definitively apportioned between authorities, a firmly established administrative hierarchy with the head of the state at the apex; specialised corps were created, authority was depersonalized, and individual officials were assigned explicit duties with personal responsibility both to their superior and to the law. . . . This insistence on personal action and personal responsibility is one of the hallmarks of the best French administrative tradition (Chapman 1959, pp. 26-27).

The French approach to administrative reform at this time can be summarized thus: *(a)* Administrative reform was considered an essential part of sweeping reforms in the polity. *(b)* Reforms followed revolution and took place during postrevolutionary difficulties, so that reforms conceived earlier were no longer practicable or desirable. *(c)* The general framework was untouched and the personnel remained relatively intact; reforms imposed from above and by outsiders were made acceptable by fundamental changes in ideology, the charismatic appeal of the principal reformer, and the sheer need to survive. *(d)* The new ideology was backed by formal changes, reorganizations, new forms of administrative unit, and discipline. *(e)* Though the main instrument was the law, the ideology brought new concepts of legitimacy and the innovation of codified administrative laws. *(f)* The reforms were retained because they were judged to be successful; certainly they were an improvement, despite their military overtones.

Prussia.   An interesting comparison can be made with the situation in Prussia following its defeat at Jena by Napoleon. Until that event, Prussia, not France, had been considered the pacemaker in administrative performance. Its administration was held as the example worth copying. But efficient practices, professional competence, discipline, honesty and devotion to duty had not been enough to offset superior numbers, abler leadership, better timing, quicker communications, novel methods and newer equipment. After the Seven Years War, the Prussian bureaucracy had been reformed by opening the higher echelons to the bourgeois, further centralization, and severe restraints on official freedom. Strict discipline had been enforced, work planned, responsibilities neatly defined, detailed professional codes compiled. This had contrasted markedly with administrations elsewhere, displaying action and orderliness until the Jena defeat revealed the other side of the coin—narrow and preconditioned outlook, overindulgence to old, incompetent comrades, and inflexibility.

The Jena defeat brought social reforms, but once the immediate threats to the polity receded, others did not follow. In administration, Stein and Hardenberg ignored Napoleon's reforms except in police and urban affairs. They replaced collective decision-making with a bureaucratic hierarchy; central control over local administration was strengthened through the *Landrat* and District Officer. In essence, the autocracy was barely touched by either these reforms or the 1848 Revolution. Concessions followed the latter in the form of a Constitution, representative assembly, and broadened base of political power. But the monarchs still dominated the governmental system, and the aristocracy ruled the public bureaucracy until the unification of Germany brought changes.

The Prussian approach over a longer period differed markedly from that of the French: *(a)* The reformers were part of the system, not outsiders. *(b)* The reforms were imposed from above and generally originated at relatively high levels. *(c)* The reforms were concessional, *i.e.*, they were unavoidable if the regime was to survive in war and revolution. *(d)* The reforms were pragmatic and empirical, lacking ideological motivation. *(e)* The reforms were resisted in principle but wholeheartedly supported after introduction. *(f)* Whether or not the reforms were judged a success, they were retained in deference to the supreme ruler in whose personal image government was conducted.

Russia. Unlike Germany, which became more liberal after 1870, the Russian Czar resisted any attempts to interfere with his absolutism. Within the huge Romanov empire, he was the largest single landowner, employer, and trader. He maintained extensive military, police, and espionage forces. The centralized bureaucracy, noted for its rigid protocol and procedures, was repressive and corrupt. The minimum demands of opponents to the regime, such as an eight-hour day and effective factory legislation, were considered challenges to the whole order. The revolutionary program of the *Communist Manifesto* was anathema. By the turn of the century, the crumbling of the autocratic edifice was evident in economic chaos, social disturbance, mass emigration, military defeat, and the 1905 revolution. The authorities were still strong enough to resist pressures for reform, and the opposition was too divided to succeed. The concessions made by the regime hardly affected the bureaucracy. But the 1913 economic depression and World War I certainly did. The state assumed new functions, took over much of industry, and administered the economy for war purposes. But the administration was unable to perform effectively; administrative chaos added to military defeat and political crisis. By the end of 1916, everything was virtually out of control. The first stage of the 1917 Revolution was relatively peaceful. The monarch was deposed and the representative assembly, conceded in 1905, took over the state apparatus while new leaders emerged in the government and militia. The Revolution was welcomed, with little resistance. But the revolutionaries were divided over what to do next; as the different groups began to act on their own initiative, the central controls began to break down. In October, the Bolsheviks made their forceful bid for power by seizing the key points. Their control of the state apparatus, military, and urban centers was disputed, and the effectiveness of the bureaucracy was diminished by desertion and passive resistance. Civil war, foreign invasion, and the revolts of minorities and peasants overshadowed ideas about administrative reform.

The Bolsheviks jettisoned their preconceived ideas of reform. In Marxist ideology, the state, as a tool of the bourgeoisie, had no place in the future society. During the dictatorship of the proletariat, the state would wither away as direct administration and collectivism gained ground. It was needed only for the repression of opponents by the majority of former wage-slaves. In 1917, however, the Bolsheviks were a minority imposing themselves on the majority. They had little idea what a dictatorship of the proletariat was supposed to achieve. They had so concentrated on conspiratorial tactics that they were not prepared for the responsibilities of government. They relied largely on the institutions they captured. They kept the state and retained the Czarist bureaucracy. Opponents deserted or were purged and their places either left vacant or filled from loyal supporters and neutral technocrats. The state apparatus was extended by nationalizing industries and land. Some Czarist measures were even reintroduced by the Bolsheviks for more effective control. These were improvisations while the new regime fought for its life.

Only after law and order returned to the country were ideas of administrative reform revived. Innovations made by the Bolsheviks were abandoned in favor of older forms. Experiments in direct administration and workers' control failed. In 1918 and again in 1921, Lenin admitted that the workers could not administer the state until they had been trained to do so. In *State and Revolution* he had already admitted that bureaucracy as such could not be destroyed. But it could be transformed, and to some extent this had taken place. The bureaucracy was in the grip of the Bolsheviks. The extension of the state apparatus had not altered radically the nature of governmental functions but opened new avenues for educated party cadres. Democratic centralization became the policy by which much of the administrative system of the previous regime was legitimized and perpetuated in the new regime. The remainder disappeared, and innovations such as economic planning, party control of the state apparatus, and new institutions (Council of People's Commissars, Central Executive Committees and the Central Bureau of Complaints and Statements, for example) were adopted along with less successful experiments.

In Prussia reform was preferred to revolution, but in Russia revolution was preferred to reform. The situation had declined to a point where nothing short of root-and-branch reforms would suffice. The Bolshevik approach can be summarized as follows: (a) Reform followed revolution. (b) The revolutionaries came largely from without the system. (c) Dissension among the revolutionaries as to the nature and extent of reform enabled the most radical to seize power by force and impose their uncompromising solutions. (d) Preconceived ideology collapsed when faced with reality. The state bureaucracy was not abandoned but strengthened. (e) Concentration on political ends and conspiratorial means left the revolutionaries without any alternative to the existing apparatus, even though they were pledged to abandon it. (f) The need for continuity foiled early attempts at revolutionary administrative changes. (g) Administrative reform was subordinated to other ends. (h) Dislocation limited action. (i) The reformed administration was accepted as a price of political revolution.

Great Britain. Absolute monarchy in Britain had come to an end with Cromwell. Thereafter power was exercised by the upper classes, which monopolized all influential positions although a few monarchs made spirited attempts to retain some freedom of action. The British situation differed from that in continental Europe in other ways too. The upper classes were not rigidly exclusive. The possibilities of invasion and revolution were not seriously considered until the nineteenth century and then without much conviction. Energies were absorbed in economic development rather than public administration. The pressures making for administrative reform elsewhere in Europe were less extensive. The common law tradition proved too strong for elaborate codification. The public bureaucracy rarely extended beyond London, as functions performed by central administrations in Europe were administered in Britain by strong autonomous local authorities. Doctrines of individualism and governmental nonintervention were also popular. A severe jolt was required to awaken the upper classes to the need for reform of the political and administrative systems, particularly an incompetent military, venal local government, an inhuman judicial system, and an inflated bureaucracy.

Between 1770 and 1870 the complacency of the upper classes was disturbed by foreign defeats (America, Napoleon, Crimea); fear of revolution (1830, 1848, 1870); riots (Peterloo, Luddites, Irish, Chartists); consequences of the agrarian and industrial revolutions (rural depopulation, urbanization, trade cycles, disease); and significant changes in the social structure. The course of reforms parallel to these events is chronicled in considerable detail elsewhere (see *Bibliographic Notes* and Finer 1956). By 1906, Parliament had been cleansed, and elections were honest, the judiciary was unimpeachable, local government was democratized and reputable, and the bureaucracy was fast developing a world-wide reputation. The transformation has been variously attributed to moral revolution, religious revival, Nonconformist conscience, middle-class influence, Victorian morality, crusading idealists, social reformers, and an exceptional period of systematic empirical research. Of importance was the upper-class attitude that perpetuated a self-image of gentlemen and amateurs brought up to rule, to give unselfish public service, and to shoulder the nation's burdens. This type of aristocratic rule, charismatic patrimony, worked well as long as the upper classes felt secure of their position, but once threatened they fought as hard as any aristocracy in warding off challenges; they gave away only what they could not keep. They divided opponents by exploiting differences among them. In crisis, they appealed to national unity and patriotism to reduce social demands. Little could shift them when they were determined to do nothing. Paradoxically, traditional forms have tended to last longer in Britain than in the former European absolutist monarchies. The British administrative style still reflects leadership by aloof amateur generalists, socially integrated with other elites and suspicious of trained professionals who have emerged from the ranks.

The British approach can be summarized as follows: (a) Administrative reforms were pragmatic; they had no ideological motive and few ideological trimmings. (b) Reforms were implemented to forestall more radical changes. (c) They were largely an internal affair, considered as technical details to be worked out by experts to meet a particular situation. (d) They were narrowly conceived, little attention being given to experiences and practices elsewhere. (e) They were incremental measures, the minimum necessary to solve specific problems. (f) They depended on individuals acceptable to the upper classes rather than on mass movements. (g) They were easily accommodated and incorporated into the system once they were accepted as unavoidable, though they met some passive resistance from reactionaries.

United States of America. The Americans started with a clean administrative sheet at federal level. They had the opportunity of creating a new organization, adopting the latest methods, and insisting on the highest personal standards. They chose to limit federal functions, which grew relatively slowly too. Isolationism and limited frontier wars reduced the need for a large standing militia, and economic liberalism dominated the open frontier. The major role in supplying supporting services fell on the states and on local governments, but gradually the federal government became a sizable employer and contractor. As elsewhere at this time, the aristocracy filled the upper echelons of the bureaucracy. Public morality was high; loyal, able, and devoted people filled public offices. Clear lines of control and responsibility were defined. The emphasis was on economy, ensured through periodic retrenchments, parsimonious remuneration, and critical self-analysis. Politics ruled, and the bureaucracy was used to advance party interests. The aristocratic exploitation of privilege and position came to be challenged by Jacksonian democracy, which held that all men should be entitled to hold public office and eligible therefore to exploit the privileges of office. Whatever its merits, it gave a theoretical justification for the spoils system.

The spoils system aided party cohesion and political stability. It also served to strengthen federalism, open the bureaucracy, and spread power. Habit, machine maneuvers, the alliance of politics and economics, and partisan advantage perpetuated it. The Civil War and postwar retrenchment exposed its shortcomings, and a series of public scandals revealed the detrimental effects on public morality. Civil War idealism and other mass movements carried over into reform movements that were aided by general alarm at public waste. Between 1865 and 1883 there was a ground swell of support for administrative reform, spearheaded by groups excluded from political influence by the spoils system and by moralists who wanted to raise public standards of morality. Their first real success at federal level came with the Pendleton Act, 1883.

The American approach was as culture-bound as the others that have been considered: (a) American tradition was innovative and experimental, stressing mobility and expectation of change, not (aristocratic) stability and caution. (b) Rapid change was absorbed by an expanding economic frontier, flexible social structure, and diversified, fragmented political processes; revolution was unlikely once the great majority identified themselves with the existing social system. (c) Reforms originated from both within and without the bureaucracy and found acceptance with equanimity. (d) Reforms had to be reconcilable with the role of the bureaucracy in the political process; administrative rationality alone was insufficient. (e) Within the political boundaries, officials were reform-conscious. (f) Reform movements stimulated public interest and prompted continuous efforts at administrative betterment.

Comparing these five different national approaches to bureaucratic reform, the following observations can be made: (1) Administrative reform is related to the specific cultural environment. No single approach is correct or better than any other. (2) Culture-bound approaches may not be exportable or, if they are, only to countries sharing general cultural features. (3) Though specific reforms may appear pragmatic and empirical, they are manifestations of ideological and ethical values. (4) Reform and compromise are related; the more fluid, flexible, and adaptable the system, the more easily reform can be accommodated and the less likely is revolution. (5) The differences in themselves are revealing—for instance, whether reforms are imposed from the outside or considered something that only insiders can understand; whether reforms are unavoidable concessions or minimum compromises. They raise more questions than they answer. How are reforms accommodated? What are the motives of reformers? Why are reforms considered necessary? What is the relationship between reform environment and strategy? To what extent are different approaches compatible? Which is better—continuous reform of an unobtrusive nature or sudden flurries of root-and-branch transformation? Should reformers act before acceptance or should they prepare the ground in advance?

UNAVOIDABLE REFORM—
THE NEWLY INDEPENDENT STATES

To manage public affairs today without resort to administrative reform entails either total disregard of efficiency, public opinion, and internal cohesion (a luxury that few regimes can afford) or a remarkable capacity to absorb change without incurring sharp divisions of opinion. The status quo is always behind what needs to be done. No sooner have the nerve centers responded to an altered situation and transmitted the new requirements than further changes overtake the solutions. For example, by the time new capital equipment has been installed and staff and clientele have gotten used to it, an advanced model has appeared, and the whole difficult process must be repeated. In trying to steer between the need for stability and continuity and the requirements of change, two main approaches are available. One waits for a crisis before taking any action. No excuse is needed for investigation and the occasion can also be used to tackle other matters that have long been suspected of needing attention. The public is reassured by the appointment of prominent, trusted, intelligent persons to investigate and to recommend reforms that might prevent repetition. During the inquiry the guilty parties can hastily make amends and anticipate the reform proposals. The assumption is that people can be trusted to do the right thing most of the time and that only in exceptional cases do reforms have to be imposed on incompetent administrators. The other approach endeavors to anticipate and prevent crisis through continuous inquiries by watchdog bodies armed with trouble-shooting powers. They can employ whom they want, choose their own study areas, and pressure offenders into adopting reforms. They have a vested interest in reform, if only to justify their existence, and must always be looking for trouble spots and promoting innovation.

The two approaches together can be extremely effective instigators of administrative reform. They require a pool of people trained to think objectively about administration and a supporting staff acquainted with the latest developments in administrative theory and practice. It is just those countries that most need administrative reform that are least equipped for it—the newly independent states that have emerged since World War II.

The fact of independence alone makes administrative reform imperative. A new state can no longer rely on foreign administrators and their imposed methods but must build its own indigenous administration borrowing what it can from the departing rulers and improvising the rest. Even when the colonial servants stay on to assist the new state and the former colonial power can point to the progress made under its aegis, the transition is traumatic. The new state has rebelled against that colonial rule, or the colonial power has decided to withdraw in view of impending rebellion, or the colonial power cannot afford to maintain its rule because of cost or international pressure, or the new state has been created to solve an international problem. The state can have a long precolonial history of nationhood, an indigenous culture barely touched by colonialism, and a strong desire to preserve some aspects of traditionalism, or it can be an artificial creation without any real basis for independent existence. Each is differently affected by colonialism; each is at a different stage of modernizing; each has its own peculiarities. Each will have to find immediate solutions to the following administrative probems:

1. Lack of sufficiently experienced administrators able to cope with independence.
2. Overhaul of the administrative system bequeathed by the colonial power, its organization, practices, and enshrined values.
3. Suspicion of all those who cooperated with or assisted the previous regime and jettisoned traditional culture sufficiently to be isolated from the great majority of citizens. They, for their part, demand access to vacancies on the basis of past experience which may be inadequate, inappropriate, outmoded, or similarly questionable on other grounds.
4. Demands to implement far-reaching development plans and national aspirations, and to enter new spheres of governmental activity, entailing a rapid expansion of public administration and the introduction of novel forms of public enterprise besides fundamental structural, institutional and behavioral changes in all social sectors.
5. Exaggerated bureaucratic powers, status, privileges and rewards, a legacy of colonial rule that may prove too costly for the economy, too strong for adequate political control, too damaging for nation-building, too cherished for balanced development.
6. Transition pains, accompanied by a decline in administrative performance, an inability to carry out new policies, breakdowns in law and order, non-cooperation, passive resistance, turmoil.
7. Public distrust of government; bad public relations; unresponsive and autocratic officials; citizenry unschooled in public affairs, bureaucratic ritual and officialese; inability to mobilize public involvement and cooperation.
8. Decline in public morality with departure of colonial rulers. Bad example set by new political leaders; nonsuppression of illegal activities, bribery, and corruption; absence of impartiality and abstract justice; collapse of professional self-respect and service motivation; revival of traditional practices.

9. Re-emergence of divisive forces, fragmenting public administration, intensifying rivalry, mutual suspicion, and non-cooperation.

10. Absence of proper planning basis through sheer lack of data, unreliable statistics, untrained people, unstable environment and no predisposition toward planning.

11. Too few successors, due to weak middle management and poor infrastructure, overdependence on small experienced elite too overworked to train successors or too distrustful and insecure to delegate to their staff or permit strong men around them.

12. Offers of overseas aid and assistance (with or without strings attached) of variable quality and aptness.

Each one of these problems would tax any administration. Meeting them all at once in most uncertain circumstances and with no past experience as a guide, the new state can only feel its way, reacting to events rather than controlling them according to an overall master plan. The present level of knowledge about administration in these new states does not allow adequate understanding, analysis, or prediction, let alone direction, of events. The solution in every case entails some kind of administrative reform, and the approach taken depends on the nature of the indigenous culture, the weight of tradition, the quality of the new leaders, the type of political regime established, the strength and diversity of internal and external opponents, and the availability and mobility of resources.

Reviewing the progress actually made by the newly independent states, their approaches fall into some regular patterns. (1) One small group of countries has made no pretense at administrative reform at all, either because the inherited colonial administration was deemed adequate and in fact has met whatever requirements were thrust upon it, or because the new leaders have become like their colonial predecessors and have seen no reason to alter the system bequeathed to them. (2) A second group has improvised reforms when the occasion has warranted. Theirs has been a purely pragmatic approach, relying on hunches and improvisation. In some cases the word "reform" was unknown for nobody consciously recognized his actions for what they were but only as a solution to a pressing problem. (3) A third group has consciously planned reforms and established formal machinery for the initiation and evaluation of reforms. These countries have established royal commissions, committees of inquiry, administrative reform commissions, ministries of administrative reform, and the like at national level, or they have invited continuing teams of investigation and consultants from outside (United Nations, former colonial ruler, or the United States) to review overall conditions. At a lower level, they have civil service commissions, interdepartmental committees, parliamentary committees, Organization and Methods teams, institutes of productivity, training centers, and similar bodies dealing with specific aspects. These may be integrated with national planning and terminal plans. (4) Finally, there have been exceptional cases where reform was imposed from the outside either because the state virtually collapsed and only outside assistance could keep it in existence, or because the state was felt to be so backward that nothing but outside assistance could lead it toward modernization.

Similarly the administrative reforms attempted fall into regular patterns: *(a)* Structural overhauls were concerned solely with formal arrangements, largely based on organizational theory and models of ideal-type bureaucracies. *(b)* Attitudinal changes dealt solely with informal arrangements such as the image of public administration, motivation and morale, service orientation, work values, status, and professional ethics. *(c)* Policy-making improvements included statistical aids, rational decision-making, efficient communications, performance evaluation, operations research, and scientific management. *(d)* Technical aids ranged from the simple replacement of muscle power with machine power to complex technological development in automatic data processing. *(e)* Administrative methods benefited from training, creativity, impariality, egalitarianism, depoliticization, delegation, and individual (as opposed to collective) responsibility. *(f)* In finance, special measures were taken to improve budget design and estimating and to prevent misappropriation and illegal expenditure, while steps were taken toward a merit system in staffing. *(g)* Some functional areas (defense, social services, economic development, and law and order) came in for more attention than others; some areas of the machinery of government (public corporations, local government, district administration) received priority. *(h)* New machinery was created to handle citizen grievances against the administration. What they were trying to do was to telescope some hundreds of years of the older states' experience into less than a decade, at the same time adopting all the latest innovations. In this, most were doomed to failure. They attempted too much too quickly and fell victim to their own maladministration. Failure only made matters worse by impeding progress, spreading disillusionment, creating new problems, and inciting reactionaries. Usually efforts would slacken, but sometimes failure would act as a greater spur. When reform virtually collapsed, more efficient elements, especially the military, might feel obliged to take over the whole system.

The success of administrative reform efforts depended on certain basic factors:

1. *A Predisposition Toward Reform.* In most new states there was abundant enthusiasm at the outset for the new regime and whatever reforms the new leaders deemed necessary.

2. *Political and Social Stability.* In some new states removal of the law and order imposed by the colonial regime was sufficient to expose suppressed hatreds that soon erupted into civil strife. Confronted with insurrection, the new regime had difficulty in absorbing reforms. To meet current crises the new leaders had to act quickly, without time to focus on new tasks on which the future might depend.

3. *Restraint.* After a long struggle for independence, there was a natural tendency to expect too much too quickly and to exaggerate what independence could achieve. Only on taking office could the new leaders know the sober reality, but they may have already been trapped by their overcommitment to new national symbols likely to waste precious resources.

4. *Information.* The new leaders needed access to the facts of governing, denied to them before independence by the colonialists and possibly afterwards by jealous officials or opponents within the bureaucracy.

5. *Literacy.* The confining of education to a small elite narrowed the possibilities of reform; crash mass education programs could detract from other equally important prerequisites of reform such as power supplies and communications.

6. *Consolidated Budgeting.* Some new states found their finances

in the same disorder as the precontemporary bureaucratic states; that is, the government did not have full control over revenues and expenditures. It was difficult to appropriate resources for national plans, let alone administrative reforms, when estimated revenues fell below expectations through leakages in collection and when planned expenditures were ignored by autonomous organs, expedient politicians, and powerful vested interests.

These prerequisites depended to a large extent on the nature of the colonial administration, especially whether its rule was imposed through traditional political mechanisms or by subordinate local administration based on foreign ideas and practices. Autocratic and repressive, it stressed symbols of ascendancy (for example, foreign flag, uniforms, identity cards) and incorporated indigenous elites. The interests of the colonial power overshadowed local interests; it could disguise its main motives by referring to civilizing and modernizing missions. The result in many cases was the exploitation of local resources, the curtailment of public services that entailed heavy investment, and the neglect of long-term needs by transient governors.

No matter how peaceful the local scene might appear, there were undercurrents of resentment against foreign rule. The principal objective of the colonial administration was to maintain law and order and root out trouble-makers. Their heavy-handed actions at times gave rise to justifiable grievances and smoldering anger. To protect colonial administrators from threats of violence, the administration was over-centralized, overformalized, and excessively detailed. For further protection, they maintained barriers between themselves and the indigenous people, encouraging a lack of trust and confidence within as well as without the colonial apparatus. They were further isolated by language differences and worked through intermediaries. As the lowest levels were staffed locally, the rulers really did not know what went on below and were largely ignorant of local criticism even if they cared about it. The more confident colonial regimes established representative institutions and other forms of indirect local participation in government, but still without access to real power.

The administration could not entirely prevent the formation of underground movements whose ultimate aim was the expulsion of foreign rule. Their leaders were forced into conspiratorial roles until the independence movement could emerge into the open. Their concern with revolutionary tactics excluded practically everything else, including considerations of what would have to be done if they were successful. The amount of support given to the underground and the extent of its infiltration into the administration were unknown despite loyalty tests. The administration's resources could always be used against it. For instance, infiltrators could use the communications network and connive at the disappearance of supplies. The rulers could only strengthen their controls in an endeavor to prevent the spread of conspiracy. The recognition of independence as a goal could come about only when the colonialists could envisage the local peoples actually ruling themselves, an attitude related to how closely the latter resembled the mother country. When the differences were wide, there might be no alternative to rebellion. Otherwise, the timing was chosen by the colonialists and transition planned and carried out so that the new state could still be dependent on the old country; at the other extreme, the colonial power could depart without regard to local circumstances, leaving chaos behind. In the main the governmental institutions that remained were a compromise between local and colonial desires, satisfactory to neither, and burdened with excessive circumlocution, unchecked bureaucratic growth, and amateurism.

Several different groups were responsible for administrative reforms during and after transition. First, there were the expatriates, the servants of the old regime who stayed behind to help the new leaders. Although they might be fond of the country and its people and feel responsible for its successful start, they had their own futures to consider. Encouragement from their own country and the new state, as well as attractive terms of employment, had to be balanced against insecurity. Relatively few chose to stay on, and they were not an unqualified success. Second, servants of an international body supervising the transition, though officially neutral observers, might assume a more positive role in advising, training, planning, and innovating. Time, however, was not on their side, and they did not necessarily possess the requisite qualifications. Third, the indigenous servants of the former regime were propelled into top positions simply because there was no one else. Not all of them were ready to take on larger responsibilities, however, and their collaboration with the colonialists might disqualify them in the eyes of the new political leaders who had suffered in the past at their hand. Fourth, leaders of the underground and the independence movement assumed the major responsibilities. For some, charisma could not overcome deficient education; while others, educated in the mother country or elsewhere, could never quite readjust to their homeland. They, too, fell victims to their own propaganda. When they faced the reality of office and saw their sweeping plans for social and economic development fail, they had to fight growing disillusionment. To cling to power, desperate leaders adopted the methods of the previous regime. Fifth, the leaders called in overseas experts, again not entirely a success. Some should never have been sent anywhere, while many others proved to be too culture-bound or too rigid in approach or ideology to understand the countries to which they were sent. There were also those who knew exactly what they were doing and what had to be done, but who were not given the support they needed by either their own government or the new states. They left behind plans, projects, and blueprints aplenty that might one day be taken up, but few people capable of understanding them, let alone translating them into practicalities.

With few exceptions, the process of administrative reform usually began before independence. Colonial powers felt obliged to give local leaders some experience in governing, perhaps educating them in the mother country. The colonial rulers might be instructed to search for local replacements and to institute crash training programs. Plans for reorganization and the consolidation of statutes might be discussed. But these preparations could be nullified by the unexpected nature of transition, which left no alternative other than continuing colonial arrangements. Much, again, depended on the relationship between the bureaucracy and their new overseers. The privileged elite in the previous regime had to accept a position subordinate to political upstarts who, in turn, had to learn how to guide the bureaucracy differently from a conspiratorial organization. Both bureaucracy and political elite, being unrepresentative, might be unresponsive to popular pressure, together exploiting power for personal advantage. Both might be ambitious and idealistic, with high expectations perhaps encouraging high performance and providing the images necessary for modernization. Both might imitate their incompetent and corrupt predecessors and be incapable of deciding on major issues. Both might underestimate the importance of sound public administration or the need for administrative reform. The process of administrative reform might therefore stop shortly after independence, but the impetus and excitement of independence might push continuing reform experiments. Thereafter, much would depend on bureaucratic response. In totalitarian regimes, officials were cowed into obedience, key positions were filled by loyal functionaries, and representative institutions were used as sounding boards and rubber stamps. By contrast, officials in bureaucratic polities ignored their new political overseers, whom they viewed as opportunists, ignorant demagogues, and corrupt self-seekers. But these extremes were rare. Most managed to work out a modus vivendi between politicians and officials. Sometimes politicians thrust reforms on unwilling officials; other times, officials thrust reforms on unwilling politicians who feared a genuinely efficient bureaucracy.

The optimum time for reform was during the honeymoon period when people were prepared to cooperate in a unique opportunity for reconstructing society. Thereafter, the longer the delay in introducing radical changes, the more difficult it was to justify them. Even when forceful action was taken at the outset, no one could predict the course of reform or the nature of changed circumstances in which it was implemented. Mistakes were made. Enthusiasm for reform waned as the practical difficulties became more apparent, and the resistance strengthened. Despite the ballyhoo surrounding reform attempts, little might be accomplished. Meanwhile a new generation barely able to recall colonialism would have to choose between accepting what had been done and finding a place within the existing system, or rejecting past efforts and advocating further attempts at transformation. Administrative reform can form part of the battleground between the radical younger generation and radical diehards of the first generation rulers, and the establishment supported by young conformists and opportunists. After a down swing, reform may re-emerge in a virulent form as the generations struggle for power. Bursts of reform might recur in generational cycles.

The major debate still revolves around the strategy for tackling administrative reform. The enthusiastic reformers, including young intellectuals who have studied administration in foreign countries, want a concerted attack on a broad front. They point to the examples of the Hoover Commissions in the United States of America, the Glassco Commission in Canada, and the general surveys conducted in the Philippines, New Zealand, and United Kingdom. They argue that improvised patching up of the machinery of government is no substitute for a thorough review of governmental administration within its environmental context, conducted by high level quality staff aware of the need for continuing efforts. The benign reformers, while acknowledging the validity of the argument, point to the practical difficulties, such as the lack of political support for wholesale investigations by outsiders into governmental processes; the scarcity of financial and human resources for conducting large-scale surveys that would be immune from the surrounding malaise; and the likelihood that such efforts would be wasted because the recommendations would be beyond absorption capacity and those actually implemented would be distorted and piecemeal, unless preceded by vast social and political changes. Reform advocates, they say, should lower their sights and be satisfied with limited gains in high priority areas. They should press for an adequate supply of umpires, trouble-shooters, bottleneck-breakers, procedural reformers and structural advisors (Appleby 1956, p. 52) within the administration and concentrate on the most promising areas, such as development administration or planning or fiscal administration. They should promote reform consciousness among those actually responsible for carrying out general administration.

The experience of the newly independent states emphasizes that, stripped of controversy, publicity, propaganda and gloss, what really counts in administrative reform is what the indigenous people themselves actually accomplish in permanently improved administrative performance. If outsiders impose their ideas, the situation is no different from what it was under colonialism. If outsiders implement their ideas but whatever they do collapses when they leave nothing is achieved. Foreign ideas and practices may need the accompanying foreign culture, which the indigenous people may be unwilling to accept. Every people is jealous of its own culture, which is its unique way of adapting to its environment. It will strive to preserve that culture unless it is convinced, through the same learning processes by which the culture is transmitted, that changes must be made. A distinction must be made between root-and-branch reforms in cultural pattern and superficial reforms accepted by a modernized elite that cannot enforce its will on anybody else. The modernized elite and the foreign experts may agree on reform programs but unless they can convince the masses, the reforms will be meaningless. Below the surface, far-reaching reforms in cultural patterns at the grass roots may be more important, but may still contrast with the values in modernized societies. However unorthodox reforms and practices may appear, the results in improved administrative performance may be much higher than if foreign examples had been copied. The cultural background is too important to be assumed.

THE ANTICIPATION OF REFORM—AUTOMATION

Administrative reform is timeless. The forces that prompt reform are always operating. The present contains the seeds of future reforms. For instance, while technological progress has improved the quality of life, it has also brought some fearful consequences such that in every age there have been people who have considered the price of progress too high. The hope of mankind is to be able to anticipate the results of technological innovation. With more information about current changes—causes, evaluation of good and bad points, resistance—it may be possible to prepare for the future and improve the quality of forecasting. Such is the motivation behind much of the work by social scientists in planning, social engineering, management science, public opinion research, psychological warfare, and planned change. Administrative reforms can perhaps be anticipated if the consequences of the wide-scale adoption of any of the technological innovations of the past two decades (*e.g.*, transistors, synthetics, space travel, supersonic flight, new vaccines) are followed through as far as possible. In this case study, automation has been selected.

Automation seems to be the obvious choice for administrative scientists, as it seems already to be heralding a Second Industrial Revolution. It worries small organizations which fear they will be driven out of existence, school-leavers and their parents who wonder which jobs and skills will become obsolete during their working life, managers and supervisors who feel their status threatened, semiskilled employees and craftsmen who are concerned about the security of their employment, and all those involved in industrial relations. Automation covers a number of different things—automatic production processes, change machines and transfer devices, automatic control devices and self-regulating machines, automatic data processing and "think" machines—that collectively are beginning to transform many industries and services, including the nature of administration itself. It is therefore an administrative reform in a much more obvious sense than other technological innovations such as the typewriter, which transformed clerical work, or the telephone, which transformed administrative methods.

This new form of administrative reform is accelerating, and soon every aspect of administration in modernized societies will be affected. Automation enables administrators to (1) substitute capital for high cost labor and supplement scarce labor; (2) improve the quality and quantity of products; (3) overcome problems of hazardous human work; (4) undertake new experiments, services, and products; (5) meet excess demand, backlog of work, and outstanding orders; (6) integrate work processes for more effective performance; (7) standardize goods and services; (8) economize on nonlabor costs; (9) relocate plant and activity; (10) enable work beyond human capacity to be undertaken; (11) centralize decision-making, forecasting and simulation; (12) make information more accessible; and (13) appear innovative and enterprising. These advantages may be exaggerated while the corresponding disadvantages may be unknown or vague, hardly competitive with the propaganda disseminated by producers of automative machinery. The only obstacle to its further spread would appear to be ignorance of its potential. But experience has been variable. There have been amazing successes, but there have been disastrous failures too, cases where large, costly automative machines have been left idle or have performed, expensively, simple tasks better done in conventional ways. Automation may enable man to explore space, work the seabeds, and eliminate hazardous tasks, but it also involves high safety risks and dependence on faultless construction and operation. Stripped of fantasy, the science-fiction writers who predict a grim future for man subject to automative machines that out-think him, or forecast a paradise where automative machines do all the work, may be indulging in the kind of long-range speculation that is needed.

The moral aspects of automation are rather confused. Automation is justified because production should be higher, quicker, and more efficient; clients should be served more efficiently, speedier, and more uniformly; administration should be more rational. On a higher plane, justification is found in higher living standards, more leisure time, greater freedom to enjoy the fruits of one's labor, and the reduc-tion, perhaps the elimination, of physical labor. On the other hand, machines may be preferred to men because they are easier to handle. They do not strike, absent themselves without reason, ask for pay in-creases, or have psychological problems. They do not become tired or bored, and they make fewer mistakes, never forget, and require no retraining (Buckingham 1961, p. 40). Men can be freed from burden-some labor to devote themselves to better things without diminishing output. But men are better than machines still in many areas; even if they were not, they might still be cheaper to employ than machines. The greater use of machines only accelerates the demand for labor in designing and constructing machines, controlling their operations and repairing defects, and distributing the products. Man must work in order to keep his physique in shape and to fulfill his urge for activity, and even if these can be accomplished during leisure time, there is no guarantee that he will do so. The moral implication is that the work ethic should be replaced by an aristocratic concept of leisure as advocated by the elite of ancient Greece, for whom slaves (= machines) did the work. Is technology or man the independent variable?

Automation will eventually transform society and most social in-stitutions. Already it is transforming the workplace (whether factory or office), and soon it will transform the classroom and the home. It is transforming employment patterns, skills, apprenticeship systems, and the occupational composition of the labor force. It will soon transform the education system, consumer expectations, location of industry, transportation, and leisure pursuits. It is transforming working conditions, organizational situations, functions, managerial decision-making, and career expectations. It will soon transform research methods, the status of the social sciences, planning techniques, and libraries. It is transforming occupations, professional qualifications, job requirements, conditions of employment. It will soon transform the social structure, ownership patterns, class divisions, and locus of power. Automation is thus something quite different from the acceleration of change. Once it has been adopted, things can never be the same again. It would be utopian to expect that automative machinery could be abandoned after people had experienced its advantages.

Those who support or object to automation are fairly easy to recognize. In support are obviously all those who stand to gain appreciably from the spread of automation: *(a)* manufacturers and merchants of automative machinery; *(b)* employers with high-cost labor (in terms of remuneration and productivity), permanent labor deficiencies, and dangerous productive processes; *(c)* organizations experiencing a steep rise or identifiable long-term increase in demand; *(d)* monopolists who can meet the costs by exploiting their hold over the market; *(e)* producers of standardized services and products; *(f)* large-scale organizations which can afford to amortize the investment over a correspondingly longer period; and *(g)* innovative managers and specialists whose personal careers will be enhanced. Against are: *(a)* manufacturers of conventional machinery who are unable to switch production and to maintain demand; *(b)* employees whose skills and training have become obsolescent and who see no immediate alternative employment; *(c)* leaders of employee organizations whose membership must decline and eventually disappear; *(d)* small businesses and *(e)* conservative managers unable and unwilling to adapt to innovations. So far there have been relatively few clashes, partly because the two groups have been able to avoid one another altogether except in local skirmishes; partly because the preparations for automation have given both sides ample time to adjust; partly because an inflationary world economy has given sufficient alternatives to absorb dislocation, again except in local circumstances; and partly because both sides have been prepared to compromise. The countries in which automation has taken hold had already implemented social welfare policies capable of dealing with localized disturbances and cushioning the worst effects of temporary dislocation.

The political battles over automation have thus been somewhat tame. But as automation spreads, more people will be directly affected and resistance will stiffen. The politics of automation will toughen and pressures will mount for public authorities to intervene and settle the major issues. First, both sides will demand firmer guarantees concerning full employment, economic expansion, political and social stability, and financial security. One side will seek protection against wildcat strikes and other disputes that could threaten to halt automated plant, while the other side will seek protection against dismissals and downgrading. Protection will also be sought by small businesses, craftsmen, unemployed professionals, and traditional industries. Second, public authorities will be called upon to decide the extent of investment in automation, regulations, licensing, and the provision of public utility services for automated plants. Third, other public services will need extensive revision. For instance, the education system will have to be overhauled, particularly in regard to adult education and retraining. Higher incomes and increased leisure will increase the demand for such public facilities as parks and nature reserves and greater public assistance for cultural and entertainment activities. Public bodies will have to investigate the effects of automation on health and society; if the shift system spreads, the public authorities will have to revise their ideas about opening hours, public transportation, and protective services. Each of these will involve political struggles cutting across existing party lines.

At the organizational level, too, the politics of automation will intensify. Power will shift from the rule-of-thumb managers to those who understand automation, programming and planning, and management services. These in turn, will lose some of their power to the scientists, technicians, and researchers. The advantages of size and centralization will encourage combination and integration. As amortization becomes more important, the elimination of uncertainty through tie-ups with competitors, suppliers, and consumers will be encouraged. White-collar unionism will overtake blue-collar unionism, general or industrial unions will replace craft unions, professional organizers will replace the elected union official. These tendencies will be resisted by those who stand to lose by them and even by those who might be expected to gain most from automation, namely, employees who work in hazardous places.

So much can be anticipated from current trends. But tomorrow's innovations, accidents, and achievements cannot be known. There are severe limitations on the preparations that can be made for automation. Naturally, it is easier to prepare for the short-run than the long-run. The result of past experiments are available, and expectations about current and contemplated projects are known. Automation does not occur in isolation, but presupposes comprehensive planning. Advanced preparations are being made by organizations and by the manufacturers and merchants of automative machinery, public authorities, and universities. What is badly needed is an international sorting house to collect scattered information and to promote projection studies. It should not prove difficult to select one body or group of bodies in every country to carry out functions similar to those required of the United States Secretary of Labor under Section 102 of the Manpower Development and Training Act 1962 (Public Law 87-415), to

> evaluate the impact of, and benefits and problems created by automation . . . establish techniques and methods *for detecting in advance* the potential impact of such developments; develop solutions to these problems . . . promote, encourage, or directly engage in programs of information and communication concerning manpower requirements, development and utilization, including prevention and amelioration of undesirable manpower effects from automation [italics added].

The further application of automation will not be decided by philosophers but by economists at organizational level and politicians at national level. So far the swiftest application has been in areas—security, national prestige, retaliatory power—where economic costs have been secondary. Otherwise profit has been the main consideration, and the most profitable areas have not necessarily coincided with communal needs. The question that will receive attention is whether profit should continue as the main criterion or be supplanted by other criteria such as opportunity cost, elimination of physical labor, and the relief of domestic drudgery. The availability of capital will remain the dominant factor in any event. Even though automation will become cheaper, it will continue to have a profound effect on economic structure and stability, foreign exchange (especially if the principal automative merchants continue to be American), and trade practices. In the future, the pace of application may have to be controlled through subsidies, tax rebates, concessions in foreign exchange trans-actions, duties, and even temporary bans on production and import of automative machinery.

Automation has caused concern mainly for its impact on employ-ment. So far, little local displacement of labor has occurred because automation has been too costly to adopt on a large scale and has been largely supplementary, not substitutive. Displaced employees have been found work elsewhere within the plant, or strong employee organizations have forced employers to retain unproductive surplus employees. Future policies will have to ensure that alternative employ-ment is available, more particularly that *local* unemployment does not persist. Of the four main causes of local unemployment, nonreplace-ment and attrition can be corrected by introducing alternative em-ployment in the area or moving the unemployed elsewhere. Immobility is more difficult to cure, and the remedies are varied and politically contentious (for instance, fair employment practices, government pur-chase of owner-occupied accommodation, subsidized rents, attack on early school dropouts). The last cause—changes in required skills—presents the additional problems of job expectations, career pat-terns, training, and preservation of handiwork crafts. From the employment angle, automation may be a mixed blessing. On the one hand, it may open new avenues for the employment of people at present excluded from work, particularly physically handicapped per-sons and mentally retarded adults who may be better adapted to machine-minding once the physical labor has been removed. Or society may be able to afford to do without so many people at work and narrow the lower and upper age limits of the labor force. On the other hand, automation will entail far-reaching changes in demands for skill with more emphasis on adaptive than fixed skills, on the ability to absorb, organize and interpret information than manual dexterity, on universalistic professional skills than employment requirements, and on new skills than conventional methods (Bright 1958). The day will come when employees will have to unlearn much of what they have been taught. This will raise serious questions about the education system, industrial training, job selection, the older worker and manpower forecasting.

Working conditions will change with the spread of automation, as already seen in the erection of new buildings, clean and thermostatically controlled not for employees but for the machinery they operate. Noise factor may be eliminated with better sound-proofing and similarly problems of routinized work, monotony, stress, and job interest may be solved in time. Other trends can be expected. (1) Hours of work are likely to be reduced and will not be so confined to daylight hours. (2) Remuneration will become increasingly divorced from production or direct human effort. Piece rates will give way to national standard wage patterns. (3) Job evaluation and performance will lose much of their value. (4) It will be harder to progress on the basis of experience on the job. (5) Work relations will be humanized much more. (6) Emotional stress will rise in the transition stage, and labor relations may be embittered by mishandling on both sides. Employee organizations may obstruct and sabotage automation. They may fail to protect their members, and the employees may take independent action. Such failures have occurred in the past where management has acted unilaterally and where employee organizations have been badly led. More common has been a mutual arrangement whereby both sides have sought the best deal for employees, usually at the expense of unrepresented third parties (consumers, taxpayers, overseas clientele). In the future, it may be necessary for the government to intervene to protect third parties, to prevent employees from being entirely dependent on the bargaining skill of their leaders and the concessions of their employers, to provide mediation and arbitration, to police agreements, and to prevent unofficial individual action.

Even with automation, people will still be judged largely by the work they do. As in automated processes this becomes difficult, so people will tend to identify themselves more with the place of work or the name of the employer. With standardization of working conditions, status symbols or minute differentiations between levels of work will become more important, and the recognition of craftsmanship and workmanship will decline. Where automation tends to increase routine, employees are likely to create their own variety on the job, (e.g. loafing, talking, militant unionism), which may call for more relaxed supervision or for facilities to relieve boredom. Perhaps increased job turnover can be expected too, within a bureaucratized personnel framework. In terms of social stratification, automation may therefore lead to greater rigidity, but social values may change and a person's employment may not count so highly in social status.

The total impact of these trends on administration will be far-reaching without transforming the nature of administration itself. But administrative *processes* are likely to be altered radically, and principal changes will probably include (1) transformation of financial and personnel administration, production control and stores, sales and record-keeping; (2) integration of units, combination of processes, centralization; (3) greater rationalization at all levels, with increased emphasis on planning and continuity, and more insistence on conformity to plans; (4) expansion in the use of management sciences both in programmed and nonprogrammed decisions; (5) reduction in the number of levels of responsibility; (6) greater responsibility for first-line supervisors (whose job will no longer be to see that people work but that the machines work and are properly attended); and (7) automation used as an excuse to implement unrelated administrative reforms.

If these predictions are correct, the structure of administration will alter radically. Top administrators will have to know how to use the new management aids and learn to deal with increasingly complex problems and more centralized organization. The most profound reforms will be found, however, at middle management level where much of the routine decision-making will be taken over by the computers and those skilled in the new management sciences. Much specialized policy-making will be integrated and/or resumed by top administrators. Intermediary agents at central and regional locations will be bypassed unless they find other functions to perform that cannot be handled better elsewhere. On the other hand, top administrators may be more prepared to delegate to middle managers who speak the same technical and administrative language. Functions formerly performed at middle management level will be pushed downward into the top ranks of the supervisors and local managers below the programmers, research analysts, and automative specialists. Technical competence will assume a greater importance at this level, as will human relations.

During these transformations, administrative philosophy will change, too. As it becomes possible to integrate administration, less stress will be placed on administrative subdisciplines. The maximum use of information and resources may well further entrench such administrative values as efficiency, productivity, rationality, impartiality, and betterment. Certainly there will be more stress on a scientific and quantitative approach. Administration may well divide between problem-solvers and functional specialists, with perhaps a tendency toward parochialism in the sense that processes may become more important than product. The bureaucratic model with its emphasis on stability, rational-legal authority, and hierarchy may be modified by stress on adaptation (through creative-innovative processes), collaboration (conflict avoidance, inculcation of harmony), horizontal differentiation, and problem-solving, which may be accommodated within the bureaucratic framework or may lead to new forms of organization. Education will be a life-long process, and administrators will have to be retrained more often. Above all, the individual may gain, for he will no longer be considered an appendage to a machine or a work-hand but a potential source of innovation.

Even in such pure conjecture, some points of significance for administrative reform do arise. First, administration, like politics, is an art of the possible. As it is impossible to tell which current developments are likely to tend to administrative reform, it may be pointless to follow up every possibility. Even if the few possibilities can be detected at an early stage, the unknowns are so many that it would be far simpler to let things develop and tackle the problems as they arise. This is, in fact, the crisis approach to reform, and it can be countered by the anticipating watchdog approach, made easier by the advent of automation. Second, speculative attempts to anticipate the future can expose existing defects that otherwise pass unnoticed. Third, existing information exists that, if properly coordinated and analyzed, can lead to successful prediction. Events which now trap the unsuspecting could be forecast in advance and plans prepared accordingly. Fourth, it may be possible to anticipate reforms and to rationalize reform processes, and ultimately, to institutionalize reform. Some researchers, like Simon, are currently thinking on these lines and conducting feasibility tests (see *Bibliographic Notes*).

CONCLUSION

Cases of administrative reform past, present, and future indicate that there are elements of universality. Reform, by its very nature, is controversial and it becomes more controversial the greater the number of people affected. Their attitudes are related to personal disposition, general political outlook, class background and interest, and the extent of personal involvement. It may not be possible to predict with complete accuracy the stand that will be taken by a particular individual but a pretty shrewd guess can be made; in time the guesswork may be eliminated as far as a group response is concerned. Culture is the all-important variable that tends to be taken too much for granted. Universals deduced from case studies may be no guide to action if cultural diversity is of much greater importance and if the universals change over time. Reformers share little in common except a belief in betterment by human action, and their reforms do not always produce the expected results.

These fairly obvious conclusions do not provide a practical handbook suitable for all occasions. Nor do they lead to general theories about society or human behavior. Yet the term "administrative reform" continues to conjure up visions of perfection and order. If these cases show anything, it is that reform may detract from such goals and that as a universal panacea it is extremely limited. Administrative reform may be nothing more than the shock effect of cold water thrown over a drunkard—it may sober him up but it will explain little about how he became intoxicated, the motives causing him to drink excessively, the effect of his disorderly behavior, and the course of rehabilitation necessary for permanent cure. It may not cure but at least it does not kill.

The cases may not reveal anything particularly profound about administrative reform, but they do suggest many avenues of further research. They are only a beginning; they raise more questions than they answer. They may not have been good examples, being too diverse, too broad, too dated. Other cases, such as an expanded account of administrative reforms undertaken in a newly independent state or a detailed study of a public inquiry leading to reforms, might produce different perspectives of greater practical value. It may be that the crucial factors cannot be recorded by case studies. Reformers may fear that revelation of their motives, intentions, plans, and difficulties might defeat their current attempts at reform or stiffen the opposition, and anything recorded after the event may fall into research and methodological difficulties. The results to date are encouraging. Already it is possible to discern a common cycle of reform processes, a check list of obstacles impeding reform, and glimpses of a possible theory of administrative reform, which are the main focus of attention in the remaining chapters.

BIBLIOGRAPHIC NOTES

Excellent case studies of administrative reform can be found in collections of essays, case study programs, and extended articles in major academic journals (see the *General Bibliography* following the last chapter). Wartime experiences prompted many to record their experiences of unusual problems in times of stress (*e.g.,* Leighton 1945) and these were followed by the reminiscences of former colonial rulers and technical experts concerned with establishing law and order in newly independent states (*e.g.,* Goodsell 1965). Retired businessmen and public officials have been more reticent, presumably because they cannot (or are forbidden to) relate the full story of the reforms in which they have participated. Governments and large-scale organizations have been generous in publishing the results of internal inquiries and evaluative summaries of efforts to overcome maladministration. The growing profession of management consultancy is accumulating valuable records even if these must remain confidential for the time being. The case studies selected for this listing are more general, to illustrate universal features of administrative reform.

The generalized account of administrative reform in the premodern bureaucratic empires is based largely on Eistenstadt's analysis, based in turn on an extensive literature listed in his book. In addition, use was also made of E. Balazs, *Chinese Civilization and Bureaucracy* (New Haven, Yale University Press, 1964); Braibanti 1966; Liu 1959; S. J.

Shaw and I. F. Hank, *Ottoman Bureaucracy* (Bloomington, Indiana, Comparative Administration Group, 1967); and K. A. Wittfogel, *Oriental Despotism* (New Haven: Yale University Press, 1957).

The precontemporary bureaucratic state has received fairly wide coverage in the history of public bureaucracies of European and English-speaking countries (*e.g.,* Finer 1956), though for specific reforms or periods of reform they are rather weak on details. General accounts are contained in Barker 1944, Chapman 1959, and Marx 1957. The administrative aspects of the French Revolution are somewhat obscure, and consistent accounts have to be gleaned from diverse sources, such as Lord Acton, *Lectures on the French Revolution* (London: Macmillan, 1930); G. Lefebvre, *The French Revolution,* 2 vols. (London: Routledge and Kegan Paul, 1964); R. Postgate, *Revolution from 1789 to 1906* (New York: Harper, 1962); A. de Tocqueville, *The Old Regime and the French Revolution* (New York: Doubleday, 1955); and general histories of France during the Napoleonic Wars. The Prussian situation, in contrast, has been well recorded by R. A. Dorwart, *The Administrative Reforms of Frederick William I of Prussia* (Cambridge: Harvard University Press, 1953); H. Jacob, *German Administration Since Bismarck* (New Haven: Yale University Press, 1963); and H. Rosenberg, *Bureaucracy, Aristocracy and Autocracy: The Prussian Experience 1660-1815* (Cambridge: Harvard University Press, 1958). General histories of Prussia and Germany and of their armies also refer to administrative reforms.

As with the French Revolution, the administrative aspects of the Russian Revolution and the Czarist and Bolshevik regimes before and after 1917 have been neglected. The great Russian novels do provide moving illustrations of the Russian bureaucracy and how the administrative culture has been altered. For the details, reference has been made to J. A. Armstrong, *The Soviet Bureaucratic Elite* (London: Stevens, 1959); J. R. Azrael, *Managerial Power and Soviet Politics* (Cambridge: Harvard University Press, 1966); R. L. Braham (Ed.), *Soviet Politics and Government* (New York: Knopf, 1965); E. H. Carr, *The Bolshevik Revolution,* 3 vols. (London: Macmillan, 1950-53); W. H. Chamberlin, *The Russian Revolution 1917-1921* (New York: Macmillan, 1935); M. Fainsod, *How Russia is Ruled* (Cambridge: Harvard University Press, 1964); D. Granick, *The Red Executive* (London: Macmillan, 1960); J. M. Hazard, *The Soviet System of Government* (University of Chicago Press, 1957); V. I. Lenin, *State and Revolution* (New York: International Publishers, 1935); L. Schapiro, *The Communist Party of the Soviet Union* (New York: Random House, 1959) and *The Government and Politics of the Soviet Union* (London: Hutchinson, 1965); S. M. Schwartz, *The Russian Revolution of 1905* (University of Chicago Press, 1966); A. B. Ulam, *The Bolsheviks* (London: Macmillan, 1965). A disappointing feature of the fiftieth anniversary of the Russian Revolution was that works produced for the occasion added little to what was already known about the administrative aspects.

The British Civil Service still awaits a worthy detailed history. Quantity does not compensate for lack of quality. Good accounts are contained in D. N. Chester and F. M. G. Willson, *The Organization of British Central Government 1914-1956* (London: Allen and Unwin, 1959); E. Cohen, *The Growth of the British Civil Service 1780-1939* (London: Allen, 1941); E. N. Gladden, *The Civil Service: Its Problems and Future* (London: Staples Press, 1948); R. K. Kelsall, *Higher Civil Servants in Britain* (London: Routledge and Kegan Paul, 1955); J. D. Kingsley, *Representative Bureaucracy* (Yellow Springs, Ohio: Antioch Press, 1944); W. A. Robson (Ed.), *The Civil Service in Britain and France* (New York: Macmillan, 1956). The best are historical articles which appear in *Political Quarterly* and *Public Administration*. The Federal Civil Service of the United States of America is better served by the L. D. White series, *The Jeffersonians* (1951), *The Jacksonians* (1954), *The Federalists* (1956), *and The Republican Era* (1958), all published by Macmillan (New York), and by Van Riper 1958. Otherwise, the literature suffers from failings like those of the British writings, but valuable material can be found in the *Annals of the Academy of Political and Social Science*, *American Political Science Review*, *Public Administration Review*, and *Public Personnel Review*.

With the establishment of new states every year, there seems to be no end to publication possibilities in development administration. The imperial legacy is recorded in J. Almada, *Colonial Administration by European Powers* (London: R.I.P.A., 1947); M. B. Brown, *After Imperialism* (London: Heinemann, 1963); W. R. Crocker, *On Governing Colonies* (London: Allen and Unwin, 1947); J. S. Furnivall,

Colonial Policy and Practice (London: Cambridge University Press, 1948); L. Hazard, *Empire Re-visited* (Homewood: Irwin, 1965); J. A. Hobson, *Imperialism—A Study* (London: Allen and Unwin, 1938); R. Maunier, *The Sociology of Colonies*, ed. by E. O. Lorimer (London: Routledge and Kegan Paul, 1949); J. Plamenatz, *On Alien Rule and Self Government* (London: Longmans, 1960); A. P. Thornton, *The Imperial Idea and its Enemies* (London: Macmillan, 1959); and I. Wallerstein, *Social Change—The Colonial Situation* (New York: Wiley, 1966). The constant threat of military rule after independence is analysed by H. Daalder, *The Role of the Military in Emerging Countries* (Mouton: 1962); J. J. Johnson, *The Role of the Military in Underdeveloped Countries* (Princeton University Press, 1962); and S. E. Finer, *The Man on Horseback* (London: Pall Mall Press, 1962).

The post-independence problems of new states are the concern of most current journals, especially *Community Development, Comparative Studies in Sociology and History, Economic Development and Social Change, Human Organization, International Development Review, International Social Science Journal, Journal of Administration Overseas, Journal of African Administration, Journal of Modern African Studies, Social Forces, Social Problems*, and *World Politics*. Studies with direct bearing on governmental and administrative problems include H. F. Alderfer, *Local Government in Developing Countries* (New York: McGraw-Hill, 1964); G. A. Almond and J. S. Coleman (Eds.), *The Politics of Developing Areas* (Princeton University Press, 1960); G. A. Almond and S. Verba, *The Civic Culture* (Princeton University Press, 1963); R. E. Asher (Ed.), *Development of Emerging Countries* (Washington D. C.: Brookings Institution, 1962); Esman 1963; M. J. Esman and F. C. Bruhns, *Institutional Building in National Development* (Philadelphia: University of Pennsylvania Press, 1965); L. P. Fickett, *Problems of the Developing Nations* (New York: Crowell, 1966); Finkle and Gable 1966; Hanson 1959; J. H. Kautsky, *Political Change in Underdeveloped Countries* (New York: Wiley, 1962); M. Kriesberg, *Public Administration in Developing Countries* (Washington D.C.: Brookings Institution, 1965); LaPalombara 1963; J. LaPalombara and M. Weiner (Eds.), *Political Parties and Political Development* (Princeton University Press, 1966); L. W. Pye, *Politics, Personality and Nation Building* (New Haven: Yale University

Press, 1962); L. W. Pye (Ed.), *Communication and Political Development* (Princeton University Press, 1963); L. W. Pye, *Aspects of Political Development* (Boston: Little, Brown, 1966); N. Raphaeli (Ed.), *Readings in Comparative Administration* (Boston: Allyn and Bacon, 1967); F. W. Riggs, *The Ecology of Public Administration* (Bombay: Asia Publishing House, 1961); F. W. Riggs, *Administration in Developing Countries* (Boston: Houghton Mifflin, 1964); E. Shils, *Political Development in The New States* (The Hague: Mouton, 1966); W. J. Siffin, *Politics and Planning* (Bloomington, Ind.: Comparative Administration Group, 1966); Siffin 1957; P. E. Sigmund (Ed.), *The Ideologies of the Developing Nations* (New York: Praeger, 1963); Swerdlow 1963; Symonds 1966; Waterton 1965; R. L. Watts, *New Federations: Experiments in the Commonwealth* (Oxford: Clarendon Press, 1966); R. E. Wraith and F. Simpkins, *Corruption in Developing Countries* (London: Allen and Unwin, 1963); K. Younger, *The Public Service in New States* (New York: Oxford University Press, 1960).

Country studies can be divided into three major areas.

(a) Middle East and North Africa. Many of the new states in this area retained their traditions under foreign rule, and the influence of the Ottoman Empire and Islam is noticeable throughout the area. General area studies have been completed by R. Dankwart, *Politics and Westernization in the Near East* (Princeton University Press, 1957); R. E. Ashford, *National Development and Local Reform* (Princeton University Press, 1967); M. Halpern, *The Politics of Social Change in the Middle East and North Africa* (Princeton University Press, 1963); M. Harari, *Governmental Problems of the Near and Middle East* (Englewood Cliffs: Prentice-Hall, 1962); D. Lerner, *The Passing of Traditional Society: Modernizing the Middle East* (New York: Free Press of Glencoe, 1965); W. R. Polk (Ed.), *Development Revolution* (Washington D.C.: The Middle East Institute, 1963). The situation changes so rapidly that country books are soon outdated. Those with a more lasting content include R. E. Ashford, *Political Change in Morocco* (Princeton University Press, 1961); I. Bashir, *Planned Administrative Change in Lebanon* (Beirut, 1965); G. Grassmuck and K. Salibi, *Reformed Administration in Lebanon* (Ann Arbor: University of Michigan Press, 1964); M. Berger, *Bureaucracy and Society in Modern Egypt* (Princeton University Press, 1957); M. Khadduri, *Modern*

Libya (Baltimore: The Johns Hopkins University Press, 1963); J. B. Kingsbury and T. Aktan, *The Public Service in Turkey* (Brussels: I.I.A.S., 1955); G. Stevens, *Reform and Power Politics in Iran* (New York: Foreign Policy Association, 1951).

(b) Africa. Whatever social unity binds the Middle East and North Africa, no semblance exists in Africa south of the Sahara. Much of the literature is still contributed by outsiders such as T. L. Hodgkin, *Nationalism in Colonial Africa* (New York University Press, 1957); but there is a significant increase of home products such as A. L. Adu, *The Civil Services in New African States* (London: Allen and Unwin, 1965). There are few country studies which have not been outdated by events. The West Coast has attracted most attention with Apter 1955, 1961; L. F. Blitz (Ed.), *The Politics and Administration of Nigerian Government* (London: Sweet and Maxwell, 1956); J. P. Mackintosh, *Nigerian Government and Politics* (London: Allen and Unwin, 1966); R. O. Tilman, *The Nigerian Political Scene* (Durham: Duke University Press, 1962).

(c) Asia. Few Asian countries were affected by Western colonization as much as African countries were. Not only is there more literature but much of it is contributed by indigenous authors. Country studies dominate but general studies include Braibanti 1966; Braibanti and Spengler 1961; D. E. Smith (Ed.), *South Asian Politics and Religion* (Princeton University Press, 1966); and E. F. Szczepanik (Ed.), *Symposium on Economic and Social Problems of the Far East* (Hong Kong University Press, 1962). The bulk of country studies deals with the Indian subcontinent, with the notable exceptions of N. Dang, *Vietnam: Politics and Public Administration* (Honolulu: East-West Center Press, 1966); R. S. Milne, *Government and Politics in Malaysia* (Boston: Houghton Mifflin, 1967); R. O. Tilman, *Bureaucratic Transition in Malaya* (Durham: Duke University Press, 1964); D. E. Smith, *Religion and Politics in Burma* (Princeton University Press, 1965); and W. H. Wriggins, *Ceylon: Dilemma of a New Nation* (Princeton University Press, 1960). Pride in India's long established administration is evident in the *Indian Journal of Public Administration* and in the writings of both Indian and foreign observers (*e.g.*, Appleby 1953, 1956). Of particular importance here are Braibanti and Spengler 1963; A. Chanda, *Indian Administration* (London: Allen and

Unwin, 1958); Epstein 1962; and E. N. Mangat Rai, *Civil Administration in the Punjab* (Cambridge: Harvard University Press, 1963). The different path of Pakistan's administration has been recorded by M. Ahmad, *The Civil Service in Pakistan* (Karachi: Oxford University Press, 1964); Birkhead 1966; Braibanti 1966; H. F. Goodman, *The Civil Service of Pakistan* (New Haven: Yale University Press, 1964); and Inayatullah 1962. For completeness, reference should also be made to Thailand's journal of public administration and the studies of F. W. Riggs, *Thailand* (Honolulu: East-West Center, 1966), and W. J. Siffin, *The Thai Bureaucracy* (Honolulu: East-West Center, 1966).

For sake of comparison, attention should also be paid to Latin American experience as recounted by R. N. Adams (Ed.), *Social Change in Latin America* (New York: Vintage Books, 1960); D'Antonio and Pike 1964; H. E. Davis (Ed.), *Government and Politics in Latin America* (New York: Ronald Press, 1958); F. G. Gil, *The Political System of Chile* (Boston: Houghton Mifflin, 1966); J. O. Hall, *Public Administration in Uruguay* (University of Pittsburgh Press, 1954); B. L. St. John Hamilton, *Problems of Administration in an Emergent Nation* (New York: Praeger, 1964); J. Johnson (Ed.), *Conformity and Change in Latin America* (Stanford University Press, 1967); M. Needler, *Political Systems of Latin America* (New York: Van Nostrand, 1964); L. V. Padgett, *The Mexican Political System* (Boston: Houghton Mifflin, 1966); and G. B. Siegel, *The Vicissitudes of Governmental Reform in Brazil* (Los Angeles: University of Southern California, 1966). Several Latin American countries possess journals of public administration in Spanish (*e.g.*, Chile) or Portuguese (Brazil).

The subject of automation, like development administration, is producing a literature that soon will exceed the capacity of any reader to keep pace with the flow. Already it is beginning to monopolize some management journals (*e.g.*, *Management Science*). Some publishers seem to think that there is an inexhaustible market, and as a result there are many bad books and precious few good ones that face the philosophical issues. J. Diebold's *Automation: The Advent of the Automotive Factory* (New York: Van Nostrand, 1952) still remains the classic and has since been joined by his *Beyond Automation* (New York: McGraw-Hill, 1964). Among those found particularly useful in this study were R. A. Beaumont and R. B. Helfgott, *Management,*

Automation and People (New York: I.R.C., 1964); Becker and Murphy 1957; R. A. Brady, *Organization, Automation and Society* (Berkeley: University of California, 1961); J. R. Bright 1958; Buckingham 1961; S. Demczynski, *Automation and the Future of Man* (London: Allen and Unwin, 1964); D.I.S.R., *Automation* (London H.M.S.O. 1956); J. B. Jacobson and J. S. Roucek, *Automation and Society* (New York: Philosophical Library, 1959); O. Lipstreu and K. Reed, *Transition to Automation* (Boulder: University of Colorado, 1964); F. C. Mann and L. R. Hoffman, *Automation and the Worker* (New York: Holt, 1960); J. Rose, *Automation: Its uses and consequences* (Edinburgh: Oliver and Boyd, 1967); E. B. Shils, *Automation and Industrial Relations* (New York: Holt, Rinehart and Winston, 1963); H. A. Simon, *The New Science of Management Decision* (New York: Harper, 1960); H. A. Simon, *The Shape of Automation* (New York: Harper, 1965).

FIVE

The Process of Administrative Reform

Administrative reform is a continuous activity that takes place in such varied circumstances that meaningful generalization is difficult. The reforms themselves may be minor or major, public or private, passing events or permanent transformations. They may achieve their purposes or they may have no clearly defined goals to achieve. They do not appear in a vacuum nor are they miracles. They are the result of a particular situation. In contrast to change, which may be unforeseen, reforms are man-made and deliberate. They have identifiable beginnings and their progress can be followed through a series of stages until the reform is rejected, compromised, transformed, or implemented in its original form. The end is not so clear-cut—they may be postponed and then reappear in the same or different form in a different place or they may be reactivated long after their originators and first advocates have been forgotten. It is possible, therefore, to identify the origins of a reform and the stages through which it progresses, and to analyze the factors that aid or impede progress. Causes have effects and effects have causes; they are different views of the same thing.

Of the various attempts that have been made to define stages in the process of reform, two are particularly significant. Goodenough, following Wallace (1956) in analyzing revitalization movements "aimed at redesigning the pattern of community life, if need be by radical alterations of public culture, and thereby transforming the way people feel about themselves" (Goodenough 1963, p. 286), identified six major phases: (1) *inspiration*, the initial reformulation of the new social order, which usually comes to some individual in a flash of insight into social and moral problems; (2) *communication*, whereby the visionary reveals his ideas to others and seeks their cooperation, perhaps embellishing these ideas and attributing them "to science, to the writings of past scholars, or to an apparent miracle" (p. 295); (3) *organization of converts*, through which the prophet reaches a wider audience; (4) *adaptation to resistance*, wherein "even mild disapproval or lack of enthusiasm is likely to be interpreted as evidence of hostility toward the movement and its aims" (p. 297); (5) *enacting a program*, "in which concrete steps are taken systematically to alter the conditions of life, and to forge a new order" (p. 298); (6) *routinization*, when the program and its results are successful and the new pattern of living becomes routine. The Wallace-Goodenough classification can be applied to reform movements centered on identifiable leaders but it is not suitable to other types of reform.

Mosher covers some of these other types of reform, although somewhat at the expense of mass reform movements (Martin 1965, Mosher 1967). He finds that there are six major sequential steps: (1) *increase of tension*, when within the administration dissatisfaction and frustration intensify, and various unsuccessful proposals for change are made; (2) *spark*, "some particular event or combination of events which temporarily unhinges the equilibrium and makes possible the serious consideration of basic organizational change" (Martin 1965, p. 142); (3) *reorganization studies* of what should be done, widely or narrowly defined, carried out by investigatory groups whose methods and style determine "the accuracy, validity, and wisdom of findings and recommendations," "the acceptability and persuasiveness of the recommendations," and "the relevance and the invulnerability of the findings" (p. 146); (4) *the reaching of decision*, "the consultation, negotiating, and decision phase," which may coincide with the previous stage or await feasibility considerations; (5) *feasibility studies*, which consist of translating recommendations into practical administrative techniques and planning implementation; and (6) *implementation*. Mosher's classification is confined to alterations in formal arrangements and does not embrace reforms confined to informal aspects of administration. It does, however, direct attention to specific administrative stages that the more general Wallace-Goodenough classification considers minor. Both these classifications are used in this chapter, where they are combined and rearranged to cover the general field of administrative reform and to incorporate the classifications of social change made by Lasswell (1963) (intelligence, promotion, prescription, invocation, application, appraisal, termination, which are analyzed according to participants, perspectives, arenas, base values, strategies, outcomes, and effects); Pages (Bennis, Benne, Chin 1961, p. 178) (recognition, diagnosis and action); and Parsons (Parsons and Smelser 1956) (dissatisfaction, symptoms of disturbance, coping with tension, tolerance of new ideas, translation of new ideas into practicalities, implementation of innovations, and routinization of innovations).

AWARENESS OF NEED

Everyone can list things that need improving in this imperfect world. The length of the list depends on one's knowledge and social contacts. The difference between the highest common factor (change) and the lowest common multiple constitutes the area of reform. Because no one consciously thinks about all the things that are wrong in the world, it is only after proposals for improvement have been made that differences in perception and values are revealed and reform can be distinguished from change by the presence or absence of resistance. The first stage in administrative reform concerns differences in perception, that is, where people cannot agree that administration or certain administrative features should be improved. This awareness of need differs from the second stage, in which those who agree on the need for improvement cannot agree on the best methods for achieving their main objective.

The symptoms of administrative ill-health are not obvious to those who know nothing beyond the administrative culture into which they were born and have lived all their lives. They can conceive of nothing different because there is no feedback to suggest that something is wrong or needs correction. When there is such feedback, nobody is motivated to think of improvements and to push them in the face of apathy and opposition. People see only what they want to see, governed largely by stereotypes, personalization, oversimplification, and political quiescence. The accent is on reassurance. Administrative action is used to suggest vigorous activity through "noisy attacks on trivia," "prolonged, repeated, well-publicized attention to a significant problem which is never solved," the use of rhetoric in administrative instructions, and the deflection of criticism into purely moral and ceremonial channels (Edelman 1964, pp. 30-40). Such an administrative culture may not be stagnant. It can be quite dynamic, adjusting and adapting to changing conditions, and everyone can be quite satisfied with its operations, warts and all, if they know no better or if, to achieve something administratively better, they have to sacrifice something else (*e.g.*, unity) that they value more. The insiders do what they have to do, assuming impossible responsibilities and impractical demands. Sometimes they succeed but more often they fail. An outsider would instantly perceive the outward signs of administrative ill-health such as, for example, postponement of controversial problems, lethargic and unhelpful staff, empire-building, manufacture of useless work and excessive *paperasserie*. Further diagnosis might show that routine and trivia have swamped creativity and innovation; that institutional arrangements are unable to adjust to changing conditions while staff cannot cope with unusual situations; that freedom to experiment organizationally or otherwise does not exist; that revolutionary thinking about current problems is discouraged; and that energy, understanding, curiosity, sustained effort, and cooperation are lacking, as are enough good caliber people, quality tools, adequate accommodation, and internal security. Insiders fail to disclose these situations because they *are* insiders or because they are too committed to reveal the truth. To keep the system going, they may have to hide their inner beliefs and defend the indefensible, which has the same net effect as unawareness.

Whenever insiders meet with outsiders mutual comparison leads to awareness of needs. But the ability of insiders in isolation to realize shortcomings must not be undervalued. After all, innovations must begin somewhere. Tensions, inconvenience, injustice, and inequality are all factors in an existing situation that prompt awareness among insiders. Modernized societies have institutionalized awareness in leadership roles—that is, those occupying elite positions in bureaucratic structures are expected to recognize the shortcomings of the social system (at least that part for which they are responsible) and either to devise means for remedying failings or to provide machinery and employ others who can do so. When things go wrong, people instinctively turn to their leaders for remedial action; if they think that their leaders are to blame or are incapable of devising solutions or having solutions devised, the leaders are unlikely to retain their elite positions for long. In short, a basic requirement for leadership, administrative and otherwise, is the ability to anticipate common recognition of deficiencies and, if possible, to prepare solutions to impending problems. If they cannot be their own reformers they may have to enlist the aid of reformers or be replaced by others who do.

Briefly, administrative reform is needed where administrative change is insufficient to keep an administration abreast of developments, and performance gaps appear—that is, "a significant discrepancy exists between what it is doing and what it 'ought' to be doing" (Downs 1967, p. 191). More specifically, administrative reform is needed in the following circumstances:

1. When the administration is obviously failing to meet the demands put on it. Things do not get done at all or are done in a manner below previous or potential standards of performance. For example, there are growing delays in decision-making. Clients complain about lower standards. Somewhere there has been a breakdown in self-adjustment. The administration has not been able to keep up with the times, as in the case of self-made men who refuse to change their habits or whose narcissistic involvement prevents their accepting any changes (Ginzberg and Reilly 1957, p. 26).

2. When the administration, though meeting current demands, is not equipped to tackle extra demands. The impact of growth takes it by surprise so that it never rids itself of improvisation or an atmosphere of temporariness. Extra demands spell crisis while external crisis means catastrophe. For instance, a peacetime army collapses under the slightest pressure of war. Seasonal fluctuations in work load put everything out of order, and at no time does the administration appear capable of catching up with itself. Alternatively, the administration may be working at peak capacity at all times; though it meets all

demands, it loses the good will of the staff as strain, tension, and sheer tiredness take their toll.

3. When the administration with reserve capacity is unable to anticipate future demands. It concerns itself only with the immediate, lacking the research facilities, communications, and creativity to anticipate the future and to prepare accordingly. For instance, no successors are being developed to replace incumbents when they retire. Future commitments are not evened out over a period of time or there is inadequate preparation for major development projects.

4. When the administration that does have reserve capacity and the ability to anticipate future demands does not adopt the most effective methods. It is out of touch with the latest developments in its field. This is the opportunity-cost concept applied to administration.

Obviously no administration can possibly meet such standards of perfection embracing the distribution and use of internal power, mobilization of energy, avoidance of conflict and waste, maintenance of adequate communications internally and with the environment, adoption of new values and skills, understanding of basic objectives and motivations, encouragement of natural change, and methods for overcoming resistance and interference. No administration has the resources and none can overcome unavoidable time lags. Consequently, any administration can be improved and reformed.

But tolerance of maladministration is high. Most people either do not realize that anything is wrong or do not know how to right things. Despite greater emphasis on education and training, they have only the vaguest notions about how society works or what is involved in administration. They live narrow, parochial lives and worry about their own immediate personal problems. They aim for a secure, carefree, settled existence and avoid involvement with other people's affairs if they can. They may demonstrate active support for others who promise to better their lot, but token acknowledgments do not occupy much of their time or thoughts except when crisis looms. They pay little heed to pleas urging them to concern themselves with general social problems.

This attitude is not merely apathy or selfishness, but a continuation of the role they have always played in history, a product of socialization (or perhaps an indication of the failure of socialization to break through individual and group defenses), a result of specialization and differentiation that force the individual to confine himself more to his own expert field, and an individual response to the bewildering complexity of modern life. If the majority live out "their lives in conventional fashion, using and profiteering from the innovations of others, mostly unknown and long dead, but adding nothing to the social heritage [acting] as social functionaries, complex human puppets who behave and think and feel mainly in the ways established for them . . . too sensitive to social pressures, too much concerned with their status, and too conventional regarding duties and social obligations to be able to concentrate their time and energies on tasks not sanctioned by society" (LaPiere 1965, pp. 126-27, 137), then few individuals rise above their immediate situation to reflect on wider issues. Even then, much of their effort is futile or irrelevant or detrimental because of their lack of adequate knowledge.

The odds are against awareness. Socialization questions deviance and reinforces any natural inclination to accept the status quo. Individuals who question the accepted are accused of treachery and shamed into conformity; if not, passions are so raised that power can be exercised to isolate them from society or to compel their future obedience. Beyond this, experience has shown that not all changes are beneficial. Until the unknowns diminish, it seems wise to wait. The known is preferred to the unknown, the established order (or disorder) to a questionable utopia. People opt for acculturation, that is, the successful innovations of others. Rather than innovate, they borrow ideas, institutions, and techniques that have proved advantageous elsewhere. This caution has saved man from destruction and untold misery, avoiding the chaos that would result if every innovation were adopted. However, its value is offset by the support it gives to the irrelevancies and absurdities used to belittle all innovation.

People's general tolerance for the inconveniences of maladministration is no reason to suppose that they are not unaware of the need for improvement. As consumers, employees, parents, clients, taxpayers, tourists, conscripts, patients, and investors, they are on the receiving end of maladministration. As discontent increases and anxieties mount, the majority may well come to perceive the need for remedial action. Case studies show that when the status quo is upset by any of the following factors:

(a) *political:* war, international crisis, changes in regime, constitutional revision, electoral victory;

(b) *economic:* poverty, depression, devaluation, bankruptcy, changes in economic system, redistribution of wealth;

(c) social: changes in class system, redistribution of power, greater mobility, revaluation of morals, prejudice, literacy;

(d) *demographic:* population pressure, closer settlement, urbanization, insignificance of the individual;

(e) *cultural:* modernization, technological advancement, shrinking isolation, crime,

there comes a point when the individual no longer accepts the traditional framework. This is particularly true of people under stress or in danger. Their awareness is sharpened by threats to life and health, by discomfort from pain and fatigue, by loss of means of subsistence and enforced idleness, by threats to family and friends, by ridicule, by capricious and unpredictable behavior of those in authority, and by abuse of expected standards of administrative behavior (as when children are separated from their mothers or when excessive cruelty is condoned). Then, sometimes in the unlikeliest of places, a voice of protest is raised, a grievance is aired, dissatisfaction is expressed, and suppression of nonconformity fails.

Once the complaint is voiced, there is no telling to what extent it is shared. The complainant may be isolated or he may have put into words the feelings and thoughts of the inarticulate. He may see mistakes, faults, or corruption where others do not, either because he is more perceptive or because he has more access, information, education, or contact than others. He may, of course, imagine mistakes, faults, or corruption because of seeing only a small part of the administration or not being aware of the full circumstances. He may be an actor, an active participant in the guilty administration, responsible for its shortcomings or in a position to influence events. On the other hand, he may be a completely dissociated outsider with a nose for trouble or a professional change agent.

There are many reasons why complainants may fail to repeat their charges. They may be conscious of their own limitations and acknowledge the narrowness of their view; with this, they may consider that other people's shortcomings are none of their business. They may be self-conscious and shy of causing a disturbance. They may fear the consequences of annoying others—personal attack, ostracism, social degradation, perhaps self-exposure. They may lack public conscience, moral indignation, courage; or they may have courage but no way of influencing an autonomous administration. Some may fear being implicated or suspected of collusion. The atomization of the mass society and the cult of the expert between them strengthen the natural tendency to confine oneself to one's own business and to speak out on other matters only in private.

More reliance may be placed on the group, a collection of like-minded individuals who meet together formally in associations or informally at private gatherings to indulge in the art of conversation, the uninhibited flow of which eventually embraces the partially submerged thoughts, observations, and complaints of the individual. Their mutual exchange of views may clarify matters and, more often than not, strengthen one another's case. Such intercourse may reveal the need for administrative reform, confirmed by combining knowledge and sharing experience. Interaction within the group may overcome individual inhibitions and lead to greater preparedness to do something. Through individual and group contacts, complaints and other symptoms of uneasiness about administrative performance filter through to those involved. When they fail to react to feedback, the complainants may follow up their frustrations by enlisting the aid of other bodies—political parties, pressure groups, research workers, intellectuals, academics, opinion leaders, mass media, etc.—to exert further pressure for improvements.

In highly organized societies, grievance procedures may be institutionalized. A direct link between administrators and administrated may be provided by intermediaries such as public relations offices, tribunals, civil liberties councils, and ombudsmen, whereby the malfunctioning of the administration in individual cases may be pointed out by a third party without necessarily revealing the identity of the complainant. Similarly, ideas for administrative improvement may be institutionalized, and justifiable complaints may be revealed in the course of investigating the feasibility of new ideas. Sometimes the two processes are combined; but where they are, elites can abuse the intermediaries by employing them to seek out dissenters for identification and imprisonment. But there are many other bodies in society willing to pursue members' grievances and ideas. Possibly the United States is richest in such bodies, among which can be included the National Economy League, RAND Corporation, Public Affairs Research Inc., American Management Association, International City Managers' Association, National Tax Association, Public Affairs Institute, and American Public Welfare Association.

Finally, recognition may come from outside the society. Observations by visitors, diplomats, experts, reporters, and students may set reformatory zeal into motion. Even when a country endeavors to minimize its outside contacts, modern telecommunications span the world and foreign broadcasts may be heard in freak weather. Reforms may be forced upon a country by its allies or required as a condition of a treaty, pact, aid program, or other international transaction with strings attached.

Recognition of need requires no uncommon talent though it presupposes a sensitivity to maladministration. Even if most people possess such sensitivity, they can choose to do nothing, to ignore it, or to permit it to be numbed by the passage of time, apathy, indifference, security, and even greed when maladministration works to their personal advantage. It is easy to complain. It is much harder to diagnose or to suggest remedies, steps that present more intellectual challenge and require relevant knowledge and creative thought.

FORMULATION OF GOALS AND OBJECTIVES, STRATEGY AND TACTICS

Without relevant knowledge and creative thought, recognition of need as voiced in complaints may be so much wasted effort. Symptoms may be misinterpreted; facts may be taken in the wrong sequence; only part of the whole may be seen. The knowledge brought to bear may be irrelevant, insufficient, or inapplicable. Even if complaint is justified, unless some suggestions for remedial action are formulated, nothing will happen. What is further required is an element of creativity and pure thought or innovation, and beyond that a practical feel for the situation so that the remedies proposed are workable. The greatest reformers have combined two sets of talents—innovation and administrative-political skills—but a distinction should be drawn between the formulators and the implementors. In neither case is it a matter of simply thinking long enough or hard enough, or otherwise all administrative problems could be thought away. Similarly, if solutions depended on combining different thoughts bereft of preconceptions, then one could mix together free thinkers from different disciplines and wait for results. No doubt persistent thinking, constant trial and error, and stimulating contact are helpful, but they do not account for all invention or unpredictable creativity. The accumulation of knowledge stimulates different combinations and new approaches within the limits of understanding and experience. Wide dissemination of ideas, the conjunction of differences, freedom to explore experience, expectation of innovation, and the deprivation of essentials are other environmental factors that promote invention. They only work insofar as they react in the minds of individuals.

In formulation, individuals originate or imitate. Imitation is much the easier process, for all the individual has to do is to find out what others have done when confronted with similar situations. Invention involves originality. Between imitation and originality come the cases where the individual believes himself to be original, although unknown to him his proposals have been made before in a different place; or where the individual consciously imitates others, but supplies sufficient thought of his own that the end result is original. Barnett (1953) has analyzed the incentives to invention, which he classified into self-wants (psychological drives, credit for cleverness, wish to be different, exclusiveness, love of inventing, desire to improve, ego satisfaction, self-vindication), dependent wants (coincident wants, compensatory wants, entrained wants), and desire for change (variety, creative urge, strong challenge, discomfiture, desire for quantitative variation). They seem just as applicable to imitators as to innovators and say nothing about the mental processes that result in productive not reproductive patterns, or about willingness to go beyond satisficing solutions to optimizing solutions.

Much more important than the incentives to formulate is the immediate fate of formulated proposals.

> Many new ideas are stillborn, and countless others are ephemeral and perish without a trace. Some are only casual thoughts; others become cornerstones of faith. Some affect only the innovator himself; others, millions of individuals. Some are bitterly resented, others are welcomed. For some the welcome comes early, for others it is tendered late (Barnett 1953, p. 291).

Although inventions may lack advocates because no one, not even their originators, is willing to sponsor them or persevere with them, reform proposals invariably have advocates or "experts in persuasion" (p. 298). These may be the originators and the imitators (spontaneous reformers) but are more likely to be people convinced by the proposals and prepared to identify with them for their own purposes (derived reformers). Advocates, like complainants, may be found within or without an administration and at any level within an organization.

> Although the praise or blame for reforms is directed at corporate bodies, such as political parties and administrations, the real advocates must take the shape of individual human beings who represent them and individually subscribe to their programs. Bureaucrats and other public servants therefore make up an important category of paid advocates of change who, like investors and professional publicists, are interested as much in the fact of acceptance as they are in the social consequences of it. In other words, getting the idea across is a job for them . . . (Barnett 1953, p. 298).

Advocates also include opportunists "who adopt an alien behavior for the impression they hope to make upon their fellows" (p. 305) and conservatives who, instead of promoting the new, promote the status quo to nonconformists. How far the reformers succeed initially not only depends on the nature of their proposals but also on their personal characteristics, such as status, prestige, sex, reputation, ingenuity, and personality.

Barnett throws light on why some people are more prone to accept innovation than others. First, the individual must believe that novelty really will satisfy a want better than existing means. Second, he is predisposed by his experiences, personality traits, and receptivity. Some individuals are permanently dissatisfied, but not with everything —they have a selective dissatisfaction. In short, there is no category of "acceptors" or of "rejectors." These terms cannot be used to impose

> a dichotomy upon humanity. They do not designate absolutes. No one is wholly or persistently an acceptor or rejector. He is simply more or less so than is somebody else and with reference to a specific idea. For any given novelty the incidence and the rapidity of accept-ance may be high or low in a certain society; but there will always be some individuals who lag behind others in giving their approval to it and some perhaps who never do. There are relenting as well as die-hard conservatives, slow and reluctant as well as quick and eager acceptors. Our attention must be focused upon the relative place-ment of individuals anywhere along this continuum, whether they fall at its extremes or in contiguous sectors. Relatively speaking, there are acceptors and rejectors all along this line; and at any given moment that is the pattern which presents itself in spite of the fact that the rejectors of today often become the acceptors of tomorrow. That shift merely changes the proportions, not the pattern of ac-ceptance versus rejection. (Barnett 1953, p. 380.)

He identifies four categories of acceptors of innovation (who are also likely to embrace reform): (1) The Dissident are nonconformists and rebels who are alienated from certain aspects of their culture and maintain a mental distance between themselves and the things they dislike (p. 381). (2) The Indifferent are prepared to accept new ideas because they have not dedicated themselves irretrievably to a custom or to an ideal of their society. They conform to existing conventions and participate in them (p. 385), but they are not enthusiastic. They passively accept. (3) The Disaffected begin as active participants in certain aspects of their culture but later acquire a distaste for them as a result of a disillusioning experience (p. 389). (4) The Resentful are jealous of others' successes and accept change because they have less to lose. New ideas and proposals are "used by the have-nots to gain the prizes that others have and which they covet" (p. 403), not for the purposes for which they were originally conceived. Obviously, the haves resist changes that will deprive them of their advantages, seeking to block or divert reforms with compromises, while the reformers implant and cultivate resentment against the haves (p. 404). The haves possess the initial advantages, and in administration can appeal to habit and the difficulties of changing personal working habits (p. 169), to the need for the security of the status quo, to the existing cooperative spirit and personal relationships, to commitments that have been made, and to the anxiety and even antagonism roused by the effect of change on self and status.

In this general setting, some individuals, reflect on the nature of maladministration and formulate specific proposals for improvement. They share a conviction that perceived wrongs should be righted. They remain discontented with some aspects of their environment until their remedies are implemented. Reform to them is an article of faith, "an act of imagination which attracts, fires, holds and elaborates [their] loyalties."

> This involvement is less through words than through images which bind together the real and the ideal, the fact and the hope, the hate and the love, the present and the future, the rational and the non-rational, the organizational and the personal. The image joins the object symbol and the metaphor, the thing and its comparison (Meadows in Swerdlow 1963, p. 100).

This moral commitment to reform, intensely held, is suspected and rarely shared or appreciated. More often, it is ridiculed and its apostles treated with contempt (sometimes justly, when reformers have nothing but their moral indignation). Missionary zeal needs to be accompanied by a strong sense of compassion, a consideration that the individual counts, the courage of independent conviction that transcends the mediocrity of group thinking, a high order of intellectuality, technical skill, administrative ability, and a sense of politics. As few people possess these talents, reform is the work of a minority.

Meadows perceives reform as the work of elite groups such as the dynastic elite in a traditional society, the middle classes in a private enterprise system, revolutionary intellectuals in a totalitarian country, colonial administrators in a colonial regime, and nationalist leaders in a newly independent state (Swerdlow 1963, pp. 91-4). Jennings (1960) classifies the "few superior individuals" who are great reformers into those who are driven by a deep-seated drive for power over others and by the need to maintain that power at all costs (princes); those of unbounded reserves of energy and iron will power, which allow them to resist the values and norms that society usually instills in weaker people (supermen); and those possessed by a sense of mission to which they dedicate their total selves (heroes). He believes that the princes are eclipsing the supermen and heroes, princes "who wish to dominate not out of strength but weakness, known by talent and ability to shift quickly and gracefully from persuasion to cajolery, flattery to intrigue, diplomacy to promises or horse-trading, or to concoct just the formula to provide escape from disaster." LaPiere (1965) attributes reform to social deviants, innovators, advocates, and adoptors, "freed from the conventionalizing effects of social ideology and of organizational membership" (p. vii); others disagree that reformers are social deviants (Rogers 1962). Here three observers have arrived at the same conclusion, though their assumptions seem contradictory.

No matter how few reformers there may be, it is unlikely that they will propose identical solutions. No two persons have identical experience, knowledge, thoughts, or values concerning administration. Though they examine the same social phenomenon, they view it differently. "People will define the meaning of a situation differently, they will come up with different evaluations, they will derive or impute different norms and certainly they will feel about the situation in many, many different ways and intensities" (Swerdlow 1963, p. 87). One believes that power is too concentrated, another that power is too fragmented. One believes that there is insufficient participation in policy-making, another that there is too much. Theoretically, the scope of administrative reform is limited only by human ingenuity. In reality the range of possibilities is narrowed by the givens in a generation; no matter how fast changes are occurring there is relatively little room in which reformers can maneuver, but enough room to get in one another's way. The damage that could result is restricted by the reformers themselves. Most reformers think only in incremental steps. Formulations are tailored to observable trends, and when unexpected resistance is met, the reformers alter their proposals, compromise with their main critics, and, if necessary, retreat a little. They are more

tender-hearted and less direct than radical reformers and revolutionaries. But such concessions do not imply that they have relinquished
the pursuit of wider ultimate aims.

The fundamental objective of administrative reform is the improvement of administration, variously described as the cure of maladministration, the attainment of efficient performance at minimum expenditure
of resources, and the development and implementation "of whatever
changes are required to enable administrative organs to execute public
policies in an effective and responsible manner" (Finan and Dean 1957).
Mosher identified four major subgoals: (1) *changing of operating policies and programs,* covering expansion of scope and extent of programs, shifts in program emphasis, and shifts in loci of power; (2)
improvement of administrative effectiveness, through (a) increased
control at the top and thus presumably better coordinated operations,
(b) decentralization of decision-making and operations, (c) increase in
productivity and/or improved quality (efficiency), (d) reduction of
costs in carrying out going programs (economy), and (e) the application of administrative principles (Martin 1965, p. 138); (3) *higher
quality personnel,* and more effective staff performance; and (4) *anticipating outside criticism or threat.* Other subgoals are less rational;
whatever their ostensible objective, they are more personally motivated
until they veer off into the erratic. From the range of objectives and
goals it is possible to draw some interesting conclusions:

1. Reform objectives are not necessarily objective and reform proposals are not necessarily subjective.
2. Complex radical reforms need more time and instruction to
   implement than simpler incremental reforms.
3. Initial steps in reform implementation are judged more critically
   than later stages, once expectations and promises seem to be in
   the process of realization.
4. Reforms are more likely to be accepted (*a*) if they are tailored
   to local circumstances, implemented through existing institutions, and invite local participation; (*b*) if existing institutions
   and practices are not condemned out of hand, that is, if attention is given to extolling the virtues of reform rather than the

defects of the unreformed; and (c) if they are based on critical rather than uncritical nonoperationalism.

5. It is easier to draft proposals and plans than to execute them. The wider the range of reform sources the more likely that the proposals will not coincide.

Formulation connotes the idea of prior preparation—that administrative reforms are organized, engineered, and planned beforehand. No doubt some preparation of this kind is done before reformers embark on a course of action. The International Institute of Administrative Sciences has attempted to outline several procedures for preparing and implementing administrative reforms (see *Bibliographic Notes*). Much writing on the subject gives the impression that more preparation is done than actually is the case. For every example of a well-executed reform, there are probably others where reform was more the result of accident than intent. Sometimes in crises administrators hit upon solutions that happen to coincide with the optimum rational choice. Often reform has been mere temporizing.

In formulation—the search for root causes of maladministration, the feasibility of reform, the extent of support, the appropriate tactics, and the provision of an escape route should reform fail—the insider has advantages over the outsider and reform from the inside is likely to be more successful than reforms imposed from outside. But sometimes the outsider is in a better position because he is not personally involved and has no personal working relationship to consider. On the other hand, he is at the mercy of the more advantageously placed insider who may deny him the really significant information without which his formulations are irrelevant.

The very art of preparation, and certainly any declaration of intent, changes the situation. It forewarns possible opponents who may thereupon block access, plant misleading information, or anticipate reforms. While outwardly denying the need for reform at all, they may be implementing reforms of their own or so altering things that previously conceived reforms cannot be implemented without radical revision. The reformers may take so long in their preparations that it may be a tactical blunder to persist with plans based on the initial observations. To overcome these pitfalls, reformers take three main approaches: (*a*) reforms are announced and implemented almost simultaneously; (*b*) reforms are planned over a period of up to five years; and (*c*) reforms are implemented according to a long-term plan, which is broken into subsidiary plans and several stages and levels of action, the master plan being revised constantly as circumstances change.

The reformers' overall strategy is to win over vested interests, opponents, and neutrals if possible while strengthening support. Accordingly they may have to disguise the real aims and purposes of reform behind vague general catchwords such as "liberty," "peace," "justice," and "prosperity," which no one can oppose. Reformers may deceive opponents and supporters alike by backing unsympathetic persons in authority in order to influence, guide, or control the course of events. In so doing they may have to compromise over objectives to win greater support. In any event, they have to divert resources from direct advocacy to splitting the opposition. Should those tactics fail or appear unlikely to succeed at the outset, there remain the bludgeon—a direct frontal assault with the opposition struggling to the bitter end—and the rapier—a backdoor entry when the opposition is off guard. Tactics vary according to circumstances, levels of objectives, and the nature of resistance where it can be gauged. Resistance may be weak initially, intensify during the struggle, and slowly fade as defeat is accepted. It may commence strongly but suddenly fade away as the reformers gain the upper hand. One thing is certain, that where reform threatens the existence of a group or even one individual, the fight for survival will be bitter. The struggle for reform is not particularly pleasant, and extreme penalties are not uncommon. People are destroyed, reformers and their opponents alike.

IMPLEMENTATION OF REFORMS

No catalogue of ways and means can guarantee the potential reformer that his selection among the possibilities will be correct or that he has the talents necessary for implementation. Unlike the new householder who fails to choose the right plants from a seed catalogue, the administrative reformer cannot start anew after initial failure. If he is not damaged by his failure, then the reforms he advocated are discredited, perhaps for all time.

To make people accept something against their will is difficult. A climate conducive to reform must exist, and the introduction of a reform requires a sense of timing if that climate is to be maintained. For instance, shock tactics more often than not rebound by producing an exaggerated defensive reaction. The surprise release of a hitherto secret condemning report, or the dramatic and unsuspected announcement of radical reversal in policy may have an effect opposite to that intended. People have not been prepared to expect something new or to identify themselves with the new. On the other hand, overconcentration on preparation may cause the reformers to miss their opportunity.

The selection of techniques for implementing a reform depends on a host of factors, the most important of which are the formulated objectives, the extent of reform contemplated, the nature of existing transformations within society, and the reformers' intentions—to proceed with or without general support, with or without the use of force, and through existing channels or otherwise. It is not always easy to distinguish between reform objectives, reforms, and techniques for implementing reforms. For instance, reorganization, planning, joint consultation, watchdogs, and policy analysis fit into all three categories (see *Bibliographic Notes*). Four methods of implementation only have been selected for special attention here simply because they illustrate different sets of factors at work within the administrative situation and are in themselves contrasts in approach.

Reforms Imposed Through Political Revolution. All administration is conducted within a given political context. Political institutions, from intergovernmental councils to local cell groups of political parties, have a decisive influence in the conduct of administration. Beyond the short run, no administration can exist without the concurrence of political office-holders and, through them, tacit support from the community. Administration is part of the political consensus. In more tangible form, administrators are constantly aware of the political decisions that determine their actions and of their political contribution to society. They must abide by the law and follow accepted political practices, such as the political parties' solicitation of financial support and their own solicitation of political favours. At any time their very existence may be threatened by political action, such as a declaration of war, the outlawing of specific social activities, or the imposition of crippling taxes. Concern with the political environment is well illustrated in the daily conversations of administrators and their search for information about the effect of political events on them.

Usually changes in the political context are easily absorbed by administrators, except perhaps in the upper reaches of public administration where politicians and administrators confront one another. Political changes are likely to induce sweeping administrative reforms beyond this area only during a radical transformation of the power elite, as, for instance, a violent revolution, particularly if the new elite is ideologically motivated and inclined to totalitarianism. The purpose of capturing political power is expressly to transform social institutions and the whole way of life of the citizens. The case studies showed how the violent replacement of imperial dynasties and aristocratic power elites by professional revolutionaries drawn from the educated middle classes, in combination with technocrats, bureaucrats, and professional administrators of coercive power, also recruited from the lower classes, changed the whole direction of governmental administration, public controls on private administration, and the working habits of all concerned.

Only in uncommon circumstances is it necessary to implement administrative reforms through political revolution. Under pressure, the ruling elites refuse to change the prevailing order and so lose their ability to command loyalty from the rest of society. They rouse an opposition intent on destroying their position and they antagonize many other people who belong to neither camp and are usually politically responsive, obedient, or passive. The ruling elites, through personal ties, dominate the economic, political, military, bureaucratic, social, business, and possibly cultural and religious hierarchies. They permit no opposition and use their powers to suppress any disagreement. Adverse reaction can only be expressed in secret underground movements, the spread of which is prevented by repression and coercion. Their example of violence is easily copied, and the weapons of suppression are easy to convert into the weapons of retribution. Despite the outbreak of violence the elites refuse to change their policy or grant concessions. Between the rulers and their opponents an unbridgeable gap appears. The elites become increasingly isolated, sometimes quite ignorant of what is happening outside their own narrow circle. The means they employ to maintain themselves may be undermined by the infiltration of opponents, so that at the first sign of trouble the whole edifice collapses.

The flash point of the revolution may be an insignificant incident that develops into a matter of principle. Only when the elites fail to control the situation is it realized that they can be swept away altogether. Revolutionary fervor spreads as the failure of the elites is demonstrated by external defeat in war, diplomacy, or trade, and internal crises in finance, famine, inept use of force, civil disobedience, and general strikes, any one of which is exploited (and may have been planned) by the revolutionaries. The political regime may be so rotten that it collapses overnight with little resistance. Leading elite members may be banished or arrested, and their property seized, while a new elite assumes leadership and prepares the reconstruction of social institutions. Under pressure the rulers may agree to capitulate and leave voluntarily, calling upon their supporters to assist the new rulers. Alternatively the elites, or that remnant unwilling to step down, and their loyal supporters, may decide to fight back. In the ensuing civil war, both rulers and revolutionaries may call on outside aid and seek international support. If the neighboring countries decide to take advantage of the civil war to invade and take spoils or side with one of the factions, then the civil war can easily escalate into an international war.

Two main courses are open to successful revolutionaries. They may grant amnesty to the remnants of the former regime (who may settle down in good faith or remain a potential fifth column, a persistent opposition, a reminder of past glory should the revolutionaries fail in creating the new order) or they may deal harshly with their opponents. In any event, the revolution is a traumatic experience in the life of the nation. It may lead to such moral revulsion that people may be willing to settle for peace at any price. On the other hand, bitterness may reach such a pitch that even after peace is restored, the new regime may be faced with passive resistance or the possibility of another round with either those who want to put the clock back or those who want to go much further forward.

In transforming social institutions, the revolutionaries may find themselves handicapped by their memories of the revolution, its destruction and dislocation, and postrevolutionary divisions on where to begin reconstruction. Rarely do they start with a clean sheet. Many prerevolutionary institutions have survived, perhaps almost intact. The revolutionaries have built up their own dependable organization, able to function separately from prerevolutionary institutions yet perhaps incapable of assuming the leadership of the latter. As a higher degree of continuity than anticipated probably exists between the two regimes, the original plans may have to be drastically overhauled. People take time to adjust to new developments; in the case of revolution the cultural lag may last for over a generation. A reaction to the revolution itself may be a temporary tendency to glorify the past and to resist the new. In such circumstances, the new elites may opt to continue the old ways rather than rush through far-reaching changes. Where possible, people return to what they were doing before the revolution, and gradually normality is restored. At first, therefore, revolutionary events may not directly touch administration except in the public sector; paradoxically, a reactionary, corrupt, and inefficient public bureaucracy may be relied on as a catalyst in implementing social reforms and imposing administrative reforms on private bodies. However, sooner or later the destruction of the old order, the transformation of elites, the trauma of revolutionary events, the historic example of the revolution itself, and the driving force of the revolutionaries will produce administrative reforms of great magnitude.

Political revolution is a particularly dramatic technique by which administrative reforms are imposed on administrators from the outside. It is admittedly a marginal device. Administrative reform is only a minor part of the transformation of the social order and may be more the result of other radical changes than the deliberate objective of the revolutionaries. However, similar dramatic transformations within the context of administration can also lead to far-reaching administrative reforms. The impact of automation in technology has been described. In history, the Black Death and similar ravaging plagues brought far-reaching changes and with them important administrative reforms. What happens is that one of the givens suddenly and unexpectedly can no longer be taken for granted. Unless administrators adjust quickly to the new situation, their survival is jeopardized. Either they reform or their administrations collapse under them. The lesson is that administrators should neither assume too much nor overcommit themselves to a given that may turn out to be unreliable after all.

Reforms Introduced to Remedy Organizational Rigidity. The principal instrument of contemporary administration is the bureaucracy, whose institutionalized behavior pattern embodied in legal codes may have a life of its own independent of the people who staff it at any particular time. The network of legal-rational authority, hierarchical organization, recorded decisions, defined responsibilities, specialization, and professionalism ensures a stable foundation which gives the bureaucracy its ability to survive in most unlikely circumstances. Providing the staff keep a watchful eye on the formal framework to see that in fact it does not become completely independent of them and that they adjust it to changing conditions, the bureaucracy can operate normally where other kinds of organization cannot. Organizational flexibility—the ability to adjust the framework—must cover the re-arrangement of work processes, improvements in viability, preparedness to switch production, promptness in altering the combination of resources, eagerness to promote efficiency and administrative and technical rationality, and willingness to revise rules and codes.

Organizational flexibility is impeded for a variety of reasons, of which the following are fairly representative:

1. The very success of an organization—in meeting expectations, production targets, sales records—may breed complacency and a tendency to stand by the well-tried formula. For example, a cigarette firm may try to repeat an unexpected spectacular success by copying the previous recipe and using the same slogan or design or flavor despite failures with each succeeding name brand. The original targets may have been set too low or its clientele may want a different product but is unable to make any impact. Hence success is no indication that an organization is flexible or that it is not in need of administrative reform.

2. Because of technological, social, ideological, or other factors,

an organization may be overcommitted to given objectives or too dependent on particular ways of doing things; it is in a rut, unable to deviate from a set path.

3. An organization lacking adequate safety margins may leave itself no room to maneuver. It is open to the danger of over-reaching itself or of being unable to cope with the unexpected.

4. No organization is immune from built-in technical inflexibility, time-lags, and rigid scientific laws.

5. The customers do not want anything different.

6. The administrators may be isolated and in ignorance of what is really going on below. Such isolation may be imposed from below or it may be physical or social or cultural.

7. The administrators may be uncreative, even dogmatic, in their reluctance to experiment. Such undue caution may be due to their peculiar characteristics (personality, age, disinterest, complacency) or to administrative processes that result in such persons being appointed (seniority rules, bad selection, deficient training).

8. Excessive bureaucratization (whereby the means become the ends) may result in red tape, empire-building, circumlocution, indifference, authoritarianism, ritualism, and inertia, all making for an extreme reluctance to change direction.

9. Greater size may contribute to inflexibility because of the greater number of people with vested interests in preserving the status quo by not permitting large-scale organizations to fail or other organizations to establish themselves in the same field.

10. Norms may not change with circumstances. Once set, adhered to, and conveyed to newcomers, they tend to stick.

11. Collusion in all kinds of informal agreements with rivals, joint producers, and suppliers, along with binding contracts, impede rapid adjustment.

12. Formal rules, by their very nature, lag behind developments.

Taken together these factors give a good indication why so few organizations have managed to survive over the years.

When an organization becomes too rigid, and stresses and strains appear, internal demands for administrative reforms increase. Flexibility is reintroduced internally. First, administrators are constantly reshuffled. No one is permitted to remain in the same job long enough to stamp his personality on the organization. New men are tried all the time. Second, more emphasis is placed on research and projection. Third, steps are taken to prevent excessive rigidity in structure and regulations. Fourth, initiative, creativity, suggestions, and innovations are encouraged by example, and by incentives and promotional schemes. Fifth, boredom is combatted through job turnover, rotation, and joint ownership schemes. Sixth, greater responsiveness is promoted by public relations, consumer research, and complaint units.

The list of reforms could be extended to cover all internal measures initiated by administrators either unanimously or after bloody infighting which caused some to leave, others to be dismissed or demoted, and a few to lose any effective power for the future. This is the usual method of implementing administrative reform and the one most frequently described in textbooks on administration and in popular executive-type fiction. Less frequent are the reforms forced on administrators from above, by owners, members, directors, and higher executives in private bodies, and by politicians and public representatives in public bodies; from below, by middle management, specialists, and other subordinate staff exercising countervailing power; and from outside, by employee organizations, trade associations, racketeers, and the like.

If carried too far, flexibility can land the bureaucratic organization in a tangle of overlapping jurisdiction, duplication of functions, haphazard procedures, insecurity, and anarchy. Things are too fluid, so that the bureaucracy is in danger of disintegrating. The solution is greater bureaucratization. Many newly independent states want to make their elite cadres more flexible while bureaucratizing many administrative practices at lower levels. Contradictory trends within administration are not unusual (*e.g.*, centralization in budgeting versus decentralization in accounting; centralization in collective bargaining versus decentralization in recruitment), and the result may be the introduction of administrative reforms that make for greater flexibility or a higher degree of bureaucratization at the same time but in different areas.

Reforms Through the Legal System. One of the most obvious ways of getting somebody else to do what one wants them to do is to have a law passed. The law, in fact, is becoming an increasingly important method for implementing administrative reforms. It is the foundation of much public administration, and, not surprisingly, the first systematic studies of administration were undertaken by public lawyers. Even today, public administration is still an integral part of legal studies in Western Europe where administrative law is highly developed. The rule of law presupposes that executive action must receive legal sanction and that any administrative activities undertaken without a basis in law are *ultra vires*. The result is that in most nations public administration is bound by complex laws that sometimes determine the smallest details. The starting point of reformers in these states is the law; their reforms are in large measure attempts to change the law. The process to which they submit is designed to encourage the maximum opposition and delay, but once they pass this obstacle, their reforms become the new law, the new enforceable standard backed by the majesty of the state.

Less obvious but no less pervasive is the amount of public law that applies to private administration, that is, to the administration of nongovernmental activities. If account is taken of all the laws that determine private administrative practices, private bodies have little more freedom than public authorities in the way they can conduct their affairs. There are company laws, restrictive practices laws, antimonopoly and antitrust laws, consumer protection laws, labor and employment laws, factory, office and workplace laws, safety laws, and so forth, quite apart from the whole realm of governmental control over the economy (Grove 1962) and professional practice. Like administrative law, the public law of American capitalism is both enabling and restrictive, though it is less directive (Martin 1965, p. 71). Reformers in private bodies are likely to run up against the law sooner or later, even if it does allow greater administrative discretion and barely touches organizational arrangements, procedures, and administrative philosophy.

However unsuitable, disagreeable, or objectionable, the law has to be obeyed until it is changed. The law also bestows rights and obligations likely to lead to court action at any time. In trying to change the law, the reformer undertakes a difficult task, because of its sacrosanct quality gained through past adherence and the mystique of the ritual. He must convince the legislature, which means the government and the majority parties. The pitfalls in trying to achieve administrative reforms through political processes can be illustrated by any case study of an administrative reform that has run the political gauntlet. Civil service changes, machinery of government overhauls, local government reorganizations, budgeting alterations, and procedural reforms have all fallen victim. One of the most spectacular examples was the 1936 Report of the President's Committee on Administrative Management, which the President accepted without anticipating the bitter political acrimony that followed. The substantive issues at stake became intertwined with seemingly irrelevant arguments that had little to do with the merits of the case (Einaudi 1959, Jacob 1967, Karl 1963, Polenberg 1966), while the proposals also fell foul of technical difficulties, such as drafting, legislative timetable, and promulgation.

Even if amendments to the law are successful, they still have to be implemented by those to whom the reforms are directed. At this stage it may be found that the law is ambiguous, thus defeating the intentions of the reformers. Worse still, it may be ignored, by-passed, or misapplied. It is then up to the reformers to take court action to ensure proper compliance, as an administrative action is not *ultra vires* until declared so by a competent legal tribunal. If the law is too detailed, it will need frequent amendment (or else it will fall behind needs) and it may hinder administrators unnecessarily. If it is too general, it may permit anything to be done in its name. In any event, lawmakers cannot anticipate everything. Disputes will arise and court action be threatened. If disputes do reach the court, judicial decision may be unrealistic, impractical, or otherwise unfavorable to administrative reforms. The only recourse then is to overrule the judges by further legislation. The risks of administrative reformers are many, but in their favor are the assumption of good faith on the part of all parties and the fear of exposure by those who deliberately ignore the law.

Despite the complications, reform through law is worthwhile. From the public viewpoint it has the advantage of publicity. When reform movements make known their intention of seeking legislation, opposition groups can form and resist such notions. In deciding whether to accept in principle the proposed legislation, the government will seek opinions, leak information to judge reactions, and endeavor to obtain expert assistance in drafting. Once the proposed legislation has entered the political arena, only secret emergency sessions in the legislature will prevent publicity. Similarly, once administrative action has been questioned in court, only closed proceedings will prevent further communication. In contrast, administrative reform through budgeting or financial methods is a closed process, known only to the immediate participants (Wildavsky 1964). Perhaps after the event (too late to make any difference) something will be known about the bargaining that accompanies the slashing of a budget. How actual figures are arrived at remains secret, whereas it is possible to know why particular words or phrases appear in laws or court decisions. But there is less danger that financial arrangements will become symbolical rather than meaningful in the way that some regulatory law does (Edelman 1964).

Reforms Through Changes in Attitude. Each of the methods so far considered has involved mainly formal changes. Lasting reforms cannot depend on the superiority of power or the coercion of nonbelievers. Ultimately those who resist reforms have to be won over in spirit as well as body. Their attitudes must change or be changed. It is not enough to devise perfect paper organizations if nobody knows what to do with them or they are made to serve wrong purposes. To change people's behavior, "it is necessary to change also their thinking and their attitudes, to anticipate and to seek out anxieties, to talk difficulties out in a kind of mental therapy" (Dimock 1959, p. 239). This is easier said than done. Some attitudes are conditioned and fixed long before people are caught up in administrative work, but others are shallow impressions derived from the administrative situation in adult life. For instance, attitudes of disrespect, hostility, resentment, inferiority, and intolerance are readily conveyed and copied unthinkingly by newcomers. Unless steps are taken to combat false images, they harden into reality for those who believe in them. It is particularly important to reformers that resistance to their proposals not be irrational and that, after implementation, the results be sufficient to change attitudes. Over a century ago, Mill warned that "no great improvements in the lot of mankind are possible until a great change takes place in the fundamental constitution of their modes of thought."

Behavioralists have tended to blame too much the bureaucratic organization for bad attitudes that obstruct change and reform. Self-development, it is argued, is hampered by such organizations, and the individual shows his resentment in dysfunctional activities and resistance to innovation. More emphasis should be placed on the informal side of work relations. The organization should be viewed as a second home in which the individual should enjoy his work and feel that his contribution is important. He should be given greater opportunity for creative freedom, individual dignity and democratic decision-making. Participation unfreezes attitudes, encourages positive responses, permits more balanced interactions, and reduces resistance. It also involves the participants in responsibility for successful decisions and satisfactory outcomes. In practice, participation may not be feasible or profitable or meaningful (Mosher 1967) and may even strengthen resistance if the most conservative elements hold out or if differences in opinion are exacerbated by direct confrontation. No doubt in an innovative atmosphere where people are receptive to change, the human relations approach will produce results and speed the implementation of reforms. But as the problem of attitudes goes beyond the individual's response to his working group, more formal methods are likely to predominate for the time being.

Example is foremost among the methods for changing obstructive attitudes when face-to-face approaches have failed. The reformers practise what they preach. If they are in no position to effect their own proposals, they seek to persuade the pace-setters and style-leaders. An increasingly popular method is formal education and training whereby people are taught to change their attitudes. Unfortunately, when the trainee returns to his place, he may forget everything he has learned or be confused when his new attitudes are unsuited to the facts of his working environment. When the end result is considered more important than motivation, rewards and incentives are offered for apparent changes in attitude. Other methods, such as trial runs, experiments, compensation, and coercion, may backfire by reinforcing existing attitudes. Reform may demand greater effort and higher standards of performance, in which case it is advantageous for the individual to stick with the status quo and take refuge behind predisposition, habit, prejudice, and irrationality.

Changing attitudes is one of the most difficult and most crucial things to achieve in the whole process of administrative reform, for there is no telling when former attitudes may return. When the reformers have achieved what they intended, they themselves become a source of resistance to further reforms. Cohen (1964) emphasized the importance of social influences, particularly group norms, social conditioning, socialization mechanisms, and personality disposition, in shaping responses to reformers. He had some useful tips for communicators concerning the way they should design their messages and present the most favorable image of themselves so as to attain maximum response. He believed that outward conformity can eventually lead to inner change, but he also warned that changed attitudes may not persist.

Whatever methods are adopted by the reformers in gaining their objective, it is perhaps trite to add that they should remain united if only to prevent differences between them from being exploited by their opponents. Their cause should emphasize social purposes even if personal ambition, self-interest, orderliness, and organizational objectives are also involved. They should also generate confidence in what they do, bearing in mind prevailing mores and cultural environment. For instance, if the reformers intend to reduce overstaffing, they should be aware of population pressure, urban drift, high unemployment and disguised underemployment, distribution of taxable income, and the state of social services. In overcoming resistance, they need to exploit all avenues of influence, including such strategic positions as confidential secretaries, consultants, and informal opinion-makers who may exercise considerable power without having any formal authority. In the final analysis, it is mastery of the political arts that counts—awareness of inarticulate dissatisfaction, access to innovators and imaginative formulators, knowledge of power distribution and the rules of social interaction, understanding of prevailing values and norms, calculation of feasible alternative approaches and their costs and limitations, and appreciation of bureaucratic defense mechanisms, and the strengths of the prevailing system and the vested interests who support it.

EVALUATION

Whatever the costs of implementation and dislocation involved in administrative reform, the end result must be some kind of permanent transformation for the better, in terms of the reformers' objectives. Temporary relief from administrative shortcomings, however welcome, is unsatisfactory and does not constitute reform. Any reform that cannot meet the test of permanence fails unless it is superseded by a more radical reform. As for other criteria by which the success or failure of an administrative reform can be determined, the literature is weak. Running through much of the writing about administrative reform is the assumption of success—once resistance to reform was overcome, everything after that went according to plan. If success is not assumed, then adverse effects are discounted or the facts selected to minimize failure and maximize success. There seems to be one absolute standard—whether the reformers secured sufficient authority to prevent their opponents from blocking implementation. Otherwise, we are too dependent on the self-evaluation of reformers.

Attempts to evaluate administrative reform according to other criteria involve serious methodological problems. First, reform is not an end in itself. Should its success be measured by its contribution to the ultimate objectives of administrative performance? In this respect, how can one evaluate mixed results or results that indicate no improvement or some decline? How much of these end results can be attributed to the reform? Even if reforms improve end performance, what if the end products do not contribute to social efficiency or the public interest?

Second, what constitutes success in reform? Is it the full realization or achievement of the reformers' original objectives or is it partial fulfillment after the reformers recognize that they must settle for something less? Is it any improvement on the status quo, irrespective of costs?

Third, how much of the success can be attributed to the reformers, directly and indirectly? How much would have been achieved anyway? How much is due to factors beyond their control? How is unexpected assistance calculated? Is the success merely on paper or have the reformers established built-in desires to ensure continuation? How much of the reform is accidental, unforeseen, unpredictable, though the reformers claim the credit?

Fourth, is it possible to determine the intentions of any particular actor, and is it not misleading to infer them from the consequences of his action? Is it possible to allow for differences between declared and real aims, between positive and negative aims? How are abstract aims (*e.g.*, justice, health, education) to be considered?

Fifth, what time limit should be allowed if results are not immediately forthcoming? What about delayed reactions and cumulative effects? What about implementation after the originators have left the scene? How long do the seeds of reform take to grow and ripen?

Sixth, what of those who copy reforms from elsewhere or who implement reforms that have failed elsewhere?

Seventh, how justified is the separation of the moral from the scientific if the successful reformer has "to cut corners, to lie, or at least distort the truth, and to engage in some back-stabbing?" (Tullock 1965, p. 31).

Eighth, how can charisma be measured when the reformer has personally won over his opponents through patience, cheerfulness, tact, and laconism?

Ninth, sometimes reform objectives are merely to explore, advise, and stimulate, as there may be no preconceived appropriate goal.

Finally, could the reform effort have been used more profitably in other directions? What were the better alternatives and were they considered? Could more have been achieved at very little extra cost if the reformers had not stopped where they did?

Rarely does the nature of the evidence allow researchers to attempt answers to these methodological problems. Such factors as motivation, morale, and subconscious feelings are beyond recall soon after the event. Rarely do reformers keep a full diary of events. In search of greater accuracy, researchers must be prepared to enter areas in which revelations are harmful and persistent inquiry is discouraged. But to stop short at this point is to court bias and contradiction. To evaluate only part of the evidence is hardly satisfactory or satisfying; researchers understandably refrain from generalizing on inadequate or incomplete evidence. Hence efforts are being made to make meaningful generalizations without accumulating all the relevant evidence and to refine research methods.

But there is a brighter side. Abortive reforms are easy to identify. The achievements of reformers are also observable, and it is possible to compare the end results with the original aims. For example, if their objective was the creation of new "thinking units" or a department of science or a central personnel agency to recruit staff according to merit, then it is relatively easy to ascertain whether such groups were created and to what extent they reflected the reformers' proposals. Productivity and the general level of services can be measured, as most organizations endeavor to ascertain their performance according to known criteria (though these may not be the most accurate or reliable of guides). Costs and expenditures are readily available, particularly in the public sector. On the basis of these and other known facts, researchers are endeavoring to measure organizational efficiency, social costs, the efficacy of decision-making, the quality of policy-planning, morale, job satisfaction, organizational loyalty, centralization, specialization, and so forth. Though much work still has to be done, every year we are in a better position to measure the accuracy of claims made by reformers. Nor is it difficult to discover whether vice, corruption, and waste have been eliminated and whether behavior patterns have altered. The records and working papers of reformers and of organizations responsible for surveys of administration are available. The accumulation of this material should in time provide solutions to methodological problems. Nevertheless, evaluation depends largely on its purposes—the questions in which the evaluator is most interested, such as contribution to development, increase in local skills, improvement in social welfare, higher level of satisfaction, greater dynamism (or self-sustained growth), and rate of circulation of new ideas. The results will differ correspondingly. Because expectations change, past efforts tend to be undervalued.

Unless administrative reforms are evaluated, the process is incomplete. To take the reformers at their word is unscientific, certainly distorting. They should be judged by their deeds alone. Their contribution may be quite marginal. Their egotistical stance may detract from the "hewers of wood and drawers of water" who work unobtrusively in the background, yet have a greater impact on the course of events than fleeting reforms. People must be prepared to change themselves, and it is here that the main emphasis should be placed, not on the various antics of the reformers. Perhaps the only lasting criterion is the contribution of reform to the capacity to eliminate the need for further reform.

CONCLUSION

Throughout the reform process, the advantage lies with those who recognize that an administrative problem exists. "They have an important voice in the way in which the problem is formulated and in the extent to which it is communicated to others" (Mailick and Van Ness 1962, p. 38). Reformers can make little headway if nobody else recognizes that a problem exists or if others disagree with their formulation of it. Similarly the reformers may lose the initiative if it is perceived that their proposals are merely peripheral to the real problem and its deep-seated causes. Once reformers perceive administrative ills, they enter a process fraught with pitfalls and dangers in which they may end up their own worst enemies. If they are not prepared to finish the process, they may never get another chance. If they do finish, they may wonder whether the effort and struggle was worth the end product. The time factor and the nature of resistance are unknowns at the outset. The whole process is a costly gamble, especially if the reformers have never thought about the nature of the obstacles.

BIBLIOGRAPHIC NOTES

As this and the remaining chapters draw heavily on sources already listed, only new material is included except when previous references are particularly important, as Barnett 1952; Bennis, Benne, and Chin 1961; Goodenough 1963; LaPiere 1965; and Mosher 1967 are throughout this chapter. In *awareness of need* the underlying argument is similar to that of "where the shoe pinches" in democratic theory, and the symptoms of distress are taken from the signs of maladministration given in most textbooks on administration. Similar approaches have been used in B. Chapman, *British Government Observed* (London: Allen and Unwin, 1963); B. Crick, *The Reform of Parliament* (London: Weidenfeld and Nicolson, 1964); H. Daalder, *Cabinet Reform in Britain 1914-1963* (Stanford University Press, 1963); Fabian Society Tract, *The Reform of the Higher Civil Service* (London: Gollancz, 1947); and W. J. Stankiewicz (Ed.), *Crisis in British Government: The Need for Reform* (London: Macmillan, 1967), which all deal with the failings of the British machinery of government.

In *formulation of goals and objectives, strategy and tactics*, the analysis was aided by the discussion of invention and creativity in W. J. J. Gordon, *Synectics: The Development of Creative Capacity* (New York: Harper and Row, 1961); and the diffusion processes in E. M. Rogers, *Social Change in Rural Society* (New York: Appleton-Century-Crofts, 1960) and his *Diffusion of Innovations* (New York: Free Press of Glencoe, 1962). The publications of the International Institute of Administrative Sciences provide sources of administrative reform: R. J. Burton and E. B. Strait, *The Central Machinery of Government: Its Role and Functions* (1954); H. O. Dovey, *Handbook of Organization and Methods Techniques* (1953); W. A. Gill, *A Performance Analysis System* (1953); T. D. Kingdom, *Improvement of Organization and Management in Public Administration* (1955); B. Kronvall, *Appropriate Forms* (1953); D. C. Stone, *National Organization for the Conduct of National Economic Programmes* (1954).

Other forms of administrative reform have been analyzed elsewhere.

(a) Reorganization: Blake and Mouton 1962; Blau and Scott 1962; Buck 1938; Crozier 1964; Emmerich 1950; Galloway 1950; Ginzberg and Reilley 1957; Guest 1962; Karl 1963; Langrod 1965; Mosher 1967; Polenberg 1966; Weiss 1966.

(b) Planning: Bennis, Benne, and Chin 1961; Bernays 1955; E. Devons, *Planning in Practice* (London: Cambridge University Press, 1950); Hanson 1966; F. A. von Hayek, *Road to Serfdom* (London: Routledge, 1945); R. A. Lester, *Manpower Planning in a Free Society* (Princeton University Press, 1966); W. A. Lewis, *The Principles of Economic Planning* (London: Allen and Unwin, 1956); Lippitt, Wat-

son, and Westley 1958; Mann and Neff 1961; D. Novick (Ed.), *Program Budgeting* (Cambridge: Harvard University Press, 1965); E. V. Rostow, *Planning for Freedom* (New Haven: Yale University Press, 1960); M. E. Sharpe (Ed.), *Planning, Profits and Incentives in the USSR*, 2 vols. (White Plains, N. Y.: I.A.S.P., 1966); J. Tinbergen, *Central Planning* (New Haven: Yale University Press, 1964); B. F. Wootton, *Freedom Under Planning* (London: Allen and Unwin, 1945).

(c) Joint Committees: Argyris 1962, 1964; Bales 1950; Bass 1960; Blake, Shepard, and Mouton 1964; Gouldner 1965.

(d) Watchdogs: S. V. Anderson (Ed.), *Ombudsmen for American Government?* (Englewood Cliffs: Prentice-Hall, 1968); W. Gellhorn, *Ombudsmen and Others: Citizens Protectors in Nine Countries* (Cambridge: Harvard University Press, 1967); D. C. Rowat, *The Ombudsman: Citizen's Defender* (London: Allen and Unwin, 1965).

(e) Policy Analysis: Ashby 1956; Barish 1951; Beer 1959, 1964; Braybrooke and Lindblom 1963; Brookings Institution 1961; Dror 1968.

(f) Revolution: Adams 1913; H. Arendt, *On Revolution* (New York: 1963); D. W. Brogan, *The Price of Revolution* (New York: Harper, 1951); L. P. Edwards, *The Natural History of Revolution* (University of Chicago, 1927); Johnson 1966; Jones, 1966; P. Kecskemeti, *The Unexpected Revolution* (Stanford University Press, 1961); W. Z. Laqueur, *The Fate of the Revolution* (London: Weidenfeld and Nicolson, 1967); L. Nalbandian, *The Armenian Revolutionary Movement* (Berkeley: University of California Press, 1967).

(g) Political process: Caiden 1965; Heeney 1958; R. Hofstader, *The Progressive Movement 1900-1915* (Englewood Cliffs: Prentice-Hall, 1963); K. Ishwaran, *Politics and Social Change,* (Leiden: Brill, 1966); C. E. Merriam, *The Role of Politics in Social Change* (New York University Press, 1936); W. A. Robson, *Politics and Government at Home and Abroad* (London: Allen and Unwin, 1967); B. S. Silberman, *Ministers of Modernization—Elite Mobility in the Meiji Restoration, 1868-1873* (University of Arizona Press, 1964); J. A. Stone, D. K. Price, and K. H. Stone, *City Manager Government in United States Cities* (Chicago: Public Administration Service, 1940); R. E. Ward and D. A. Rustow (Eds.), *Modern Political Systems* (Englewood Cliffs: Prentice-Hall, 1965).

(h) Legal Process: J. Bentham, *Constitutional Code* (London, 1832); G. C. Gurvich, *Sociology of Law* (Toronto: Longmans, 1942); Martin 1965.

(i) Executive Direction: Einaudi 1959; Jacob 1967; Karl 1963; Polenberg 1966.

(j) Changing Attitudes: Argyris 1965; Argyris et al. 1962; E. C. Bursk (Ed.), *How to Increase Executive Effectiveness* (Cambridge: Harvard University Press, 1953); Cohen 1964; Costello and Zalkind 1963; G. Fisk (Ed.), *The Frontiers of Management Psychology* (New York: Harper and Row, 1964); R. T. Golembiewski, F. Gibson, and G. Y. Cornog (Eds.), *Public Administration* (Chicago: Rand McNally, 1966); A. W. Gouldner and S. M. Miller (Eds.), *Applied Sociology* (Glencoe, Ill.: Free Press, 1965); M. Haire, *Psychology in Management* (New York: McGraw-Hill, 1964); R. L. Kahn, *Organizational Stress* (New York: Wiley, 1964); N. R. F. Maier and J. J. Hayes, *Creative Management* (New York: Wiley, 1962); Schein and Bennis 1965.

(k) Education and Training: Bradford, Gibbs, and Benne 1964, H. W. Burns, *Education and the Development of Nations* (Syracuse University Press, 1963); L. K. Caldwell, *Improving the Public Service Through Training* (Washington, D. C.: A.I.D., 1962), Chen 1960; J. J. Corson, *Executives for the Federal Service* (Columbia University Press, 1952); A. Curle, *Educational Strategy for Developing Societies* (London: Tavistock, 1963); F. I. de P. Garforth, *Management Development* (London: I.P.M. 1959); N. F. Hall, *The Making of Higher Executives* (New York University Press, 1958); F. C. Pierson (Ed.), *The Education of American Businessmen* (New York: McGraw-Hill, 1959); D. C. Stone, *Education in Public Administration* (Brussels: I.I.A.S., 1963); F. J. Tickner, *Modern Staff Training* (University of London Press, 1952); R. J. Ward (Ed.), *The Challenge of Development* (Chicago: Aldine, 1967).

(l) Mechanization: As with automation, the literature on the mechanization of administration is rapidly growing. Most devote themselves solely to the technical side and largely ignore reform implications.

The problems of *evaluation* have received scant attention except by Wasserman 1959. Criteria for evaluation are still disputed between different schools of thought, particularly between public interest (Friedrich 1952; Schubert 1960) and social efficiency (Lawrence 1966;

Rakowski 1966). Among those who do come to grips with the main issues are E. D. Chapple and L. R. Sayles, *The Measurement of Management* (New York: Macmillan, 1961); Robson 1960; L. Tatham, *The Efficiency Experts: An Impartial Survey of Management Consultancy* (London: Business Publications, 1964); Taylor 1947; United States Bureau of the Budget, *Measuring Productivities of Federal Government Organizations* (Washington, D.C.: Government Printing Office, 1964); University of Connecticut 1965.

SIX

Obstacles to
Administrative Reform

In analyzing the process of administrative reform, the administrative subculture was ignored, as were the multitude of events that crisscross it in practice. Reform was deliberately abstracted from its surroundings to concentrate on the specific stages that reformers experience in their essentially political struggle to change existing behavior patterns. The analysis assumed that the process was being undertaken in fairly sophisticated societies with governments strong enough to ward off external enemies and to maintain internal stability with sufficient continuity to allow interdependent formal organizations and voluntary associations to fulfill social purposes and exchange services. Such societies would possess a certain minimum level of administrative skills, a basis for lasting cooperation, a stable political system, and certain clientele expectations of administrative performance. Administrative skills would be backed by a social system that reconciles individual differences, an institutional system that passes on accumulated knowledge, a communications system that brings people into quick contact with one another, and a recording system that provides reliable statistics as a basis for accounting, budgeting, and planning. These were the "givens," the deep-seated social traits and strongly held beliefs, which were kept constant throughout the analysis. In practice, few countries can claim to possess these givens. To approximate to what really happens in real life, the specific givens must be examined closely and in combination with temporary factors in the administrative subculture that block progress, change, and reform.

A thorough check list of all the factors that reformers ideally should take into account would cover practically every conceivable aspect of human ecology. As so much is taken for granted without undue harm, the value of such an extensive check list is questionable. But as too much also may be taken for granted, it is desirable that a check list be made of the more important factors or at least of the most important obstacles in the path of administrative reformers. Where the precise line is between important and not-so-important is a matter of opinion, but there are outstanding universal obstacles that would appear in all lists. It is on these that this chapter concentrates. All check lists tend to be tedious; the more complete, the less stimulating they are, for each reader is looking for something that interests him personally and helps him tackle specific problems. Although people skim over what appears to them to be irrelevant to their administrative subculture, they may be blind to what is relevant. If a check list causes them to pause and question what they have always taken for granted, it will have served a useful purpose.

Resistance to reform is a complex phenomenon grounded in immovable obstacles appertaining to reform in general and to administrative reform in particular. On the highest plane, social progress, whether desired or not, is hindered by the absence of growth and innovation, by intense social conflict and lack of political consensus, by the lack of natural resources and technological knowhow, and by instability and discontinuity. Without the prospect of minimum social progress, the obstacles to reform are insurmountable and the society continues to stagnate. On the other hand, where the rate of change is so furious that nobody knows from one moment to another what is going to happen next, reform is equally out of the question until the pace of change slows down sufficiently to permit reformers to formulate and implement their proposals. In both extremes, not all the obstacles are man-made, but they so overlap and interrelate that they reinforce one another. But the same is also true of reforms. Reforms in one area will lead to reforms in other areas, and a general propensity to reform is not likely to exclude the administrative subculture. Case studies confirm the interrelatedness of administrative reforms with other kinds of reform. They also indicate how they are bound up with such general social traits as the lack of enterprise (or willingness to take a risk); the existence of an unprogressive, unenlightened power elite with a self-image of godlike infallibility; the closeness of the people through kinship ties, religion, race, density, and so forth, which makes individuals reluctant to offend one another; and a level of administrative skills so low that even the reformers are unable to plan, formulate, or execute their own proposals.

The process of administrative reform points to several other insurmountable obstacles. First, there may be nobody willing to complain about administrative defects either because the defects are perceived as virtues or because society penalizes nonconformists.

Second, there may be no effective formulators. Insufficient general knowledge may exist on which proposals can be formulated; the requisite knowledge is kept as a secret inaccessible to outsiders. Available information may be inaccurate, distorted, or otherwise unusable for reform purposes. The intelligentsia with access to the requisite knowledge may be isolated within their own society, alienated from public life either because they are feared by an anti- or nonintellectual elite or because they have withdrawn from public life in protest or disgust at political antics. They are not prepared to lower their social esteem, dignity, or status by being associated with sordid politicking or to compromise their lofty ideals for political advantage. They may be disillusioned by their own political ineptness. Their intellectuality may have no empirical bent.

Third, there may be no advocates, that is, insufficient nonconformists and role-players willing to question and re-examine values, and no leaders willing to push reforms or dramatize reform issues. The root cause may be economic, simply the lack of sufficient resources to provide universal services. When there is not enough to go round, everybody competes against everybody else to get what is rightfully his, and the premium is on those who can find the short cuts and ensure that they receive priority. In this mad scramble for what is available, corruption, favoritism, influence, and power obviously count, and the leaders and potential advocates are likely to be haves rather than have-nots. Reforms likely to bolster justice and fairness, equality, integration and nondiscrimination, freedom and national rights, equity, public or general interest, social welfare and constitutionalism are not likely to be supported by the haves, who are the only ones likely to lose by them.

Fourth, there may be no interest in improving administrative performance. Administration may be lowly valued, or low performance standards may be perfectly acceptable. Again the root cause may be economic or social—nobody really cares about maladministration as long as they personally do not lose. There may be total lack of cooperation and mutual distrust between the administrators and the administered. The administered may do all they can to outwit and defeat those in authority while the elite may have no real control over the administrative infrastructure. Any improvement in administration would be viewed as strengthening the administrators and hotly resisted in practice by everyone else. Resistance in this case is symptomatic of deep-seated social malaise and other environmental factors that shape the administrative subculture.

GEOGRAPHY

The direct impact of geography on the administrative subculture is so obvious that it is least analyzed. Man, through his adaptiveness and inventiveness, has managed to overcome nature's handicaps and to construct where necessary an artificial environment. But there are geographical obstacles which he has yet to overcome. The most important of these is physical location, more particularly physical barriers that block a society from its neighbors and from the mainstream of human progress. It lacks the benefits of acculturation—cross-cultural intercourse, continuous and easy contacts, competition, and spread of accumulating knowledge. It is shielded from some prime movers of administrative reform, such as war, invasion, occupation, and other man-made crises. Much of the time it is thrown back on its own devices unless it can overcome the physical obstacles artificially. On the other hand, some countries with easy communications deliberately create their own artificial barriers, which act in effect like physical barriers but lack the same dramatic impact just because they are man-made and fallible. In the short run it may be possible to modernize the administration of isolated societies in the Andes and Himalayas, in the deserts of the Middle East and the Arctic, or in the jungles of

Africa and Asia by conquest, coercion, and superimposition; however, any permanent transformation entails the breakdown of isolation through better communications and greater mobility. Administrative reform in many isolated societies may have to await improvements in economic conditions or may have to be imposed from the outside by autocratic means. Otherwise the resistance of traditional elites is likely to prove too powerful. In short, a first-class highway system or aviation network may be more important in the long run than any number of foreign experts who reside for short periods and in effect advise only the traditional elites.

Sheer size and diversity of topography may similarly obstruct the progress of administrative reform internally. Reforms at the center, in the capital city and major ports, may be totally unreflected elsewhere in the country; they may be quite irrelevant to branch offices and local administrations in isolated areas. This can work both ways. An isolated and virtually autonomous administrative subsystem may solve local problems in ways that could benefit the whole system, but its experiments and innovations remain unknown at large. Large countries are likely to be more difficult to reform uniformly than smaller countries, for not only do they lack easy communication, quick contact, intimate social relations, immediate feedback, and interest in national events; but they are also more difficult to integrate and to administer homogeneously, and they suffer from parochialism and competing local interests that transcend nationalism. On the other hand, a large country may accommodate diversity and permit experimentation without incurring the headlong clashes and bitter personal feuds of a small, compact society where there is no room to maneuver. For instance, Australia and Canada (or any of the large federations) accommodate much administrative variety, and their different administrative subsystems benefit from each other's experiments in reform without raising the emotion and public passions engendered in Israel and Singapore when they attempt to do the same. Smaller countries lack the space or distance to absorb the friction. It is not so much size as the concentration of population that brings different concepts and standards into conflict and demands that attention be paid to the overloading of the center and the top people, the repetition and duplication of work, decision-making performed with inadequate knowledge of the application points, inadequate coordination, and dissipation of energies on less important matters.

People who live in climatically harsh areas are too busy combating the weather to concentrate on administrative reform unless they live in artificial surroundings. Climate becomes really important when, in combination with natural resources, it influences, perhaps even determines, the pattern and nature of economic development, the extent of self-sufficiency or reliance on external trade, and the local diet. The last, for instance, affects physical growth, labor productivity, and disease resistance, which in turn are related to the proportion of workers and nonworkers, the average life expectancy, the sickness rate, and the level of human energy. Administrative reforms alone may make no perceptible impact on the deficiencies they seek to remedy. They may be peripheral and even irrelevant to the root causes, exacerbating the ills rather than curing them. The richer countries have an advantage. They can compensate for their natural deficiencies. It might be expected, therefore, that poorer countries stress economy and efficiency, conservation, and population control to bridge the gap, but in fact the richer countries have done just this and widened the gap instead. Paradoxically, the richer countries can afford to economize, to promote efficiency, and generally to encourage higher administrative performance as more important problems have been solved or settled themselves with prosperity. They are also better able to afford the dislocation of transformation and reform, to postpone current consumption so as to devote resources to experimentation, innovation, and investment, and to spare resources to develop the young (who are usually more radical and dynamic than their elders). Without the fears of overpopulation and the hazards of cheap life and labor, the richer countries—just to stay rich—may have to prevent slackness on attaining prosperity, conserve diminishing nonreplaceable resources and high-cost labor force, and encourage progress, creativity, and administrative competence. For them, the problems of disease, illiteracy, hunger, poverty, and injustice are less significant; and those of barbarism, slavery, caste stratification, unrestrained procreation, mysticism, social ignorance, hidden unemployment, and isolationism virtually things of the past.

HISTORY

Except for isolated societies that have been left to their own devices and now provide much source material for anthropologists, contemporary societies are conglomerates that have been transformed often by conquest or migration. The refusal of conqueror and vanquished to mix emphasized cultural differentiation, while persecution further strengthened national self-consciousness, easing the assimilation of self-imposed reforms but impeding the acceptance of other-imposed reforms. The free association of peoples favored acculturation and upset reforms in progress, but ushered in more lasting reforms than imposed reforms, which rarely survived the withdrawal of coercive pressure. Decolonization in recent times has illustrated how much of the colonial administrative pattern was assimilated by the indigenous peoples and how long it took for them to reject the imposed superstructure. Some have reverted back to precolonial administrative patterns while retaining the formal imperial structure, while others have incorporated the imposed values into their administrative subculture as part of their modernization. None has completely obliterated all traces of colonization or desired to, but further prospects of administrative reform vary according to emerging social forces, usually more chauvinistic.

Migration had similar repercussions as free movement within an empire. The different peoples borrowed from one another and the differences in their administrative practices were smoothed out. Some might resist incorporating foreign practices and insist on administrative autonomy but social pressures would induce them to change in time. Administrative reform in societies in which the peoples have been mixed for a long time does not involve the communal passions roused in societies in which the peoples have maintained separate identities and place cultural autonomy above national unity. In this respect Switzerland and New Zealand are favored compared with Canada, Belgium, India and Nigeria.

In the political struggle over administrative reform, both reformers and their opponents appeal to history as proving their respective cases. Reformers argue that the story of society is one of unfailing progress and liberation from nature's grasp, a continuous causal process wherein everything is in perpetual transition. Opponents of reform see no continuous improvement in man's lot but a series of cycles alternating between progress and regress. Few changes, reforms, and revolutions, it is argued, have been absolute successes. More were regressive and most were accompanied by disappointment and disillusionment. Both sides select examples to prove their case. Reforms have succeeded and failed. They have been accommodated easily and they have caused much dislocation. History is interpreted according to the needs of the time, but where reforms have a bad record of failures, new proposals are unlikely to receive the same sympathetic hearing as where the record is one of success. This would suggest that potential reformers woud do well to investigate the past not so much to learn from mistakes as to shape strategy, using historical reference to advantage.

TECHNOLOGY

"The one sure index of human advancement" and the outstanding feature of human history, is the constant progress of technology, whose obvious utility is accepted before the cultural impact is properly considered (Arensberg and Niehoff 1964). Sudden breakthroughs in technology transform administrative practices; the level of technology achieved in a society is also a good indication of administrative skills. Neither can afford to lose sight of the other without causing widespread chaos and misery. When technology outstrips administrative performance, not only is it wasted but its uncontrolled cultural impact can bring havoc. Whenever administrative capacity outstrips technology, it cannot be properly utilized. When the balance is profoundly disturbed by a dramatic development, it is sooner or later restored as technologists flounder in administrative chaos and seek to apply scientific thinking to administrative problems, or as administrators come to realize new-found opportunities opened up by technological advancement. A low-level technology is therefore a handicap to administration and a damper on administrative reform. If the rate of development is slow too, there is not the same pressure to find administrative remedies to complex social and administrative problems.

In theory, every society has an equal opportunity in the techno-logical race because the requisite knowledge is easily accessible except for the most advanced experiments and information with military application. In practice, technology requires large capital investment, extensive research, sophisticated training, and a mechanically and ad-ministratively minded people, used from childhood to tinkering with mechanical gadgets or organizing group activities. Where societies place academic study, philosophical speculation, conspicuous consump-tion, and entertaining above mechanics, utilitarianism, politics, and administration, the education system and reward structure are likely to be slanted against technology and administration. The downgrading of technological and administrative skills is an obstacle to administrative reform, whose prospects are tied to a transformation of social attitudes. The success of technology, certainly since the eighteenth century, virtually guarantees it (and administration) a higher social evaluation, but there will remain isolated societies and aesthetically dominated societies that will reject technological progress in prefer-ence to possessing an esteemed cultural heritage. These will remain obstructive to reformers.

CULTURE

Cultural influence on administration and administrative reform has already been described in the case studies. Cultural diversity is a handicap in administrative cooperation as is well illustrated in national administrations embracing diverse cultures and in international organi-zations. Administrative subcultures are quite different, and when they come together without any overriding uniformity or preparedness to compromise for mutual goals, the results are often haphazard, some-times tragically comic. For a start, people cannot communicate with one another, even when one common language is accepted and employment is confined to a select group who know that language sufficiently to be able to think in it and comprehend idiomatic expres-sions. Interpretation of ideas calls for much more than translation. Language is important simply because the bulk of reforms are achieved by talking and response to word evocation. Some languages are unsuitable for modern technology and administration. Linguistic reforms that might suit the purpose better are resisted by fervent nationalists. Language barriers and problems alone have bedevilled administrative reform in some newly independent states, particularly where previous colonial rulers divided up continents according to their own political, trade, and military interests irrespective of local wishes. Now these states are saddled with a colonial legacy without the unifying force of an imperial regime or a united nationalist movement.

Language is an expression of thoughts. The symbols each person uses to conduct his affairs—ideals, legends, myths, religious doctrines, scientism—are not neutral toward the concept of reform. A good many symbols, notably the Protestant Ethic, rationality, and progressive ideologies, are favorable; others can be obstructive. Religious doctrines, for instance, being sacrosanct, tend to lag behind the times until new prophets revise them. The pursuit of heavenly things on earth diverts resources to the spiritual world. Such concentration of effort on matters spiritual diverts attention from the practical problems of man in the here and now, and can lead to an uncaring attitude toward remedial human suffering and misery. On the other hand, man's aspiration to serve and glorify his gods may be an elevating experience that ennobles him and incites him to do good. It can be an innovating factor in exploration, construction, and administration. On balance, however, religious doctrines tend to conservatism. Men are commanded not to challenge the status quo, not to question God's will, but to accept "their lot." Religious doctrines tend to emphasize tradition and continuity, to perpetuate fear, superstition, prejudice and outdated belief systems of "what is right or wrong, what is proper or improper, what is lucky or unlucky or what is possible or impossible" (Niehoff and Niehoff 1966, p. 7). Of course, there are notable exceptions and religion may be less of an obstacle than the clergy.

Some religious moral codes are more conducive to reform than others. A distinction must be made between the ethical teachings, the behavior of the mass of followers, and the political behavior of the organized clergy. The ethics usually constitute effective administrative practice and, if adhered to, might obviate the need for much administrative reform. The motivation of some reformers, particularly in Western countries, is religious revivalism, that is, a desire to make the ideal the norm. The organized clergy, on the other hand, has rarely been a progressive force in history because of its advocacy of a theocracy, its vested interest in accumulated wealth and privilege, its exploitation of the fears and superstitions of the mass, its encouragement of religious warfare and persecution, and its reluctance to support reform. At the present time, the Catholic Church in Latin America finds its leaders bitterly divided on the direction of change and on the part the church ought to play in it as a force for social and economic reform (D'Antonio and Pike 1964). But individual members of the clergy have possessed that spark of moral indignation and compassion indispensable to all reformers and change agents, and they have been in the forefront of reform movements. Some would have been anyway, but others were fired by religion and by the ethical codes taught by it. The direct impact of religion and religious ethics on administration and administrative reform have been best analyzed for the Indian sub-continent, for the impact of the Protestant Ethic on Western administration, and for the effects of Confucianism in the administration of China and other Asian countries (see *Bibliographic Notes*).

Most other cultural factors contain obstructive features but are not in themselves dominantly obstructive. Nationalism can obstruct administrative reform if it turns into chauvinism or if nationalists fritter away scarce resources on prestige projects. Kinship ties may prevent the application of universalistic criteria. Local etiquette and values may impede acculturation. Extensive ruralism may hinder mobility. Low valuation of punctuality and regularity may diminish administrative performance. These are manifestations of the accredited reasonableness of one set of beliefs, themselves culture-bound, which render other beliefs automatically unrealistic and unreasonable. But what may appear rational and right in one environment may be quite the opposite in another. Goodenough (1963) warns that observers should distinguish between the major variables: "the private cultures of a community's members; their operating cultures; the community's public culture and the public culture of its subgroups; the material, social, and behavioral conditions which the community's members, guided by their cultural resources, try to maintain in their phenomenal world and which are their cultural artifacts and the customary routines by which they seek to produce and maintain the conditions they desire" (p. 272). Each varies in the degree to which it contains obstructive elements, but they are closely integrated and mutually enforcing. Like other anthropologists and behavioral scientists, Goodenough advocates voluntary compliance and advises that reforms should be compatible with existing practices, consistent with basic values, consistent with people's self-image, realistic, and identifiable with society (pp. 368-70). Reformers accept these cultural limitations. It is revolutionaries who seek to go beyond them.

A cultural trait that has been relatively overlooked, yet is crucial in the reform process is that of national complacency—a paralysis of the national will. The government dithers about doing anything, while the public bureaucracy lacks energy and integrity to mobilize capital and skill. Private enterprise looks for easy pickings in protected domestic markets and fails to develop exports, permitting foreign investors to do the innovating. Nobody is prepared to look below the surface. Social life turns sour. Dull and boring routine is broken only by erratic forms of escapism. Leaders act on instinct without attempting explanation or justification of their actions and hide behind secrecy, arrogance, and nonchalance. The past is denigrated and the future perceived pessimistically. Present discontents simmer. Are these symptoms or the course of decline? Or are they reflections of underlying physical and mental laziness?

ECONOMY

Administrative reform is not impossible in a barter system, but implementation is certainly eased by a money economy (as the Bolsheviks discovered after the Russian Revolution). A moneyless society without administration was described by William Morris under the apt title of *News From Nowhere*. Administrative reform, like administration, involves time, effort, and investment, scarce resources in any society, particularly in poor countries whose subsistence economy cannot afford the risk of reform failure. The paradox is that the societies most in need of administrative reforms are least able to afford them, while those that could accommodate low administrative performance have the resources for investment to put them further ahead. The process can be reversed if the richer societies deliberately forego further advances and devote their spare resources (savings) to helping the poorer societies reach a take-off point where they can afford to invest in innovations and reforms by themselves. To some extent, international aid schemes serve this purpose, but they do not prevent rich societies from continuing to invest much more in their own futures than in the poor societies, which may not reach the take-off point for some time to come. Lack of resources is then the most important economic obstacle to administrative reform, with waste of resources on nonessentials as a close second.

The objectives of administrative reform are closely related to the type of economy. In a society dominated by private enterprise, resistance to reforms would depend on the extent to which they interfered with the capitalist system, that is, whether they promised *(a)* to reduce government enterprise and the role (and expense) of the state; *(b)* to increase the amount of business going to private enterprise; *(c)* to save private enterprise money; and *(d)* to help private enterprise at the expense of the state. In a more collectivist-oriented society wherein the economy is manipulated by the government to protect and advance communal objectives, resistance to reforms might depend on their incompatibility with collective goals, national planning, prior commitment of resources, and adherence to ideological aims. In totalitarian societies, administrative reforms must comply with the idosyncracies of dictators. Reforms are least likely to meet obstruction in a society that prefers the flexibility of a middle position or a mixed enterprise economy. But overriding the general form of the economy may be development policies or crises (such as inflation and adverse trade balances), which must be given priority irrespective of the value and future contribution of administrative reforms.

Even when administrative reformers have resources and governmental support, they may be obstructed by the general lack of administrative and political skills that they need to plan and carry through their reforms. How many people with such skills are available in an economy is a function of manpower and employment policies, education, migration, citizenship and residence laws, and labor mobility. Most, if not all, societies complain of deficiencies in these areas—there never are enough good people to go around. The market is international, with immediate job conditions less important than career prospects, status, taxation, housing and educational facilities, travel opportunities and health risks. The supply is limited by social customs, local prejudices, and restrictive labor practices by professional groups and employee organizations. Particularly handicapping to reformers are strikes, refusals to readjust work norms, demarcation disputes, and disinterest in improved administrative performance. Even more serious is the extent of administrative crime or the connivance of administrators in crime at lower levels, especially in theft, corruption, bribery, falsification, frauds, and blackmail. These, like budgetary procedures, are built-in inefficiencies, deeply rooted and socially accepted which nothing short of a moral or fiscal revolution can overcome. Like adverse attitudes to work, they block administrative reform.

SOCIETY

People cling to accustomed values and institutions until something better presents itself. Then they switch, providing the new can be assimilated into current cultural patterns. LaPiere (1965) argues that society itself is an obstacle to change. Most of its arrangements are designed to preserve the status quo as much as possible. Reform is the work of the self-chosen innovating minority struggling to overcome the social bias against them. Though the social system may be naturally adaptive to change, particular features in it are highly resistant. Even organizations ostensibly dedicated to bringing about change operate to preserve their structures and contexts.

> A given organization may not succeed in preventing changes that ultimately destroy it; but to the extent that it is internally integrated . . . it resists being changed and it discourages changes in its context. Survival is . . . the motif of any organization and stability is the *sine qua non* of organizational survival (LaPiere 1965, p. 329).
>
> . . . Bureaucracy, like other forms of organization, discourages the emergence of changes from within and resists the impact of changes imposed from without . . . [It] does much to discourage the emerg-

ence of innovative individuals, and even more to retard the adoption of whatever innovations do appear . . . The inherent tendency [is] for any mature bureaucratic organization to resist change from without, i.e., to be reluctant to adapt itself to changed external conditions or to adopt innovations that are available to it (La Piere 1965, pp. 409-11).

It is this intransigence of bureaucracy in particular that has prompted Bennis (1966) to predict its disappearance in modernized society. But contemporary large-scale organizations, far from disappearing, seem to be adapting themselves to changing conditions, and administrative reformers have allowed for their resilience and used it to advantage.

As Eisenstadt's analysis of bureaucratic empires showed, each social class has a certain predisposition toward reform in general and administrative reforms in particular (Eisenstadt 1963). The elite classes support reforms that leave essentials unaltered and their position intact. The lower classes favor reforms that promise to improve their lot, so concerned are they with the struggle for livelihood; but they have been so often abused by reformers with ulterior motives that they may be exceedingly suspicious of new prophets. Not only are they fatalistic because of past abuse, but they side with their protectors in the elite classes in resisting middle class reformers. Sometimes, the very people who have most to gain from reform may well be the most resistant. But resistance may be less related to position in the social scale than to sense of security.

> It is not only the rich, and privileged and well born (the traditional elites) who feel the threats of changes and resist them. The middle class man, entrenched in his small business, farm or government job; the poor man, deriving security from familiar institutions and relationships—they also fear the uncertainty of measures that may cause changes in economic functions or social status. The more precarious their security, the more they fear change (Esman 1963, p. 28).

One might expect insecure people to support reforms that would guarantee their greater security. But examples could be found both to support and to contradict generalizations of this kind. The most that can be said is that there is a tendency in a certain direction if other factors—for example, social mobility, class identification, wealth distribution, occupational status, and civil rights—are held constant. The following are examples of such general tendencies.

1. Families with close kinship relations are more resistant to reform than atomistic families.
2. Self-contained groups are more resistant than dependent groups.
3. Rural communities are more resistant than urban communities.
4. Individuals open to more socialization influences are less resistant than individuals confined to fewer socialization influences.
5. Younger people are less resistant than older, single people less than married couples, married couples without dependents less than married couples with dependents.
6. Rigidly stratified societies are more resistant than weakly stratified societies.
7. High social mobility is less conducive to resistance than low social mobility.
8. Societies with highly elaborate rules systems are more resistant than societies with few explicit rules and regulations.
9. Isolated elites are more likely than integrated elites to meet resistance in implementing reforms. Those who have neglected reform opportunities previously are more resistant than those who have participated in reform.

Perhaps in time even these generalizations will be exposed as folklore, as have geographical determinism, social Darwinism, dialectical materialism, and sex inferiority. Age in years may not be so important as mental alertness. Social mobility may not be as important as the accommodation of the social structure to new classes, particularly the rising middle classes. Kinship ties may be less important than the acceptance of the concept of citizenship (see *Bibliographic Notes*). One of the most important social obstacles to administrative reform remains indifference to administration. Maladministration is the norm; lip service only is paid to concepts of service, efficiency, productivity, equality, universality, and other reform goals. If the clientele does not demand anything better (perhaps because it is in no position to express or enforce its expectations), administrators are unlikely to go out of their way to make their job more demanding. Further, maladministration can serve as a blessing in disguise as, for instance, in totalitarian regimes, inhumane organizations, robber economies, and slave societies, where it may act to cushion inhumanities and atrocities perpetrated by merciless elites. Unless the regimes themselves are transformed, administrative reform may be undesirable. Much the same applies to politicized administrations where the political functions are more important than the administrative functions, and to bureaucratic politics. There, administrative reform, if not defeated by its unpopularity, would be wrecked by its superficiality and irrelevance.

POLITY

Administrative reform is not only a political process, but is directly related to the nature of the polity. The extent to which reformers are successful depends on astute political tactics and manipulation of political forces within the society. The methods of implementation are geared to the nature of the political regime. In one-party totalitarian states, administrative reforms must conform with centrally approved policies and directions. In dictatorships, they must have the concurrence of the dictator, however paranoiac or stupid he may be. Once reforms are accepted, there is little open resistance to their implementation, but passive resistance may be hidden. The alternative is to bypass the center altogether and hope that no one there will find out until it is too late, or that, if they do, they will sympathize. In multiparty democracies, much administration is outside the political sphere in practice, and reforms do not need political concurrence unless the political actors wish to make them political issues. The extent to which the political processes impede administrative reform depends less on the form of the polity and more on their controversial nature and whether the reformers can avoid the political arena.

As with the social factors, certain general tendencies can be stated about the relationship between politics and administrative reform.

1. Denial of civil liberties obstructs administrative reform.
2. Written constitutions are less conducive to reform than unwritten constitutions.

3. Rigid constitutions are more resistant to reform than flexible constitutions.

4. Federal states have greater potentiality for experimenting with reforms than unitary states.

5. Strong local government systems are less resistant to reforms at local level but are an obstacle at national level.

6. When legislative and executive are controlled by the same political parties, reform meets less resistance than when they are controlled by different parties.

7. When two or more chambers of a legislature are controlled by different political parties, more resistance is shown to reform than when they are controlled by the same party.

8. When the government is composed of a single party, reform is likely to be more acceptable than when the government is a coalition, providing that party is not antireform.

9. Guaranteed tenure of office is more conducive to reform than insecurity, and long tenure more so than short tenure.

10. Ideological parties are more resistant to reforms that do not conform with their ideology than nonideological parties.

11. Resistance to reform is likely to be higher in a weak political system than in a strong one where the government can impose its will on vested interests, isolated groups, and its own militia and bureaucracy. Similarly, strong political leaders are more likely to succeed in attaining reforms than weak ones, not only in the areas directly under their control but also in anything in which they play a part.

12. Politicized administrations are more resistant to reform than depoliticized administrations. Indigenous institutions are less susceptible to reform than transferred institutions.

Resistance to administrative reforms by political leaders and political arrangements is only a reflection of underlying political attitudes. Who really wants a perfectly administered taxation system or police force? There are good political reasons why maladministration exists, why it is allowed to persist, and why apparently obvious remedies are not applied. These underlying political reasons vary from society to society but the end result is much the same—maladministration is

preferred to efficient administration. Administrative reformers, looking
from one angle, want to upset the delicate balance that exists between
contending political forces by pushing certain values that have far-
reaching political connotations (though they may be unaware of
them). Resistance soon indicates the nature of political opposition.
Taylorism when blindly applied roused the organized labor movement.
The Brownlow Committee's report in strengthening the President
roused all his political opponents at the time from Congress down to
local nature clubs. Fingerprinting, an effective police device, has been
hotly resisted by many law-abiding citizens. The introduction of type-
writers into Australian public administration was delayed long after
their value was demonstrated because of such political implications as
the displacement of labor, emancipation of women, and readjustment
of the education system. Automation poses similar political problems.

PITFALLS IN ORGANIZATIONAL REFORM

In the contemporary world, administrative reforms, if not conceived within organizations, are pursued by organizations or individuals
within organizations and are usually directed at other organizations
or other individuals within the same organization. (Hence they are so
easily confused with organizational reforms, which constitute only a
part of administrative reform.) Here the struggle for reform cannot
be clothed in ideological garb or carried by national sentiment. Administrative reform is a personal matter between people who have to work
together all day and every day and carry on whether the reforms
are successful or not. Overcoming resistance at this level entails at the
outset a thorough study of the position by the potential reformers,
paying close attention to the facts and not relying on hopeful guesses
or demagoguery. Any tendency to distort or exaggerate will eventually
rebound on them. They carefully analyze the strengths and weaknesses of the principal power-holders, decision-makers, and opinion
leaders, and meticulously select their arguments. Initial approaches
may be followed up with direct confrontation, as memoranda and
polite exchanges of correspondence cannot convey the full impact.
Discussion permits reformers and their backers to project their per-

sonality and enthusiasm, to gauge reactions, and to reassure doubters. The appropriate techniques of persuasion are selected. For instance, subtle suggestions are dropped in conversation, or articles supporting the reform are circulated around the organization, or cabals are formed to tackle dissenters individually. Psychology is important in building up a solid nucleus of support. Doubters must be reassured, opponents cajoled, convinced, enticed, if possible without threatening the stability of the organization, stiffening the resistance of vested interests and others who will suffer by the reforms, and causing lasting impairments in personal relations. Failure to think and act on these lines constitutes a self-imposed obstacle.

Most organizations are composed by chance. There is no fundamental reason why people who work together should enjoy one another's company. Reform is only one factor that will set one group against another, one individual against another. To overcome the tensions, some people wear a mask at work or act somewhat out of natural character; reform proposals may challenge the double standard. Abrupt changes in character as assumed roles are dropped in taking sides over reform proposals add to the difficulties in the way of reform. Personality clashes may be overriding; that is, reforms may be opposed just because rivals or enemies are known to be in favor. Administrative reform may be used as an issue in a greater battle or as a lever for more important things by those more politically acute than the reformers, who may find themselves being used as instruments by people who are not basically disposed to reform at all. Organizational politicians are able to divide the reformers, take the credit for themselves, or exploit the petty personal differences between reformers.

Conflicts within the organization, such as those provoked by reform, are increasingly dealt with in committees or other forms of joint consultation rather than by organizational czars. Decisions are taken collectively, the minority agreeing to abide by majority rulings. Reformers these days must be skilled at committee politics. They must try to ensure a favorable vote beforehand by, for instance, stacking the committee with known sympathizers, capturing the support of the chairman and the more influential members, tapping opinions before the meeting, and working to divide, isolate, and win over opponents individually. Mastery of procedural rules and a sense of timing are political arts that are useful in determining the most opportune time for a vote, pushing through an innocuous looking amendment, or withdrawing until a better occasion. Failure to develop such politico-administrative skills can be disastrous to the cause of administrative reform.

The task of reformers is not completed when reforms are accepted in principle. A high staff turnover in the organization jeopardizes success. The reformers and their supporters may find other employment, leaving behind no one who knows how to proceed or has sufficient faith to see the reforms through. The people who have been trained to implement the reforms may leave, thereby causing delays until a new set of people can be trained. On the other hand, turnover can diminish the opposition and ease the path of reform.

Opponents of reform encourage passive resistance and fan resentment against the new reforms until anger, hatred, and bitterness are stirred. They place innumerable obstacles in the way so that everything connected with reform is made unnecessarily difficult. They continue with the old ways. They look for every excuse to challenge, ridicule, and reverse the reforms. The reformers have to win over the informal leaders—the foreman who tells his group to take no notice of the new instructions, the manager who goes his own way regardless of what others are doing, the supervisors who assure those below that the reforms are temporary and will soon be abandoned, the veteran employee who has "seen them all come and go," and the shop steward or trade union leader who passes adverse comment on cooperation with reformers and reforms. At this stage the reformers should go into full explanations, widen the decision-making process to include the informal leaders, increase training efforts, and introduce trial runs where practicable before total commitment. Thereafter, periodic checks should be sufficient to ensure that the reforms are implemented. If they are found not to be working, it may be necessary to use force, that is, to dismiss the main opponents, coerce those who passively resist, and reshuffle the staff to overcome deceit and malingering. Failure to act tough at the required moment may be self-defeating.

The politics of organizational reform have been considered to show that *(a)* if the wider environment is held constant, the organizational environment is full of traps and obstacles; *(b)* those traps and obstacles may defeat reforms irrespective of the merits of the case; and *(c)* reformers who do not possess certain politico-administrative and organizational skills, or who cannot attract followers who do, will create their own traps or ensnarc themselves in those laid by their opponents. The moment the reformers relax their efforts, they are likely to be surprised from an unexpected quarter.

CONCLUSION

When account is taken of all the environmental, organizational, and personality obstacles to administrative reform, it is not surprising that many reforms, reform movements, and reformers fail and that those that succeed receive the attention given to them. Even in the most favorable circumstances, reform is a tricky business. This is why potential reformers study the successes and failures of past reformers, hoping to copy the successes and avoid the failures. What they may fail to appreciate is that the circumstances may so have changed since previous attempts that the more important lessons have become irrelevant. They may have to start anew, assuming nothing. For this purpose, they need to consult a check list of likely potential and probable obstacles in the context, the organizational situation, and themselves. All the signs may point to failure but they may reassure themselves that some reformers have succeeded in far worse circumstances. Skills can offset environmental traps, and the element of chance may work in their favor so that they bring off a major historical triumph. Modern societies value their innovators, instigators, trailblazers and change agents, to whose inventions all are indebted. If they had adjusted to the world as they found it, they could never have changed it. They had to be different, reaping the penalties and rewards of those who deviate from given ways.

BIBLIOGRAPHIC NOTES

There are so many obstacles in the way of reform that the wonder is not so much that so many fail but that some succeed. Geographical obstacles are possibly the most obvious and yet the least mentioned, perhaps because discussion is thought superfluous. There is geopolitics but not geoadministration. In contrast, the historical obstacles are fairly well covered in the literature, certainly in country studies such as Bonnefous 1958; F. Ridley and J. Blondel, *Public Administration in France* (London: Routledge and Kegan Paul, 1964); Mariani 1958. The administrative culture is a product of historical forces that can be used both to support and to oppose reforms (A. L. Rowse, *The Use of History* [London: Hodder and Stoughton, 1946]). The impact of colonialism is described in detail in development administration studies (sce Chapter 4). Migration and acculturation are dealt with in social change studies (see Chapter 3) and in analyses by H. Arendt, *The Origins of Totalitarianism* (New York: Meridian, 1958); Heady and Stokes 1962; Hirschman, 1967; R. Levy, *The Social Structure of Islam* (London: Cambridge University Press, 1957); Symonds 1966. Both factors merge into the cultural context, a link emphasized by Barnett 1956; Brannen and Hodgson 1965; Cleveland and Mangone 1958; G. Heckscher, *The Study of Comparative Government and Politics* (London: Allen and Unwin, 1957) and R. Hoggart, *The Uses of Literacy* (London: Chatto and Windus, 1957).

The technological factor is covered by F. R. Allen (Ed.), *Technology and Social Change* (New York: Appleton-Century-Crofts, 1957); G. M. Foster, *Traditional Cultures and the Impact of Technological Change* (New York: Harper and Row, 1962); M. Mead (Ed.), *Cultural Patterns and Technical Changes* (New York: Mentor Books, 1954); B. Russell, *The Impact of Science in Society* (London: Allen and Unwin, 1952); E. H. Spicer (Ed.), *Human Problems in Technological Change* (New York: Russell Sage Foundation, 1952). For a different angle, the works of O. Lewis are worth consulting, particularly *Pedro Martinez* (New York: Random House, 1964).

Religion as such hardly needs references here but there are some works that refer to its impact on administration. The relationship between Protestantism and the evolution of the bureaucratic organization is described by R. Bendix, *Max Weber: An Intellectual Portrait* (New York: Doubleday, 1960); M. Weber, *Theory of Social and Economic Organization*, ed. by A. R. Henderson and T. Parsons (London: Hodge, 1947); and R. H. Tawney, *Religion and the Rise of*

Capitalism (New York: Mentor Books, 1948). The impact of Hinduism and Islam on administration in India and Pakistan and the impact of Confucianism and Buddhism on administration in South and Southeast Asia are dealt with in development administration literature: P. Abrecht, *The Churches and Rapid Social Change* (London: S. C. M. Press, 1961); M. Eliade, *Shamanism* (London: Routledge and Kegan Paul, 1964); E. G. Leonard, *A History of Protestantism*, Vol. I: *The Reformation* (London: Nelson, 1965); W. A. Lessa (Ed.), *Reader in Comparative Religion* (Evanston: Row, Peterson, 1958); K. Marx, *Capital*, ed. by F. Engels (Chicago: Kerr, 1906-7); M. Weber, *The Religion of India* (Glencoe, Ill.: Free Press 1958); M. Weber, *The Religion of China* (Glencoe, Ill.: Free Press, 1960); C. K. Young, *Religion in Chinese Society* (Berkeley: University of California Press, 1961). The impact of Communist ideology is examined with all the twists and turns in the classics of Communism, but different approaches can be found in F. Borkenau, *European Communism* (New York: Harper, 1953); G. Lichtheim, *Marxism* (London: Routledge and Kegan Paul, 1964); R. C. Tucker, *Philosophy and Myth in Karl Marx* (London: Cambridge University Press, 1961); and W. L. Tung, *The Political Institutions of Modern China* (The Hague: Nijhoff, 1966).

The economists are dominant in the field of development, largely because progress has been judged in terms of material satisfaction. They have run quickly up against noneconomic obstacles and in this respect the works of R. O. Hirschman, B. F. Hoselitz, W. A. Lewis, G. Myrdal, and A. Waterston are illustrative. Others maintain that it is not so much lack of resources as lack of will or skill or development priorities that diminishes effective performance, though A. Berle, J. K. Galbraith, and A. Shonfeld have shown that the rich countries are not exempt. Otherwise, economic obstacles to administrative reform have to be gleaned from Fenn 1958; Forrester 1961; A. L. Harris, *Economics and Social Reform* (New York: Harper, 1958); Hoselitz and Moore 1963; F. C. Lane and J. C. Riemersma (Eds.), *Enterprise and Secular Change* (Homewood, Ill: Irwin, 1953); National Planning Association, *Technical Cooperation in Latin American* (Washington, D.C., 1956); H. C. Thole and C. C. Gibbons, *Business Action in a Changing World* (Chicago: Public Administration Service, 1956); and such specialized studies as C. S. Shoup, *The Fiscal System of Venezuela*

(Baltimore: The Johns Hopkins University Press, 1959) and C. H. Zondag, *The Bolivian Economy, 1952-65* (New York: Praeger, 1966).

Cultural, religious, and social obstacles, on the one hand, and economic and political obstacles on the other seem to overlap, merge, and reinforce one another. The sociologists, more than any other group, seem to realize this and are not so prone as other social scientists to approach their subject matter with single-mindedness. To the references listed in previous chapters the following should be added: Arrow 1951; M. Djilas, *The New Class* (London: Thames and Hudson, 1958); E. H. Erikson (Ed.), *The Challenge of Youth* (Toronto: Doubleday, 1965); P. H. Odegard, *Political Power and Social Change* (Rutgers University Press, 1966); R. Serenso, *The Rulers* (New York: Praeger, 1962); E. H. Tuma, *Twenty-Six Centuries of Agrarian Reform* (Berkeley: University of California Press, 1965). Theories of social change which have since been discarded are discussed in E. H. Carr, *What is History?* (London: Macmillan, 1962); Childe 1951; E. Huntington, *Civilization and Climate* (New Haven: Yale University Press, 1915); E. Huntington, *Mainsprings of Civilization* (New York: Wiley, 1945); Ponsioen 1962; W. G. Sumner, *Social Darwinism* (Englewood Cliffs: Prentice-Hall, 1963).

What constitutes a political obstacle is a matter of opinion with little demonstrable proof as yet. Controversies abound—autocracy *versus* democracy, unitary *versus* federal form of government, presidential *versus* cabinet systems, presidential *versus* parliamentary systems, division of power *versus* integration. Reflections on these lines can be found in S. P. Aiyar, *Federalism and Social Change* (London: Asia Publishing House, 1961); P. H. Appleby, *Big Democracy* (New York: Knopf, 1949); Banfield 1961; S. H. Beer and A. B. Ulam, *Patterns of Government* (New York: Random House, 1958); G. C. S. Benson, et al., *Essays in Federalism*, Claremont College Calif., 1961; H. Finer, *The Presidency* (Chicago: University of Chicago Press, 1960); C. J. Friedrich, *Constitutional Government and Democracy* (Boston: Ginn and Company, 1950); C. J. Friedrich and Z. K. Brzezinski, *Totalitarian Dictatorship and Autocracy* (Cambridge: Harvard University Press, 1965); W. B. Graves, *Public Administration in a Democratic Society* (Boston: D. C. Heath, 1950); J. A. G. Griffith, *Central Governments and Local Authorities* (London: Allen and Unwin, 1966); E. P. Herring, *Presidential Leadership* (New York: Farrar and Rinehart, 1940); R. E. Neustadt, *Presidential Power* (New York: Wiley, 1960); C. Rossiter, *The American Presidency* (New York: Harcourt, 1960); F. E. Rourke, *Bureaucratic Power in National Politics* (Boston: Little, Brown, 1965); D. Verney, *The Analysis of Political Systems* (London: Routledge and Kegan Paul, 1959); R. E. Ward and R. C. Macridis (Eds.), *Modern Political Systems* (Englewood Cliffs: Prentice Hall, 1965); L. D. White, *The City Manager* (Chicago: University of Chicago Press, 1927); and W. Wilson, *Congressional Government* (Boston: Houghton Mifflin, 1885).

The internal organizational obstacles to administrative reform are examined in the general body of literature on administration already listed in Chapter 1 and on the process of administrative reform in Chapter 4. Case studies of how administrators overcome new obstacles are provided in J. D. Barker, *Power in Committees* (Chicago: Rand McNally, 1966); E. Dale, *The Great Organizers* (New York: McGraw-Hill, 1960); M. Dalton, *Men Who Manage* (New York: Wiley, 1959); Tannenbaum, Weschler, and Massarik 1961.

SEVEN

Discovering the Quintessence of Administrative Reform

It is not possible to evolve a theory of administrative reform until a universally accepted definition exists, but it is possible to speculate and hypothesize about its nature even before there is general consensus about its meaning and while the field is novel and confused. The assumption underlying previous chapters is that consensus will be reached eventually and thereafter a theory of administrative reform will become more feasible. This, of course, may be mere wishful thinking. The survey so far suggests that the empirically defined phenomenon of administrative reform can be explained in an orderly and systematic fashion; that it can be studied scientifically; that its complicated nature can be unraveled, its processes classified, and current generalizations tested; and that theories about administrative reform can stimulate and guide further research that will validate them. When the incomplete nature of the evidence is expanded to take in the full complexity of the subject, existing generalizations may be replaced by more complicated explanations. Already, one can hazard a guess that, in common with much else in political science, these explanations will not be deductive but probabilistic, mainly tendency, causal, and teleological, and that the theories will be largely of the factor kind (Meeham 1965). They will need to be placed in a larger framework of administrative dynamics and a theoretical structure of social change that can cope with accumulating knowledge about human behavior.

The prerequisites for a theory of administrative reform already exist. There is an objective reality concerning which uniformities are discoverable. Such regularity can be expressed in explanatory (but not yet predictive) generalizations with a high degree of probability capable of verification through refined methods. The generalizations can be placed in an orderly system of constructs which is internally coherent (meeting the tests of consistency and adequacy) and joined by the thread of causality. Empirical explanation is separated from ethical evaluation in exploring administrative behavior and can be integrated with other knowledge about human behavior in general. Factual data can be observed and classified. From the inferred generalizations, hypotheses can be constructed. The hypotheses can be verified and causally and conceptually integrated.

What, then, blocks progress toward a theory? First, the absence of a proper framework of administrative dynamics or theory of change that would cover (*a*) the manipulable variables influencing the direction, tempo, and quality of reform; (*b*) the roles of reformers, conservatives and neutrals; (*c*) the costs of reform; and (*d*) reliable bases for diagnosis, formulation, implementation, and evaluation. Second, the incompleteness of existing evidence. The literature on administrative reform suffers from serious defects. Studies are unrelated to one another, lacking any common framework or definition. Too much describes the unique and is therefore unmanageable for theoretical purposes. Environmental factors and ecological relationships are largely assumed; while processes are well-treated, motivation and evaluation are neglected. The source material is not treated critically. The descriptions are superficial, perhaps as a result of compression whereby depth has been sacrificed for coverage. Evaluations are concerned more with what *should* have been done than what *was* done. Third, the nature of the subject, particularly its methodological difficulties, its subjectivity, and the extent of taboo on it. Few participants in reform can remain objective about it and even fewer nonparticipants can know what really transpired. Rarely has it been possible to reach the required depth from which valid conclusions could be drawn. Alas, many researchers have forgotten, too, Fontenelle's warning that a philosopher may not believe what he sees because he is too busy speculating about what he does not see. There may be sufficient evidence at hand for significant generalization if researchers do not set their sights on a predictable science of administrative reform, with professionally trained administrative reformers or with every administrator his own reformer. The accumulation of further evidence might produce only an aimless collection of facts (Meeham 1965, p. 183). What is now perhaps required is less a detailed definition of administrative reform than an understanding of its quintessence from which it will be possible to ascertain the relevant facts. "An understanding which leaves the activity in debt to something outside itself is, for that reason, an inadequate understanding" (Oakeshott 1962, p. 113). With accumulating knowledge and mounting interest in the subject, a theory, if there is a theory to be found, will emerge, but there is no overwhelming reason why there should be a theory to find or why such a theory should be simple enough to have any explanatory or practical value. The facts may be contradictory and the necessary methodological sophistication may not develop.

Idealistically, one day it may be possible to program a computer for administrative reform. Some theorists are already thinking in this direction. Into the machine would be fed symptoms that seemed to indicate the need for something more than planned change and all other pertinent data. The machine would check on the symptoms (possibly rejecting them or demanding further information before continuing), make a diagnosis, and select the optimum strategy for rectification. In the absence of such an invention, individuals and organizations troubled by maladministration today turn to advisers or consultants whose knowledge and experience of similar administrative failings elsewhere and of administrative processes in general they believe qualify them to diagnose and select the optimum strategy. The advantages of the machine would be its impersonality, that is, automatic reaction to the facts, absence of prejudices (unless built-in), and inanimate concern with the inquirers, its greater storage capacity or memory system, and quicker selection or processing of relevant data. But dreams aside, it may still be possible to accumulate sufficient knowledge about administrative reforms, past, present and future, that anyone so minded, after adequate study, may be able to apply it to his own situation and choose the optimum strategy. All this presupposes (*a*) that there is such a thing as administrative reform, (*b*) that it is possible to accumulate knowledge about administrative reform, (*c*) that accumulated knowledge can be applied, and (*d*) that it is desirable to apply such knowledge. Each of these assumptions deserves further examination.

Administrative reform rejects any notion that human society is governed by a hidden hand. The idea that the universe of which man is part is governed by supernatural powers against which man is powerless is still strong. Much religious fatalism is founded on it: everything is ordained by God; the Messiah will put things right when He comes. The "hidden hand" idea has appeared in laissez-faire economic doctrines (free competition), social Darwinism (survival of the fittest), and, lately, in systems analysis where it is transformed into self-regulating mechanisms, homeostatic equilibrium, and automatic adjustments. They are mechanistic rather than probabilistic views of the universe. They preach either that man should not intervene at all for his intervention can only make things worse, or that however man intervenes, his efforts are useless. They add weight to the conservative case in that they degrade interferers and muddlers and support those who wait and see. But things do not just happen; they are caused and they can be manipulated. Administrative reform, like planned change, is deliberate and collaborative. It is a concrete expression of man's mastery over his destiny in at least some of his activities.

DENIAL OF ADMINISTRATIVE REFORM

Administrative reform is denied on two different counts. *First*, it is argued that if one delved deeper and cut away the superfluous rationalizations and propaganda, one would find that the so-called reforms are really nothing more than changes in attitude. Once people change their attitudes, for whatever reasons, then they are prepared to accept, and may work for, material transformations and reversals. Administrative reform, it is claimed, is merely the outward sign of inner changes of belief that have already taken place.

It is true that changes—administrative reforms and otherwise—are only effective if people change their attitude toward the new behavior expected of them and do not continue to expect the previous patterns. If they do, then behavior will revert back and the reforms will have failed. People have to be convinced that things beyond their immediate life are important even if they cannot connect changes expected in their behavior with administrative goals. But changes cannot be imposed by commands alone.

> First of all, command is one directional. One can give orders to a subordinate but not to an associate, superior or competitor . . . Second, the power of command rests upon the receivers' assumption that evasion or disobedience will be punished. Few people can draw upon all the punishments needed to back up reliance on command as the sole means of activation. . . . Third, if command is relied on too much it can readily lose its effectiveness . . . (Gross in Lawrence 1966, pp. 450-451).

Changes are brought about when people participate in reform processes and accept the new behavior patterns. They do this when they see that changes are worthwhile in terms of personal, group, and class interests or in terms of future interests against present inconvenience. There must be a sense of purpose behind their preparedness to sacrifice. The analysis of Gross in activating national plans can easily be adapted to administrative reform. Essentially, people have to be made optimistic, or otherwise reform becomes "a cynical game of manipulation, personal aggrandizement, and parasitic security" and "the optimism of leadership becomes a play rather than an honest mood and a moral commitment" (Martin 1965, p. 293). In advanced countries, an optimistic background can be assumed as people accept change and innovation, welcome new things, and favor experimentation. But an optimistic background is not in itself sufficient to overcome a conservative disposition in specific matters or to muster enough energy to activate reforms. Administrative reform involves changes in attitudes, but then so does all social change. It is not distinguishable on this score alone.

Second, it is claimed that reform is only a polite description for the old-fashioned exercise of power. People's behavior cannot be suddenly transformed against their will without violence or at least the threat of violence. If people cannot be persuaded that the circumstances brought about by reform would be to their advantage, then their resistance can be overcome by pointing to a worse fate if they do not conform. People are seen as being inherently conservative. They enjoy the present rather than "what was or what may be."

> To be conservative, then, is to prefer the familiar to the unknown, to prefer the tried to the untried, fact to mystery, the actual to the possible, the limited to the unbounded, the convenient to the perfect, present laughter to utopian bliss. Familiar relationships and loyalties will be preferred to the allure of more profitable attachments; to acquire and to enlarge will be less important than to keep, to cultivate and to enjoy; the grief of loss will be more acute than the excitement of novelty or promise (Oakeshott 1962, p. 169).

The conservative judges change by the disturbance it entails. He knows that there are both loss and gain in reform, unequally distributed, and that losses can outweigh gains. He draws the appropriate conclusions:

> First, innovation entails certain loss and possible gain, therefore, the onus of proof, to show that the proposed change may be expected to be on the whole beneficial, rests with the would-be innovator. Secondly, he believes that the more closely an innovation resembles growth (that is, the more clearly it is intimated in and not merely imposed upon the situation) the less likely it is to result in the preponderance of loss. Thirdly, he thinks that an innovation which is a response to some specific defect, one designed to redress some specific disequilibrium, is more desirable than one generated by a vision of perfection. Consequently, he prefers small and limited innovations to large and indefinite. Fourthly, he favours a slow rather than a rapid pace, and pauses to observe current consequences and make appropriate adjustments. . . . (Oakeshott 1962, p. 172)

In administration, this view of human nature is reflected less sympathetically in what has been described as "Theory X" (McGregor 1960), the hard line in management with the accent on coercion and threat, close supervision, and tight controls over behavior. Hence the aim of reformers should be the capture of power and such "strategic leverage points" as communications, motivations, and influence. It is power which enables reformers to change other people's way of living.

Again, this argument is persuasive and contains a great deal of truth, but like the other it is only one perspective, an element of the truth but not the whole truth. Administrative reform is much more than changes in attitude or the exercise of power. It is the application of the idea of progress, one of the most compelling forces in civilized life, to one area of human activity in a deliberately selective and therefore artificial way. The very fact that men believe in it means that for them it is real and has great significance. It exists.

Its existence is confirmed by accumulating knowledge, dating back beyond the Greek founders of political science, the Bible, and the ancient bureaucratic empires. Indeed, this rich heritage makes originality difficult. If one searches diligently among the varied writings and reflections, much can be learned about administrative reform that is as relevant today as it was at the time. To this historical material can be added the ever-increasing output of contemporary scholars, particularly in directly related topics such as planned change, governmental reorganization, and technical assistance. Relevant source material can be found in all social and behavioral sciences and also in the physical sciences, particularly mathematics, engineering, and biology. From history to military tactics, from operations research to social psychology—that is, wherever administrative and organizational behavior is thought about—more light is thrown on this complex, multidisciplinary, and basically practical subject.

Correspondingly, there are many different approaches, ranging from the mathematical to the comparative. In recent years some 26 different methodological approaches and 12 different schools have been classified in political science alone (Charlesworth 1967), most of them relevant in the study of administrative reform. Some study group behavior while others direct their attention to the individual. Some believe that behind the complexity, there lurk universals that match those in the physical sciences. Others are concerned solely with applying common sense to everyday administrative problems. These efforts are supported by many disciples, which include all those hopeful of applying the results. As long as there are reformers, then there must be something to study. If there is something to study, then there must be something to learn. Already administrative change-agents are being taught by laboratory methods in groups. This is a short step to the training of administrative reformers.

Administrative reform is a significant social activity. It is concrete, visible, frequent, transformatory, and deliberate. In the 1960's alone, there has been widespread debate and detailed circulation of information of rival views on the reorganization of the United Nations Organization, the overhaul of the machinery of government in Canada, New Zealand, Great Britain, and several other countries, the rearrangement of administrative procedures in the Roman Catholic Church, the restructuring of several large international companies such as General Motors, Shell, Krupps, and Ford, the impact of behavioral research on administrative practices, particularly in staffing arrangements, and the incorporation of management sciences in policy-making, especially in defense strategy. Since World War II special organizations have been established to suggest administrative reforms in both private and public organizations, notably in Israel (State Comptroller), India (Administrative Reforms Department and Administrative Reform Commissions), Lebanon (Ministry of Administrative Reform), and Italy (Office of Reform), and other countries as diverse as Chile and Burma. Many countries possess either popular administrative reform movements or specialized professional bodies urging administrative reforms.

THE RELEVANCE OF
ADMINISTRATIVE REFORM THEORY

Reforms have taken place, are taking place, and are being planned. Indeed, it is reasonable to predict an upward propensity to reform if change continues at an accelerating pace and if crisis indicates that the rising tempo of change is not matched by the capacity to accommodate it. Even if conservatism gains ground, the social arteries harden, and further innovation is resisted, reform will persist as a progressive force urging action. Natural change, at whatever pace, is no longer sufficient. Progress is now artificially stimulated as part of the continuing scientific revolution, the reaction against laissez-faire doctrines, the reassertion of free-will theories, and the enthronement of utilitarianism. Administrative reform is part of this movement. It has become valuable in itself, not merely as a more effective practical means to attaining other objectives. "Change in all its disarray is always ahead of men's efforts to bring reason to bear, but what in another age could be treated with the philosophic urbanity of a Montaigne cries out today with a portentous urgency" (Brookings Institution 1961, p. 3). Unfortunately, it is impossible to calculate how much reform or how many reformers will be needed, from where reformers will be drawn, or what personal qualities they will (or ought to) possess. Presumably, as in the past, self-selection will dominate. Administrative reform theory would look into these matters. Certainly, it would increase rationality in reform programs, add to understanding about differences in reform approaches, systematize the richness and variety of administrative reform, and provide a common vocabulary.

From an academic viewpoint, administrative reform is not simply the application of radical proposals to cope with problems of change and stagnation. This is the surface phenomenon only. Administrative reforms are bound up with other reforms in society and other influences that interact. These influences are not equal and their effect depends on reaction which, in turn, depends on both rational and irrational factors. In the final analysis, virtually the whole universe of knowledge has to be taken into consideration. Fortunately there are levels of influence and degrees of importance. As knowledge about administrative reform expands, so the indices of relevance and evaluations of importance may change. Many different approaches can be tried, and no doubt some will bring quicker results than others in prediction, prescription, generalization, rule-making, and theorizing. If they do no more than add to the check list of factors that should be taken into account by potential reformers, they will have been worthwhile.

But they will certainly do more than this. First, they will contribute to the theory of conflict resolution by revealing much about the processes of opposition and collaboration in achieving administrative reform. They may also show the advantages as well as the disadvantages of conflict. Second, they will demonstrate to what extent decay and stagnation are the result of a failure to reform. This would be the converse side to a theory of development. Third, they will illumine action theory—if the administrative reformer is considered an actor possessed of goals, in command of alternative means, involved in a situation over which he has only partial control, and governed by values, norms, and beliefs with respect to his goals, means, and situation. Fourth, and more speculatively, they may throw light on the recognition, development, and training of potential reformers. In time, accumulated experience may point (*a*) to the prerequisites for reformers in personality, attitudes, motivation, and interpersonal skills, and the professional or technical training, knowledge, and experience required in carrying out specific reforms; (*b*) to reliable predictions about the success or failure of reform attempts and the factors that account for successful performance; (*c*) to comparability and transferability of reform experience, as related to environment, social milieu, cultural empathy, political sense, organizing ability, intelligence and missionary zeal; and (*d*) to evaluate guides to degrees of success.

In essence administrative reform is normative, rooted in values. The implied rationale is that administration really does matter, that it is not something that can be ignored or cast aside, and that an improvement in administration will pay handsomely in the attainment of other objectives. Improved administration is wanted less for itself than for the results that are supposed to flow from it, though improved administrative performance may be enough. The first aspect, that of improved end products of the administrative process, can be demonstrated and fairly accurately measured. It is possible also to measure attitudes and feelings, though not with the same degree of reliability or objectivity. The second aspect, that of improvements in the administrative process itself, has more to do with internal problems and the reduction of internal friction. The quality of everyday living and working is improved. Since more people are becoming more dependent on the cooperation of others, and a higher proportion of an individual's life is spent in formal organizations and administrative activities, improved administrative performance in itself assumes a greater importance.

Another rationale relates to the idea of progress—that man is not at the mercy of gods but can determine his own future, that with this freedom of action he should choose to improve himself. He should not waste the limited time available to him, but should use it in improving his lot, though not at the expense of others. One should leave the world having put in more than taken out. One's children should be sheltered from the tribulations encountered early in one's own life and be prepared to make sacrifices to improve their opportunities. All these feelings evidence a belief that man is evolving a higher civilization, that historical cycles move upwards. This optimistic view of history is further buttressed by ideology and doctrinal purity that has led some countries into adopting bold experiments based on an idealist view of man or utopian society. There have always been dreamers capable of capturing the popular imagination and moving people to perform heroic feats, just as there have been expropriators and vagabonds. Somewhere between the two, man has progressed toward a higher plane.

ADMINISTRATIVE REFORMERS

Who are reformers and what makes a person a reformer? With some it is a matter of personal psychology; they are the born rebels, the perfectionists, the nonconformists, the geniuses, the eccentrics. They may not be found on the political left or professing progressive views but they are not conservative, cautionary, dependent, or masochistic. They are naturally disposed to reform by some inner compulsion and are happier in the company of like-minded individuals. With others it is more environmental pressures coupled with a predisposition to sympathize with the underdog, a social conscience that revolts against exploitation, poverty, ignorance, suffering, misery, pain, and a moral doctrine favoring action and outspokenness. They may be dreamers and martyrs or responsible, compassionate, charismatic individuals willing to fight for others. They may be strategists placed in a situation in which logic demands reform.

It might be more meaningful to divide reformers into innovators, executors, and followers, each with a different set of influences prevailing. What would a thorough investigation of their psychological condition, environmental background, and motivation reveal? Would the same people when placed in different circumstances adopt different attitudes to reform? The question very much resembles that of determining why some people become coal miners or military commanders or what constitutes leadership and under what circumstances.

A different approach would be to search for the common qualities of administrative reformers. Reference has already been made to the possibility that they may hold similar beliefs about the nature of progress. Do they believe that there is only one path to truth? Do they possess an intelligence and sensitivity above the average? Is the discomfort they bear compensated by dedication, missionary zeal, militarism? What motivates them? They may be divided into (*a*) self-gratifiers, who use reform as a vehicle to satisfy personal ambition; (*b*) group-promoters, who identify themselves with a specific group (by race, religion, nationality, sex, age etc.); (*c*) humanitarians, who believe that all are of equal worth and that everything promising to improve the lot of anyone (providing no one else suffers) is worth supporting. How easily do they fall into these three categories? What personal attributes should or do reformers possess? What of their morality? (Bailey warned that "there is not a moral vice which cannot be made into a relative good by context. There is not a moral virtue which cannot in peculiar circumstances have patently evil results." [Martin 1965, p. 291]) Finally, how well do they stand up to the tactics of their opponents—the smear campaign, countervailing power, persecution?

Answers to these questions open yet another channel of inquiry. What circumstances give rise to reformers? How do they conceive their ideas? Are their major ways of knowing uncritical (dogmatic authoritarianism, mysticism, naive pragmatism) or critical (pure rationalism, pure empiricism)? Why and how do they identify tension and stress? How do they detect a willing predisposition to change? In brief, how are reformers related to their background? How are they linked with their reforms? Often they are inseparable. Optimum reforms have failed because of their advocates' shortcomings, while inadequate reforms have been accepted on the strength of their originators alone. But whatever the personal merits of reformers, environmental shortcomings may cripple reform. For instance, the nature of the political regime will largely determine the source of supply of reformers, their institutional status, and their strategies and tactics. The triangle (environment—reform—reformers) is completed by considering the impact of personality on environment. Even servile societies rebel. The human spirit is not easily defeated by circumstances.

REFORM STRATEGY

Reforms are not brought about by shouting or hard thinking or diagnosis alone. They require action relating to the substance of administration, not the forms. Ideally, the reformer "should combine in some measure the wisdom and sense of perspective of the historian and the penetrating acumen of the scientific observer, while putting into practice the skills and arts of appropriate and resolute action" (Bennis, Benne, Chin 1961, p. 187). In proceeding, he needs to select readily workable solutions only, taking into account people's reactions to maladministration, their habits and beliefs, customary forms, and behavior patterns.

Some maxims can be derived:

1. He should not attempt everything at once.
2. He should avoid being a perfectionist.
3. He should not skip over necessary intermediary stages.
4. He should develop a healthy reform climate and a predisposition toward new forms of thinking and behavior.
5. He should restrict preventable harmful consequences.
6. He should avoid blind imitation by remembering that the world is always new.
7. He should accept what he can get, settling for something less rather than spoiling future opportunities or unduly antagonizing opponents.
8. He should use available institutions as far as possible.
9. He should plan each successive stage and evaluate the previous one before attempting the next.
10. He should attempt a trial run or confine reforms to a small area before total commitment.
11. He should identify reforms with the familiar and known.
12. He should pay particular regard to feedback.
13. He should provide for self-continuing reforms and permit his original reforms to be superseded.
14. He should act on flexible plans without concealing motives.
15. He should establish a dependable reform administration,

whether formal or informal, public or private, large-scale or small-scale.

16. He should balance gains and losses, and he should evaluate mixed results.

These normative prescriptions which permeate much of the literature on administrative reform are part logic, part value, and part experience. They are useful guides but they cannot deal with all situations. For instance, they fail when it comes to organizations that have sufficient power, prestige, and reputation to prevent outside attempts at reform and yet cannot reform themselves internally because of bureaucratic inertia, weak leadership, inadequate machinery, and personal enmity. Worse still, they cannot meet the case where an administrative shortcoming (such as corruption) is not only socially accepted but institutionalized, disguised, and rationalized (Inayatullah 1962).

Where the maxims are not helpful, reformers have a difficult time deciding upon strategy. Sometimes disputes between them become more heated than the debates with their opponents. With each phase of implementation, more reformers are satisfied and switch their allegiance, leaving behind the more radical to argue further among themselves. Doubts over objectives and strategy are bound to be exposed in the charged atmosphere of reform gatherings. Opponents of reform are not always to blame for the conspiratorial leanings of rival reform groups. Assuming that the reformers are prepared to work in the open, the following are the kinds of questions that arise:

Are we sure about our diagnosis?

What are our short- and long-term objectives? What are we trying to achieve? Are conditions and goals likely to change?

Who are our main opponents? What are their strengths and weaknesses? How can we undermine them? Do we rely too much on surprise and continuous creativity?

What kind of support can we muster? How can we extend our circle of influence?

What do we hold out to our supporters? How convincing are we? How dedicated?

How can we ensure greater collaboration? What compromises and sacrifices are involved? Should we compensate those who will lose? If so, how?

Are we too rigid, overcommitted, idealist, perfectionist, over-sensitive?

Do we have too rosy a picture of ourselves and what we represent? Are we underestimating our ignorance of the difficulties?

Do we overestimate our opponents and passive resistance?

What weapons do we possess? What tactics shall we adopt? What alternatives are open to us? Which is best, the most practicable, expedient, sure or advantageous?

Whom do we most trust or least fear?

When is the best time to act? Do we wait for a crisis?

Do we plan an incident or pick an issue?

Do we use existing channels and play according to accepted rules or do we establish new channels and make our own rules?

Do we lead up slowly or explode? Do we fight to the end or leave escape routes? What reserves do we have?

Have we neglected the irrational or allowed for the unexpected?

How best do we control the direction, tempo, and quality of reform?

Do we work through reliable third parties rather than expose ourselves? When do we intervene? In what role?

Do we seek legal recognition and political support?

Must we resort to coercion and violence? At which points?

Where, when, how, and why are we having difficulty? Are we misjudging the whole business? If we fail, will the side effects still be worth the effort?

In coming to their answers, they might well heed the advice of J. S. Mill, a first-rate administrative strategist.

> As a Secretary conducting political correspondence I could not issue an order or express an opinion without satisfying various persons very unlike myself that the thing was fit to be done. I was thus in a good position for finding out by practice the mode of putting a thought which gives it easiest admittance into minds not prepared for it by habit; while I became practically conversant with the difficulties of moving bodies of men, the necessities of compromise, the art of sacrificing the non-essential to preserve the essential. I learnt

how to obtain the best I could, when I could not obtain everything, instead of being indignant or dispirited because I could not have entirely my own way, to be pleased and encouraged when I could have the smallest part of it; and when that could not be, to bear with complete equanimity being overruled altogether (Quoted by V. T. Krishnamachari 1963, p. vi.).

Mill stressed the need for a proper appreciation of a sense of timing, of knowing when to hold back as well as to push forward, when to give way to pressure and when to resist. Dror (1968), Langrod (1966), and Mariani (1958)have brought Mill's strategy up-to-date. Reforms should be attempted at several levels at the same time, designed with short-, middle-, and long-run intentions in mind, and machinery planned for overall coordination and continuity in reform processes. "What must be done is to go ahead with partial alterations, carrying out reforms at several levels at once, on whatever seems especially harmful or out of date, by a pre-established order of priority. . . . *Nothing* will undergo lasting reform unless a complex of modern, active, energetic and competent administrations is quickly brought into action." (Langrod 1966, p. 65).

Strategy is related to the scope and complexity of attaining different objectives. The elimination of corruption is probably harder to achieve than the adoption of a new investment program, and the reorganization of the whole machinery of government is harder to achieve than the reorganization of a component part. But behind these objectives there may be certain preconceptions that may be self-defeating. First, the idea of administrative improvement may have low priority, and over-attention to administration may detract from other problems that give rise to maladministration. Second, improved administration is desirable providing the end product is moral, as, for instance, the "final solution" of the Nazis was not. Third, the problem may be insoluble. Solutions may only create more difficult problems. Fourth, the improvements may serve no useful social purposes; the end product is not wanted. Fifth, administrative reform may tackle features, such as conflict, disorderliness, and competition, which are the heart of administrative effectiveness whatever their surface appearance (Grodzins 1962). Eliminate conflict—and dissatisfaction, the starting point of reform, may be eliminated too. Eliminate disorderliness—and the unusual and exceptional cannot be tolerated. Eliminate competition —and initiative, choice, and enterprise may be lost. Sixth, sometimes even administrative defects may have their long-run (or hindsight) advantages, and many administrators must have often been thankful for the gap between intention and action. Finally, reformers may overlook the extent of conservatism, conflict of interests, defects in reform proposals, short-sightedness, chauvinism and politeness which may undermine them. Few individuals stand in isolation, and their opponents are rarely unanimous. Thus strategy should be designed to provide inner conviction and to overcome overt resistance.

A further problem in strategy is the choice between using established institutions or creating new ones. The balance sheet looks something like this:

EXISTING	NEW
1. Change of attitudes difficult; saddled with past legacies; hardened bureaucratic arteries.	1. Commence with new attitudes, innovation; boldness; announcement of new policies; start from scratch.
2. Institution already a going concern; little disruption; continuity; people already trained; fund of experience; reliability and stability.	2. Teething troubles; difficulties in getting into motion; rawness; inexperienced staff; diversion of energies at first; initial dislocation.
3. Accepted.	3. Seek acceptance and reputation.
4. Integrated with environment.	4. Seek modus vivendi with environment.
5. Loyalty established; conformity assured.	5. Unknown element; a risk.
6. Problems in reorganization, replacement, overhaul.	6. New broom; ambitious; idealistic; spectacular.
7. Reform against natural inclinations, existing attitudes, beliefs, and practices.	7. Abuses in existing institutions too ingrained; possibility of new relationships in view.
8. Indifference; resistance; hostility towards reform.	8. Reform motivated; support and sympathy forthcoming.
9. Benefits of existing institutions.	9. Costs of new institutions, new techniques.
10. Costs of defects and imperfections.	10. Costs of failure; termination of experiment by abolition.
11. Reform from within; coercive reform from the top or revolution from below; possibility of civil war.	11. Reform from without; superimposition; warfare between old and new.

12. Dated; closed; stale; unresponsive; backward-looking.	12. Fresh; open; stimulating; receptive; forward-looking.
13. Accessibility to control by conservatives.	13. Accessibility to control by radicals.
14. Possibility of counter-reaction.	14. Possibility of revolution.
15. Network of support exists.	15. Danger of duplication.
16. Incremental reform; piecemeal.	16. Isolated reform ignored.

As both may share the same supposed defects and advantages, no clear preference can be expressed without reference to specific circumstances. The same point arises repeatedly. The emphasis in administration is getting things done. People are not concerned with unobtainable perfection but with any satisfactory improvement. Whereas change is welcomed for itself in advanced countries (even if by rational measures it does not improve the quality of life), administrative reform is not; until it is, it must be rationally based and emotionally acceptable.

In administrative reform, there is unlikely to be a final word as long as there are imagination, originality, and a willingness to abandon tradition when it has served its purpose. In all administrative reform plans there is always something missing; they cannot cover every conceivable circumstance. The results cannot be told accurately beforehand. If they turn out to be correct, it is little more than coincidence, because it is impossible to calculate unexpected reactions, unanticipated consequences and boomerang effects by which future action is committed and future choice limited. If the reforms are too hasty, maladministration may intensify and problems escalate. Furthermore, "any given state of human affairs is likely to contain within it the seeds of its own transformation into a new and different state" (Bennis, Benne, Chin 1961, p. 219). Reform proposals never totally fail. They change the world with their appearance. A new source of intelligence comes into being which may form the basis of a future change program. The very minimum achieved is the reaffirmation of what is considered good in the status quo.

WHAT NEXT?

In rounding off this survey of current knowledge about administrative reform, it only remains to add that slowly the quintessence of administrative reform is coming into view. It is a long way off yet. More questions have been raised in this and preceding chapters than can be answered from what is known. In a sense, this has been a diagnosis of the ills with few remedies for their alleviation except an exhortation to gather more facts, agree on a definition, and construct a better framework in which the facts can be related on the basis of a universally accepted definition. It would appear that much more needs to be done and no effort would be wasted. It is possible to agree with Bennis that

> In the United States it is my guess that industrial bureaucracies are the most radical, innovative, and adventurous in adapting new ways of organizing—far ahead, it seems to me, of the government, universities, and trade unions, who appear rigid and stodgy in the face of rapid change. Industrial bureaucracies, at least in the United States, are acting with a verve and imagination regarding rapid change which, I wager, will not only be copied but will also be a model for future organizational change programmes in other institutions (Bennis in Lawrence 1966, p. 43).

But how can such statements be confirmed? Is it true of all industrial bureaucracies in the United States or only of industrial bureaucracies in the United States and nowhere else? Could the innovations of industrial bureaucracies in the United States be copied anywhere else? These and other fascinating questions can be found throughout the study of administrative reform. Much more needs to be known, for instance, about the following aspects:

Human reaction to reform and the impact of irrationality.

Validation of existing generalizations and the construction of propositions and axioms.

Scientific approach to maladministration.

Contribution of academic study to practice.

Interrelationships between variables in the reform process.

The possibility of controlling and manipulating the variables.
Construction of a practical guide book to potential reformers.
The introduction of quantification and mathematical models.

The list could be extended much further, but these examples suffice to show the need to attract researchers into this area of administrative dynamics, to exploit the full range of approaches now available, and to explore the possibilities of an empirical theory that would be behaviorally relevant.

One last word of caution: The study of administrative reform confers no expertise or special status on the student, or relevant competence in reform work. The needs of administrative reform should continue to take precedence over the needs of its study. But further study may well contribute to the practice. It may also "quicken that sense of social inventiveness and responsibility which makes change not a burden but an adventure in the art of government and mutual adaptation in free societies" (Frankel in Meynaud 1963, p. 58).

BIBLIOGRAPHIC NOTES

The methodological issues in further pursuing administrative reform are similar to those confronting all social science. The future of administrative science is currently being examined in such journals as *Administrative Science Quarterly, American Behavioral Scientist, International Review of Administrative Sciences, Journal of the Academy of Management, Journal of Management Studies,* and *Management Science;* while the relationship between administrative science and other disciplines is being discussed in the *American Political Science Review, American Journal of Sociology, American Sociological Review, Journal of Politics* and *World Politics.* Good summaries of the present position are found in B. M. Barry, *Political Argument* (London: Routledge and Kegan Paul, 1965); Becker and Boskoff 1957, J. C. Charlesworth, *Contemporary Political Analysis* (New York: Free Press, 1967); Cowling 1963, R. A. Dahl, *Modern Political Analysis* (Englewood Cliffs: Prentice-Hall, 1963); G. J. DiRenzo, *Concepts,*

Theory and Explanation in the Behavioral Sciences (New York: Random House, 1966); M. Duverger, *The Idea of Politics* (London: Methuen, 1966); D. Easton, *A Framework for Politics* (Englewood Cliffs: Prentice-Hall, 1965); Eulau 1963; Gross 1959; H. Guetzkow, *Simulation in the Social Sciences* (Englewood Cliffs: Prentice-Hall, 1962); K. W. Karp, *Towards a Science of Man in Society* (The Hague: Nijhoff, 1961); Lasswell 1963; Macridis 1955; Meeham 1965; Merton, Lerner, and Lasswell 1957; I. de S. Pool, *Contemporary Political Science: Towards Empirical Theory* (New York: McGraw-Hill, 1967); G. L. S. Shackle, *Decision, Order and Time in Human Affairs* (London: Cambridge University Press, 1961); H. J. Storing (Ed.), *Essays on the Scientific Study of Politics* (New York: Holt, Rinehart and Winston, 1962); Znaniecki 1934.

The case against reform is best rationalized by Oakeshott (1962), but similar arguments can be found less cogently in the daily press. The difficulty of obtaining reforms in the face of conservatism is illustrated in J. M. Sanchez, *Reform and Reaction* (Chapel Hill: University of North Carolina Press, 1964) and Stanley 1965. The philosophical justification of reform has deep roots involving the nature of man, sin, obligation, and love from which thinkers in every age have constructed elaborate frameworks to justify reform in the name of such notions as liberty, equality, fraternity, and peace. Their ideas are embedded in contemporary socialization processes, religious teaching, and citizenship training whereby most youngsters learn about reform before they reach adulthood.

General Bibliography

Adams, B. *The Theory of Social Revolutions*. New York: Macmillan, 1913.

Alexander, F. *International Technical Assistance Experts*. New York: Praeger, 1966.

Allen, L. A. *Management and Organization*. New York: McGraw-Hill, 1958.

Allen, P. J. (Ed.) *Pitirim A. Sorokin: A Review*. Durham, N.C.: Duke University Press, 1963.

Annan, N. "The Reform of Higher Education," *Political Quarterly*, 38 (3): 234-252, 1967.

Appleby, P. H. *Morality and Administration in Democratic Government*. Baton Rouge: Louisiana State University, 1952.

————. *Public Administration in India: Report of a Survey*. New Delhi: Government of India, 1953.

————. *Re-examination of India's Administrative System*. New Delhi: Government of India, 1956.

————. *Policy and Administration*. University, Ala.: University of Alabama Press, 1957.

Apter, D. E. *The Gold Coast in Transition*. Princeton, N.J.: Princeton University Press, 1955.

————. *The Political Kingdom in Uganda*. Princeton, N.J.: Princeton University Press, 1961.

————. *The Politics of Modernization*. Chicago: University of Chicago Press, 1965.

Arensberg, C. M., and Niehoff, A. N. *Introducing Social Change*. Chicago: Aldine Publishing Company, 1964.

Argyriades, D. "Some Aspects of Civil Service Reorganization in Greece," *International Review of Administrative Sciences*, 31 (4): 297-309, 1965.

Argyris, C. *Executive Leadership*. New York: Harper, 1953.

————. *Personality and Organization*. New York: Harper, 1957.

————. *Understanding Organizational Behavior*. Homewood, Ill.: Dorsey, 1960.

————. *Interpersonal Competence and Organizational Effectiveness*. Homewood, Ill.: Irwin, 1962.

————. *Integrating the Individual and the Organization*. New York: Wiley, 1964.

————. *Organization and Innovation*. Homewood, Ill.: Irwin, 1965.

————., et al. *Social Science Approaches to Business Behavior*. Homewood, Ill.: Irwin, 1962.

Arrow, K. J. *Social Choice and Individual Values*. New York: Wiley, 1951.

Ashby, W. R. *An Introduction to Cybernetics*. New York: Wiley, 1956.

Austria, E., "Historical Background and Implementation of the Reorganization Plans 1955-56," *International Review of Administrative Sciences*, 23 (3): 293-317, 1957.

Bales, R. F. *Interaction Process Analysis*. Reading, Mass.: Addison-Wesley, 1950.

Banerjee, A. M. "Fifteen Years of Administrative Reforms—An Overview," *Indian Journal of Public Administration*, 9 (3): 441-456, 1963.

Banfield, E. C. *Political Influence*. Glencoe, Ill.: Free Press, 1961.

————, and Meyerson, M. C. *Politics, Planning and the Public Interest*. Glencoe, Ill.: Free Press, 1955.

Barker, E. *The Development of Public Services in Western Europe, 1660-1930*. London: Oxford University Press, 1944.

Barnard, C. I. *The Functions of the Executive*. Cambridge, Mass.: Harvard University Press, 1938.

————. *Organization and Management*. Cambridge, Mass.: Harvard University Press, 1948.

Barnett, H. G. *Innovation: The Basis of Cultural Change*. New York: McGraw-Hill, 1953.

————. *Anthropology in Administration*. Evanston, Ill.: Row, Peterson, 1956.

Barringer, H. R., Blanksten, G. I., and Mack, R. W. *Social Change in Developing Areas*. Cambridge, Mass.: Schenkman, 1965.

Barve, S. G. "The Larger Political Context of Administrative Reforms," *Indian Journal of Public Administration*, 12 (3): 352-355, 1966.

Bass, B. M. *Leadership, Psychology and Organizational Behavior*. New York: Harper, 1960.

Becker, E. R., and Murphy, E. F. *The Office in Transition*. New York: Harper, 1957.

Becker, H., and Boskoff, A. (Eds.) *Modern Sociological Theory*. New York: Dryden Press, 1957.

Beer, S. *Cybernetics and Management*, New York: Wiley, 1959.

Beer, S. *Decision and Control*. New York: Wiley, 1964.

Belshaw, C. S. "Evaluation of Technical Assistance as a Contribution to Development," *International Development Review*, 8 (2): 2-6, 1966.

Bennis, W. G. *Changing Organizations*. New York: McGraw-Hill, 1966.

————, Benne, K. D., and Chin, R. (Eds.) *The Planning of Change*. New York: Holt, Rinehart and Winston, 1961.

Bernays, E. L. *Engineering of Consent*. Norman: University of Oklahoma Press, 1955.

Biller, R. P. "Some Implications of Adaption Capacity for Organizational and Political Development." Berkeley: Department of Political Science, University of California, September 1968.

Birkhead, G. S. (Ed.) *Administrative Problems in Pakistan*. Syracuse, N. Y.: Syracuse University Press, 1966.

Black, M. *The Social Theories of Talcott Parsons*. Englewood Cliffs, N. J.: Prentice-Hall, 1961.

Blake, R. R., and Mouton, J. S. *The Induction of Change in Industrial Organizations*. Austin, Texas.: Scientific Methods, Inc., 1962.

————, Shepard, H. A., and Mouton, J. S. *Managing Intergroup Conflict in Industry*. Houston, Texas: Gulf Publishing Company, 1964.

Blau, P. M. *The Dynamics of Bureaucracy*. Chicago: University of Chicago Press, 1955.

————. *Bureaucracy in Modern Society*. New York: Random House, 1956.

————, and Scott, W. R. *Formal Organizations*. San Francisco: Chandler Publishing Company, 1962.

Bock, E. A. (Ed.) *State and Local Government: A Case Book*. University, Ala.: University of Alabama Press, 1963.

————, and Campbell, A. K. (Eds.) *Case Studies in American Government*. Englewood Cliffs, N. J.: Prentice-Hall, 1962.

Bonnefous, E. *La Reforme Administrative*. Paris: Presses Universitaires de France, 1958.

Boulding, R. E. *The Image*. Ann Arbor: University of Michigan Press, 1956.

————, and Kahn, R. L. *Power and Conflict in Organization*. New York: Basic Books, 1964.

Bradford, L. P., Gibbs, J. R., and Benne, K. D. (Eds.) *T-Group Theory and Laboratory Method.* New York: Wiley, 1964.

Braibanti, R. J. *Research on the Bureaucracy of Pakistan.* Durham, N. C.: Duke University Press, 1966.

——. (Ed.) *Asian Bureaucratic Systems Emerging from the British Imperial Tradition.* Durham, N. C.: Duke University Press. 1966.

——, and Spengler, J. J. (Eds.) *Tradition, Values and Socio-Economic Development.* Durham, N. C.: Duke University Press, 1961.

——, ——, (Eds.) *Administrative and Economic Development in India.* Durham, N. C.: Duke University Press, 1963.

Brannen, T. R., and Hodgson, F. X. *Overseas Management.* New York: McGraw-Hill, 1965.

Braybrooke, D., and Lindblom, C. D. *A Strategy of Decision.* New York: Free Press, 1963.

Bright, J. R. *Automation and Management.* Cambridge, Mass.: Harvard University Press, 1958.

Bromhead, P. "How Should Parliament Be Reformed?," *Political Quarterly,* 30(3): 272-282, 1959.

Brookings Institution. *Research for Public Policy.* Washington, D.C., 1961.

Brown, D. S. "The Ultimate Management Challenge—Creative Change," *Public Management,* December: 271-276, 1963.

Brown, R. G. S. "Organization Theory and Civil Service Reform," *Public Administration,* 43 (Autumn): 313-330, 1965.

Buchanan, J. M., and Tullock, G. *Calculus of Consent.* Ann Arbor: University of Michigan Press, 1962.

Buck, A. E. *The Re-Organization of State Governments in the United States.* New York: Columbia University Press, 1938.

Buckingham, W. S. *Automation.* New York: Harper, 1961.

Burns, T., and Stalker, G. M. *The Management of Innovation.* London: Tavistock, 1961.

——, and Saul, S. B. *Social Theory and Economic Change.* London: Tavistock, 1967.

Bursk, E. C. (Ed.) *How to Increase Executive Effectiveness.* Cambridge, Mass.: Harvard University Press, 1953.

Bush, H. C. "Transplanting Administrative Techniques," *International Development Review,* 2(2): 10-15, 1960.

Butani, K. N. "Implementing Administrative Innovations and Reforms," *Indian Journal of Public Administration,* 12(3): 673-685, 1966.

Caiden, G. E. *Career Service.* Melbourne: Melbourne University Press, 1965.

———. *Commonwealth Bureaucracy*. Melbourne: Melbourne University Press, 1967.

———. "Prospects for Administrative Reform in Israel," *Public Administration*, 46(1): 25-44, 1968.

Cartwright, D. *Studies in Social Power*. Ann Arbor: University of Michigan Press, 1959.

———, and Zander, A. (Eds.) *Group Dynamics*. Evanston, Ill.: Row, Peterson, 1960.

Chapman, B. *The Profession of Government*. London: Allen and Unwin, 1959.

Chen, T. H. E. *Thought Reform of the Chinese Intellectuals*. Hong Kong: Hong Kong University Press, 1960.

Childe, V. G. *Social Evolution*. London: Watts, 1951.

Clark, D. H. *Administrative Therapy*. London: Tavistock, 1964.

Cleveland, H., and Mangone, G. (Eds.) *The Art of Overseasmanship*. Syracuse, N.Y.: Syracuse University Press, 1958.

Cohen, A. R. *Attitude Change and Social Influence*. New York: Basic Books, 1964.

Cooper, W. W., Leavitt, H. J., and Shelly, M. W. *New Perspectives in Organization Research*. New York: Wiley, 1964.

Costello, T. W., and Zalkind, S. S. *Psychology in Administration*. Englewood Cliffs, N.J.: Prentice-Hall, 1963.

Cowling, M. *The Nature and Limits of Political Science*. London: Cambridge University Press, 1963.

Crick, B. *Essays on Reforms*. London: Oxford University Press, 1967.

Crow, R. E., and Iskander, A. "Administrative Reform in Lebanon, 1958-59," *International Review of Administrative Sciences*, 27(3): 293-307, 1961.

Crozier, M. *The Bureaucratic Phenomenon*. London: Tavistock, 1964.

Cyert, R. M., and March, J. G. *A Behavioral Theory of the Firm*. Englewood Cliffs, N.J.: Prentice-Hall, 1963.

Daalder, H. *Cabinet Reform in Britain 1914-1963*. Stanford, Cal.: Stanford University Press, 1963.

Dahl, R. A. *A Preface to Democratic Theory*. Chicago: University of Chicago Press, 1956.

———, and Lindblom, C. E. *Politics, Economics and Welfare*. New York: Harper and Row, 1953.

D'Antonio, W. V., and Pike, F. B. *Religion, Revolution and Reform*. New York: Praeger, 1964.

David, P. T. "Analytical Approaches to the Study of Change," *Public Administration Review,* 26 (September): 160-168, 1966.

Davies, E. "Reorganization of Nationalised Transport," *Political Quarterly,* 32 (April-June): 182-192, 1961.

Davis, R. C. *Industrial Organization and Management.* New York: Harper and Row, 1956.

Dessureau, J. P. "Reorganization Problems and Selection of Personnel: Quebec Provincial Police," *Canadian Public Administration,* 5(2): 180-185, 1962.

Deutsch, K. W. *The Nerves of Government.* New York: Free Press of Glencoe, 1963.

Diamant, A. *Bureaucracy in Developmental Movement Regimes: A Bureaucratic Model for Developing Societies.* Bloomington: Comparative Administration Group, 1964.

Dimock, M. E. *A Philosophy of Administration.* New York: Harper, 1958.

———. *Administrative Vitality.* New York: Harper, 1959.

Dodd, C. H. "Administrative Reform in Turkey," *Public Administration,* 43 (Spring): 71-83, 1965.

Donnelly, D. "The Politics and Administration of Planning. The Need for Reform," *Political Quarterly,* 33(4): 404-413, 1962.

Downs, A. *Inside Bureaucracy.* Boston: Little, Brown, 1967.

———. *Bureaucratic Structure and Decision Making.* Santa Monica, Cal.: RAND Corp., 1966.

Dror, Y. *Public Policy-Making Re-examined.* San Francisco: Chandler, 1968.

———. "Muddling Through Science or Inertia," *Public Administration Review,* 24(3): 53-58, 1966.

Dubin, R. *The World of Work.* Englewood Cliffs, N.J.: Prentice-Hall, 1958.

Durham, A. *Community Welfare Organization.* New York: Crowell, 1958.

Eckstein, J., and Apter, D. E. (Eds.) *Comparative Politics.* New York: Free Press, 1963.

Edelman, M. *The Symbolic Uses of Politics.* Urbana: University of Illinois Press, 1964.

Einaudi, M. *The Roosevelt Revolution.* New York: Harcourt, 1959.

Eisenstadt, S. N. *The Political Systems of Empires.* New York: Free Press, 1963.

———. *Modernization, Growth and Diversity.* Bloomington: University of Indiana Press, 1963.

———. *Essays on Comparative Institutions.* New York: Wiley, 1965.

————. *Modernization: Protest and Change.* Englewood Cliffs, N.J.: Prentice-Hall, 1966.

Elton, G. R. *The Tudor Revolution in Government.* London: Cambridge University Press, 1953.

Emmerich, H. *Essays in Federal Reorganization.* University, Ala.: University of Alabama Press, 1950.

Epstein, T. S. *Economic Development and Social Change in India.* Manchester: Manchester University Press, 1962.

Esman, M. J. *The Politics of Development Administration.* Pittsburgh: University of Pittsburgh Press, 1963.

Etzioni, A. *A Comparative Analysis of Complex Organizations.* New York: Free Press of Glencoe, 1961.

————. (Ed.) *Complex Organizations.* New York: Holt, Rinehart and Winston, 1961.

————. *Modern Organizations.* Englewood Cliffs, N.J.: Prentice-Hall, 1964.

————. *The Active Society.* New York: The Free Press, 1968.

Eulau, H. *The Behavioral Persuasion in Politics.* New York: Random House, 1963.

Fayerweather, J. *The Executive Overseas.* Syracuse, N.Y.: Syracuse University Press, 1959.

Fayol, H. *General and Industrial Management.* London: Pitman, 1959.

Felix, D. "Agrarian Reform and Industrial Growth," *International Development Review,* 2(2): 16-21, 1960.

Fenn, D. H. (Ed.) *Management in a Rapidly Changing Economy.* New York: McGraw-Hill, 1958.

Fields, B. A. "Introducing Continuous Change in Pennsylvania," *Public Administration Review,* 22(3): 134-138, 1962.

Finan, W. F., and Dean, A. L. "Procedures for the Preparation and Implementation of Administrative Reforms," *International Review of Administrative Sciences,* 23(4): 437-452, 1957.

Finer, H. *The Theory and Practice of Modern Government.* London: Methuen, 1956.

Finkle, J. L., and Gable, R. W. (Eds.) *Political Development and Social Change.* New York: Wiley, 1966.

Fitzgibbon, R. H., and Johnson, K. F. "Measurement of Latin American Political Change," *American Political Science Review,* 55(3): 515-526, 1961.

Follett, M. P. *Dynamic Administration,* ed. by H. Metcalf and L. Urwick. New York: Harper, 1941.

Forrester, J. W. *Industrial Dynamics*. Cambridge, Mass.: Massachusetts Institute of Technology, 1961.

Friedmann, G. *Industrial Society*. Glencoe, Ill.: Free Press, 1955.

———. *The Anatomy of Work*. New York: Free Press, 1961.

Friedrich, C. J. *Public Policy*. Cambridge, Mass.: Harvard University Press, 1940.

———. *The Public Interest*. New York: Atherton Press, 1952.

———. *Authority*. Cambridge, Mass.: Harvard University Press, 1958.

———. *Revolution*. New York: Atherton Press, 1966.

Galloway, G. B. *Reform of the Federal Budget*. Washington, D.C.: Library of Congress, 1950.

Garcia, C. P. "The Improvement of Public Administration," *Philippine Journal of Public Administration*, 1(1): 89-91, 1957.

Garner, J. F. "London Government and Its Reform," *Public Law*, (Autumn): pp. 256-270, 1961.

Gaus, J. M. *Reflections on Public Administration*. University, Ala.: University of Alabama Press, 1947.

Ginzberg, E., and Reilley, E. W. *Effecting Change in Large Organizations*. New York: Columbia University Press, 1957.

Glick, P. M. *The Administration of Technical Assistance*. Chicago: University of Chicago Press, 1957.

Golembiewski, R. T. *The Small Group*. Chicago: University of Chicago Press, 1962.

———. "The 'Laboratory Approach' to Organizational Change: Schema of a Model," *Public Administration Review*, 3: 211-221, 1967.

Goodenough, W. H. *Cooperation in Change*. New York: Russell Sage Foundation, 1963.

Goodsell, G. T. *Administration of a Revolution*, Cambridge, Mass.: Harvard University Press, 1965.

Gore, W. J. *Administrative Decision Making*. New York: Wiley, 1964.

Gouldner, A. W. *Patterns of Industrial Bureaucracy*, Glencoe, Ill.: Free Press, 1954.

———. (Ed.) *Studies in Leadership*. New York: Russel and Russel, 1965.

Grodzins, M. *Trends in American Living and Outdoor Recreation*. Washington, D.C.: U.S. Government Printing Office, 1962.

Gross, B. M. *The Managing of Oragnizations*. 2 vols. New York: Free Press of Glencoe, 1964.

———. *The State of the National Social Systems Accounting*. London: Social Science Publications, 1966.

Gross, L. (Ed.) *Symposium on Sociological Theory*. Evanston, Ill.: Row, Peterson, 1959.

Grove, J. W. *Government and Industry in Britain*. London: Longmans, 1962.

Grove, W. J., and Dyons, J. W. (Eds.) *The Making of Decisions: A Reader in Administrative Behavior*. New York: Free Press of Glencoe, 1964.

Groves, R. T. "Administrative Reform and the Politics of Reform: The Case of Venezuela," *Public Administrative Review*, December: 436-45, 1967.

———, and Levy, F. D. *Planning and Administrative Reform in Venezuela*. Comparative Administration Group, Bloomington, Ind., 1965.

Guest, R. H. *Organizational Change*. Homewood, Ill.: Dorsey, 1962.

Gulick, L. H., and Urwick, L. (Eds.) *Papers on the Science of Administration*. New York: New York Institute of Public Administration, 1937.

Hage, J., and Aiken, M. "Program Change and Organizational Properties: A Comparative Analysis," *American Journal of Sociology*, 72(5): 503-519, 1967.

Hagen, E. E. *On the Theory of Social Change*. Homewood, Ill.: Dorsey Press, 1962.

Haimann, T. *Professional Management—Theory and Practice*. Boston: Houghton Mifflin, 1962.

Haire, M. *Modern Organization Theory*. New York: Wiley, 1959.

Hanson, A. H. *Public Enterprise and Economic Development*. London: Routledge and Kegan Paul, 1959.

———. *The Process of Planning*. London: Oxford University Press, 1966.

Hanson, E. J. "The Changing Structure of Local Government in Alberta," *Canadian Public Administration*, 1(3): 26-31, 1958.

Heady, F., and Stokes, S. L. (Eds.) *Papers in Comparative Public Administration*. Ann Arbor: University of Michigan Press, 1962.

Heaphey, J. *Spatial Aspects of Development Administration*. Bloomington: Ind. Comparative Administration Group, 1966.

———. "Comparative Public Administration: Comments on Current Characteristics," *Public Administration Review*, May/June: 242-248, 1968.

———, and Kronenberg, P. *Towards Theory Building in Comparative Public Administration: A Functional Approach*. Bloomington, Ind., Comparative Administration Group, 1966.

Heeney, A. D. P. *Civil Service Reform*. Edmonton, Alta.: Canadian Political Science Association, 1958.

————. "Some Aspects of Administrative Reform in the Public Service," *Canadian Public Administration,* 9(2): 221-235, 1966.

Henrich, M. "The Use of Time in the Study of Social Change," *American Sociological Review,* 29(3): 386-397, 1964.

Herzberg, F., Mausner, B., and Snyderman, B. B. *The Motivation to Work.* New York: Wiley, 1959.

Heydebrand, W. "Administration of Social Change," *Public Administration Review,* 24(3): 163-165, 1964.

Hirschman, A. O. *The Strategy of Economic Development.* New Haven: Yale University Press, 1958.

————. *Journeys Toward Progress: Studies of Economic Policymaking in Latin America.* New York: Twentieth Century Fund, 1963.

————. *Development Projects Observed.* Washington, D.C.: Brookings Institution, 1967.

Hodgkinson, H. L. *Education, Interaction and Social Change.* Englewood Cliffs, N.J.: Prentice-Hall, 1967.

Horowitz, I. L. *The New Sociology.* New York: Oxford University Press, 1964.

Hoselitz, B. F. (Ed.) *The Progress of Underdeveloped Areas.* Chicago: University of Chicago Press, 1952.

————, and Moore, W. E. (Eds.) *Industrialization and Society.* Paris: UNESCO, 1966.

Hsueh, S. *Public Administration in South and South-East Asia.* Brussels: I.I.A.S., 1962.

Hudgens, R. W. "Essentials of Land Reform," *International Development Review,* 3(3): 6-7, 1961.

Hudson, W. F. S. "Local Government Reorganization in Isoho District, Zambia," *Journal of Local Administration Overseas,* 4(1): 47-50, 1965.

Hume, L. J. "Reforms in Budget Documents," *Public Administration* (Sydney), December: 309-322, 1966.

Hyneman, C. S. *Bureaucracy in a Democracy.* New York: Harper, 1950.

Inayatullah, (Ed.) *Bureaucracy and Development in Pakistan.* Peshawar: Pakistan Academy for Rural Development, 1962.

"India, Interim Report of the Administrative Reforms Commission on Problems of Redress of Citizens Grievances," *Indian Journal of Public Administration,* 13(2): 371-383, 1967.

International Institute of Administrative Sciences. "University Research and Administrative Reform," *Progress in Public Administration,* 16 (April): 1-2, 1956.

Invan, P. H., and Longham, F. W. "The Change Seekers," *Harvard Business Review*, Jan.-Feb.: 81-92, 1966.

Iserzon, E. "The Reform of Administrative Procedures in Poland," *International Review of Administrative Sciences*, 24(1): 21-32, 1958.

Jacob, C. E. *Leadership in the New Deal*. Englewood Cliffs, N.J.: Prentice-Hall, 1967.

Jagannadham, V. "Sociological Aspects of Administrative Reforms," *Indian Journal of Public Administration*, 12(3): 673-685, 1966.

Jennings, E. E. *An Anatomy of Leadership*. New York: Harper, 1960.

Johns, R. *Confronting Organizational Change*. New York: Association Press, 1963.

Johnson, C. *Revolutionary Change*. Boston: Little, Brown, 1966.

Jones, G. N. "Preventive Medicine at Work: A Hypothetical Case of Managed Organizational Change," *Philippine Journal of Public Administration*, 9(3): 241-255, 1965.

———. "Strategies and Tactics of Planned Organizational Change," *Philippine Journal of Public Administration*, 10(4): 320-342, 1966.

———, and Niaz, A. "Strategies and Tactics of Planned Organizational Change: A Scheme of Working Concepts," *Philippine Journal of Public Administration*, 7(4): 275-285, 1963.

Juviler, P. H., and Morton, H. W. (Eds.) *Soviet Policy Making and Institutional Change in the Soviet Union*. London: Pall Mall, 1967.

Karl, B. D. *Executive Reorganization and Reform in the New Deal 1900-1939*. Cambridge, Mass.: Harvard University Press, 1963.

Katz, D., and Kahn, R. L. *The Social Psychology of Organizations*. New York: Wiley, 1966.

Keenleyside, H. L. "Obstacles and Means in International Development," *International Development Review*, 2(1): 20-25, 1960.

Keith, J. P. and Batson, E. R. (Eds.) *Changing Perspectives in Public Administration*. Chicago: American Society for Public Administration, 1958.

Kiernan, V. G. *The Revolution of 1854 in Spanish History*. Oxford: Clarendon Press, 1966.

Kornhauser, W. *The Politics of Mass Society*. New York: Free Press, 1959.

Koontz, H. *Toward a Unified Theory of Management*. New York: McGraw-Hill, 1964.

———, and O'Donnell, C. *Principles of Management*. New York: McGraw-Hill, 1959.

———. (Eds) *Management—A Book of Readings*. New York: McGraw-Hill, 1964.

Krishnamachari, V. T. *Indian Journal of Public Administration*, July-Sept. 1963.

Krishnamurti, P. "The Re-organization of the Treasury System in India," *Indian Journal of Public Administration*, 8(2): 215-220, 1962.

Landau, M. "Decision Theory and Comparative Public Administration," *Comparative Political Studies*, 1(2): 175-195, 1968.

———. "Due Process of Inquiry," *The American Behavioral Scientist*, 9(2): 4-10, 1965.

———. "On the Use of Functional Analysis in American Political Science," *Social Research*, 35(1): 48-75, 1968.

———. "Sociology as the Study of Formal Organization," in *The Study of Organizational Behavior*, Papers in Comparative Public Administration 8: 37-52. Washington, D.C.: American Society for Public Administration (Dec. 1966).

———. "Theoretical Problems of Administrative Reform in Developing States: A Commentary." New York: Department of Political Science, Brooklyn College, City University of New York, March 1968.

Landers, F. M., and Hamilton, H. D. "State Administrative Reorganization in Michigan: The Legislative Approach," *Public Administration Review*, 14(2): 112-118, 1954.

Langrod, G. *Reorganization of Public Administration in Greece*. Paris: O.E.C.D., 1965.

LaPalombara, J. (Ed.) *Bureaucracy and Political Development*. Princeton, N.J.: Princeton University Press, 1963.

LaPiere, R. T. *A Theory of Social Control*. New York: McGraw-Hill, 1954.

———. *Social Change*. New York: McGraw-Hill, 1965.

LaPorte T. R. "The Recovery of Relevance in the Study of Public Organizations." Berkeley: Department of Political Science, University of California, September 1968.

Lasswell, H. D. *The Future of Political Science*. New York: Atherton Press, 1963.

———, and Kaplan, A. *Power and Society*. New Haven: Yale University Press, 1950.

Lawrence, J. R. *Operations Research and the Social Sciences*. London: Tavistock, 1966.

Lawrence, P. R. *The Changing of Organizational Behavior Patterns*. Cambridge, Mass.: Harvard University Press, 1958.

———, and Seiler, J. A. *Organizational Behavior and Administration*. Homewood, Ill.: Irwin, 1961.

Leavitt, H. J. (Ed.) *Managerial Psychology*. Chicago: University of Chicago Press, 1959.

———. (Ed.) *The Social Science of Organizations*. Englewood Cliffs, N.J.: Prentice-Hall, 1963.

Lehman, W. P. "Federal Pay Reform: Some Facets of Comparability," *Public Personnel Review*, 23(3): 177-181, 1962.

Leighton, A. H. *The Governing of Men*. Princeton, N.J.: Princeton University Press, 1945.

———. *Human Relations in a Changing World*. New York: Dutton, 1949.

Lemass, S. F., "The European Economic Community. 1. The Task of Reorganization," *Administration*, 10(1): 3-7, 1962.

Lepawsky, A. *Administration*. New York: Knopf, 1949.

Lerner, D. (Ed.) *Cause and Effect*. New York: Free Press, 1965.

Levy, M. J. *Modernization and the Structure of Societies*. 2 vols. Princeton, N.J.: Princeton University Press, 1966.

Lewin, K. *Resolving Social Conflicts*. New York: Harper, 1948.

Liddell-Hart, B. N. *Strategy*. London: Faber and Faber, 1954.

Liebenow, G. J. "Some Problems in Introducing Local Government Reforms in Tanganyika," *International Review of Administrative Sciences*, 23(1): 107-109, 1957.

Likert, R. *The Human Organization*. New York: McGraw-Hill, 1951.

———. *New Patterns of Management*. New York: McGraw-Hill, 1961.

———, and Hayes, S. P. (Eds.) *Some Applications of Behavioral Research*. Paris: UNESCO, 1957.

Lilienthal, D. E. "The Road to Change," *International Development Review*, 6(4): 9-13, 1964.

Lineberry, R. L., and Fowler, E. P. "Reformism and Public Policies in American Cities," *American Political Science Review*, September: 701-716, 1967.

Lippitt, R., Watson, J., and Westley, B. *The Dynamics of Planned Change*. New York: Harcourt, 1958.

Litterer, J. A. *Organizations: Structure and Behavior*. New York: Wiley, 1963.

Liu, J. T. C. *Reforms in Sung China*. Cambridge, Mass.: Harvard University Press, 1959.

McDonald, G. P. A. "Labour, Manpower, and Government Reorganization," *Canadian Public Administration*, 10(4): 471-498, 1967.

McEwen, W. P. *The Problem of Social Scientific Knowledge*. Totowa, N.J.: Bedminster Press, 1963.

McFarland, D. F. *Management: Principles and Practices.* New York: Macmillan, 1958.

McGregor, D. *The Human Side of Enterprise.* New York: McGraw-Hill, 1960.

MacIver, R. M. *Social Causation.* Boston: Ginn and Company, 1942.

MacKenzie, M. W. "Towards Better Government Administration," *Canadian Public Administration,* 2(2): 77-82, 1959.

MacKintosh, J. P. "Devolution, Regionalism ,and the Reform of Local Government: The Scottish Case," *Public Law,* Spring: 19-32, 1964.

Macridis, R. C. *The Study of Comparative Government.* New York: Doubleday, 1955.

Mailick, S., and Van Ness, E. H. (Eds.) *Concepts and Issues in Administrative Behavior.* Englewood Cliffs, N.J.: Prentice-Hall, 1962.

Mann, F. C., and Neff, F. W. *Managing Major Changes in Organizations.* Ann Arbor: University of Michigan Press, 1961.

March, J. G. (Ed.) *Handbook of Organizations.* Chicago: Rand McNally, 1965.

——, and Simon, H. *Organizations.* New York: Wiley, 1958.

Mariani, L. F. *Les Chemins de la Reforme Administrative.* Paris: Librairie Mariel Riviere, 1958.

Mariano, L. C. "Legislative Reform: An Analysis of Current Proposals," *Philippine Journal of Public Administration,* 3(1): 61-74, 1959.

Martin, R. C. *Public Administration and Democracy.* Syracuse, N.Y.: Syracuse University Press, 1965.

Martindale, D. *Social Life and Cultural Change.* Princeton, N.J.: Van Nostrand, 1962.

Marx, F. M. *The Administrative State.* Chicago: University of Chicago Press, 1957.

——. *Elements of Public Administration.* Englewood Cliffs, N.J.: Prentice-Hall, 1961.

Mechanic, D. "The Power to Resist Change Among Low Ranking Personnel," *Personnel Administration,* July-August: 5-12, 1963.

Mee, J. F. *Management Thought in a Dynamic Economy.* New York: New York University Press, 1963.

Meeham, E. J. *The Theory and Method of Political Analysis.* Homewood, Ill.: Dorsey, 1965.

Merton, R. K. (Ed.) *Readings in Bureaucracy.* Glencoe, Ill.: Free Press, 1952.

——, Broom, L., and Cottrell, L. S. (Eds) *Sociology Today.* New York: Basic Books, 1959.

————, Lerner, D., and Lasswell, H. D. *The Policy Sciences.* Stanford, Cal.: Stanford University Press, 1957.

Menzel, J. M. *The Chinese Civil Service.* Boston: D. C. Heath, 1963.

Meynaud, J. (Ed.) *Social Change and Economic Development.* Paris: UNESCO, 1963.

Milhaud, M. *The Historical Development of Social Policy.* The Hague: Institute of Social Studies, 1958.

Millett, J. D. *Government and Public Administration.* New York: Mc-Graw-Hill, 1959.

Mills, C. W. *White Collar.* New York: Oxford University Press, 1951.

————. *The Power Elite.* New York: Oxford University Press, 1956.

————. *The Sociological Imagination.* New York: Oxford University Press, 1959.

Milne, R. S. "Bureaucracy and Bureaucratic Reform in Malaysia," *Philippine Journal of Public Administration,* 10(4): 375-388, 1966.

Milward, G. E. (Ed.) *Large-Scale Organization.* London: MacDonald and Evans, 1950.

Mises, L. V. *Bureaucracy.* New Haven: Yale University Press, 1946.

Misra, B. B. "Efforts for Administrative Reforms Before Independence," *Indian Journal of Public Administration,* 9(3): 311-335, 1963.

Mitchell, W. C. *Sociological Analysis and Politics.* Englewood Cliffs, N.J.: Prentice-Hall, 1967.

Montgomery, J. D. *The Politics of Foreign Aid.* New York: Praeger, 1962.

————. *Sources of Administrative Reform: Problems of Power, Purpose and Politics.* Bloomington, Ind.: Comparative Administration Group, 1967.

————, and Siffin, W. J. *Approaches to Development.* New York: Mc-Graw-Hill, 1966.

Moore, G. *Social Origins of Dictatorship and Democracy.* Boston: Beacon, 1966.

Moore, W. E. *Social Change.* Englewood Cliffs, N.J.: Prentice-Hall, 1963.

————, and Cooke, R. M. (Eds) *Readings in Social Change,* Englewood Cliffs, N.J.: Prentice-Hall, 1967.

Mosca, G. *The Ruling Class.* New York: McGraw-Hill, 1939.

Mosher, F. C. *Governmental Reorganizations.* Indianapolis: Bobbs-Merrill Company, 1967.

————, "Research in Public Administration: Some Notes and Suggestions," *Public Administration Review,* 16(3), 169-178, 1956.

Murphy, M. "Budget Reforms in the Republic of Vietnam," *International Review of Administrative Sciences,* 26(4): 357-363, 1960.

Musicus, M. "Reappraising Reorganization," *Public Administration Review*, 24(2): 107-112, 1964.

Myrdal. G. *Beyond the Welfare State*. London: Duckworth. 1960.

——. "The Relation Between Social Theory and Social Policy," *The British Journal of Sociology*, 4(Sept.): 210-242, 1953.

Nascimento, K. T. "Change Strategy and Client Systems: Administrative Reform in Brazil." Ph.D. dissertation, University of Southern California, 1966.

Neal, M. A. *Values and Interests in Social Change*. Englewood Cliffs: Prentice-Hall, 1965.

Nemenzo, F., Jr. "The Press and the Government Reorganization of 1954-56," *Philippine Journal of Public Administration*, 1(3): 223-235, 1957.

Neufeld, M. F. *Poor Countries and Authoritarian Rule*. Ithaca, N.Y.: Cornell University Press, 1965.

Newman, W. H. *Administrative Action*. Englewood Cliffs, N.J.: Prentice-Hall, 1963.

——, Summer, C. E., and Warren, E. K. *The Process of Management*. Englewood Cliffs, N.J.: Prentice-Hall, 1963.

Niehoff, A. (Ed.) *Casebook of Social Change*. Chicago: Aldine, 1966.

Niehoff, J., and Niehoff, A. "The Influence of Religion on Socio-Economic Development," *International Development Review*, 8(2): 6-12, 1966.

Nigro, F. A. *Modern Public Administration*. New York: Harper and Row, 1965.

Nordskog, J. E. *Social Change*. New York: McGraw-Hill, 1960.

Oakeshott, M. J. *Rationalism in Politics*. London: Methuen, 1962.

Ocampo, R. B. "The Reorganization Program of Quezon City: Mayor-Council Relations in the Formulation and Implementation of Reform Policy," *Philippine Journal of Public Administration*, 7(3): 184-219, 1963.

Odegard, P. H. *Political Power and Social Change*. New Brunswick, N.J.: Rutgers University Press, 1966.

O'Donnell, M. *Readings in Public Administration*. Boston: Houghton-Mifflin, 1966.

Ogburn, W. F. *Social Change*. New York: Viking Press, 1950.

O'Neill, E. R. "Re-Organization and Adaptation of Industry," *Administration*, 12(1): 48-54, 1964.

Paige, G. D. *Proposition Building in the Study of Comparative Administration*. Chicago, 1964.

Papastathopoulos, C. D. "Civil Service Reforms in Greece: 1950-1964," *International Review of Administrative Sciences*. 30(4): 373-384, 1964.

Parsons, T. *The Social System.* New York: Free Press, 1951.

——, et al. *Theories of Society.* 2 vols. New York: Free Press, 1961.

——, and Shils, E. A. *Towards a General Theory of Action.* Cambridge, Mass.: Harvard University Press, 1951.

——, and Smelser, N. J. *Economy and Society.* London: Routledge and Kegan Paul, 1956.

Paternost, E. "The Reorganization of the Chilean 'Contraloria,'" *Progress in Public Administration*, 13(October): 1-3, 1955.

Penniman, C. "Reorganization and the Internal Revenue," *Public Administration Review*, 21(3): 121-130, 1961.

Peter, E. W., and Henry, E. R. "Measuring Successful Performance Overseas," *International Development Review*, 3(3): 8-12, 1961.

Pfiffner, J. M., and Presthus, R. V. *Public Administration.* New York: Ronald Press, 1953.

——, and Sherwood, F. P. *Administrative Organization.* Englewood Cliffs, N.J.: Prentice-Hall, 1960.

Philippines, Government of. "Report of the Special Committee on Reorganization of Agencies for Land Reform," *Philippine Journal of Public Administration*, 8(2): 136-142, 1964.

Phillips, E. K. "Administrative Reform in the Operation of Land Registries," *New Zealand Journal of Public Administration*, 26(1): 20-33, 1963.

Polenberg, R. *Reorganizing Roosevelt's Government.* Cambridge, Mass.: Harvard University Press, 1966.

Polk, W. R. (Ed.) *Developmental Revolution.* Washington, D.C.: The Middle East Institute, 1963.

Ponsioen, J. A. *The Analysis of Social Change Reconsidered.* The Hague: Mouton, 1962.

Presthus, R. V. *Behavioral Approaches to Public Administration.* University, Ala.: University of Alabama Press, 1965.

——. *The Organizational Society.* New York: Knopf, 1962.

Price, J. L. *Organizational Effectiveness.* Homewood, Ill.: Irwin, 1968.

Raj, S. M. "Priorities in Administrative Reforms," *Indian Journal of Public Administration*, 13(2): 235-267, 1967.

Rakowski, M. (Ed.) *Efficiency of Investment in a Socialist Economy.* Oxford: Pergamon Press, 1966.

Redford, E. S. *Ideal and Practice in Public Administration.* University, Ala.: University of Alabama Press, 1958.

Riesman, D., et al. *The Lonely Crowd.* New Haven: Yale University Press, 1961.

Riggs, F. W. "Modernization and Development Administration," *Philippine Journal of Public Administration,* 9(1): 41-57, 1967.

———, and Weidner, E. W. *Models and Priorities in the Comparative Study of Public Administration.* Chicago, 1963.

Riker, H. A. Jr. "Training the Government Administrator for Management of Industrial Development," *International Development Review,* 8(2): 13-16, 1966.

Roberts, C. A. "The Reorganization of the National Coal Board's Management Structure," *Public Administration,* 44(Autumn): 283-294, 1966.

Robson, W. A. *Nationalised Industry and Public Ownership.* London: Allen and Unwin, 1960.

Roethlisberger, F. S., and Dickson, W. C. *Management and the Worker.* Cambridge, Mass.: Harvard University Press, 1941.

Rogers, E. M. *Diffusion of Innovations.* New York: Free Press, 1962.

Rosholt, R. A. *An Administrative History of N.A.S.A. 1955-63.* Washington, D.C.: N.A.S.A., 1966.

Rubenstein, A. H., and Haberstroh, C. J. (Eds.) *Some Theories of Organization.* Homewood, Ill.: Irwin, 1966.

Russell, B. *Freedom and Organization.* London: Allen and Unwin, 1934.

Sady, E. J. "Central Agencies and Institutions for the Improvement of Local Government," *Philippine Journal of Public Administration,* 10(2-3): 242-255, 1966.

Saunders, C. B. *The Brookings Institution—A Fifty Year History.* Washington, D.C.: The Brookings Institution, 1966.

Sayles, L. R., and Strauss, G. *Human Behavior in Organizations.* Englewood Cliffs, N.J.: Prentice-Hall, 1966.

Schein, E. H., and Bennis, W. G. *Personnel and Organizational Change through Group Methods.* New York: Wiley, 1965.

Schick, A. "Planning-Programming-Budgeting System: A Symposium. The Road to PPB: The Stages of Budget Reform," *Public Administration Review,* 26(4): 243-258, 1966.

Schingel, M. S. *History of Efficiency Ratings in the Federal Government.* New York: Brookman Associates, 1966.

School of Social Welfare. *The Social Work Profession and Planned Change.* Berkeley: Group Research Project, University of California, June 1965.

Schubert, G. *The Public Interest.* Glencoe, Ill.: Free Press, 1960.

Self, P. "Reform of the Civil Service: The Future of General Administration," *Political Quarterly,* 38(2): 132-139, 1967.

Selznick, P. *T.V.A. and the Grass Roots*. Berkeley: University of California Press, 1949.

———. *Leadership in Administration*, Evanston, Ill.: Row, Peterson, 1957.

Sharma, K. C. "Development Planning and Development Administration," *International Review of Administrative Sciences,* 2: 120-129, 1967.

Sharp, W. R. *International Technical Assistance*. Chicago: Public Administration Clearing House, 1952.

———. *Field Administration in the United Nations System*. London: Stevens, 1961.

Sherif, M., and Sherif, C. W. *Groups in Harmony and Tension*. New York: Harper, 1953.

Shonfeld, A. *Modern Capitalism*. London: Oxford University Press, 1965.

———. "The Pragmatic Illusion," *Encounter*, May: 3-12, 1967.

Siegel, G. B. "The Vicissitudes of Governmental Reform in Brazil: A Study of the DASP." Ph.D. dissertation, University of Pittsburgh, 1964.

———. "The Strategy of Public Administration Reform: The Case of Brazil," *Public Administration Review*, 26(1): 45-55, 1966.

———, and Nascimiento, K. "Formalism in Brazilian Administrative Reform: The Example of Position Classification," *Internatonal Review of Administrative Sciences*, 31(3): 175-184, 1965.

Siffin, W. J. (Ed.) *Toward the Comparative Study of Public Administration*. Bloomington, Ind.: University of Indiana, 1957.

Simon, H. A. *Administrative Behavior*, London: Macmillan, 1946.

———, Smithburg, D. W., and Thompson, V. A. *Public Administration*. New York: Knopf, 1950.

Sims, N. L. *Problems of Social Change*. New York: Crowell, 1939.

Singh, I. "Reorganizing the Indian Income-Tax Department," *Indian Journal of Public Administration*, 1(3): 224-239, 1955.

Singh, J. "The Administrative Reform Reports of the States: A Content Analysis," *Indian Journal of Public Administration*, 9(3): 491-513, 1963.

Slesinger, J. *A Model for the Comparative Study of Public Bureaucracies*. Ann Arbor: University of Michigan Press, 1951.

Smallwood, F. *Greater London: The Politics of Metropolitan Reform*. Indianapolis: Bobbs-Merrill, 1965.

Smelser, N. J. *Social Change in the Industrial Revolution*. London: Routledge and Kegan Paul, 1959.

Stanley, D. T. *Changing Administrations: The 1961 and 1964 transitions in six departments*. Washington, D.C.: Brookings Institution, 1965.

Sorokin, P. *Social and Cultural Dynamics*. 4 vols. New York: American Book Company, 1947.

Spann, R. N. "The Eisenhower Civil Service and the Reformers," *Public Administration*, 34(Summer): 143-156, 1956.

Stanley, D. T. *Changing Administrations*. Washington, D.C.: The Brookings Institution, 1965.

Stein, H. *Public Administration and Policy Development*. New York: Harcourt, 1952.

Stewart, R. *The Reality of Management*. London: Heinemann, 1963.

Swerdlow, I. *Development Administration*. Syracuse: Syracuse University Press, 1963.

Symonds, R. *The British and Their Successors*. London: Faber and Faber, 1966.

Tannenbaum, R., Weschler, I. R., and Massarik, F. *Leadership and Organization*. New York: McGraw-Hill, 1961.

Taylor, F. W. *Scientific Management*. New York: Harper, 1947.

Tead, O. *The Art of Administration*. New York: McGraw-Hill, 1951.

Terry, G. R. *Principles of Management*. Homewood, Ill.: Irwin, 1958.

Thelan, H. A. *Dynamics of Groups at Work*. Chicago: University of Chicago Press, 1954.

Thompson, J. D. *Approaches to Organizational Design*. Pittsburgh: University of Pittsburgh Press, 1966.

――――. *Organizations in Action*. New York: McGraw-Hill, 1967.

――――. (Ed.) *Comparative Studies in Administration*. Pittsburgh: University of Pittsburgh Press, 1959.

Thompson, V. A. *Modern Organization*. New York: Knopf, 1961.

Tiryakian, E. A. (Ed.) *Sociological Theory Values and Sociocultural Change*. London: Macmillan (Free Press of Glencoe), 1963.

Tivey, L. "The Reform of the Firm," *Political Quarterly*, 34(2): 151-161, 1963.

Toynbee, A. J. *Change and Habit*. London: Oxford University Press, 1966.

Trist, E. L., et al. *Organizational Choice*. London: Tavistock, 1963.

Tullock, G. *The Politics of Bureaucracy*. Washington, D.C.: Public Affairs Press, 1965.

Tunnoch, G. V. "The Bureau of Government Organization: Improvement by Order-in-Council, Committee, and Anomaly," *Canadian Public Administration*, 8(4): 558-568, 1965.

United Kingdom Ministry of Reconstruction. *Report on Machinery of Government*. London: H.M.S.O., 1918.

United Nations Technical Assistance Program. *A Handbook of Public Administration*. New York: United Nations, 1961.

United States Government. *President's Committee on Administrative Man-*

agement. Washington, D.C.: U.S. Government Printing Office, 1937.

University of Connecticut, Second Annual Conference on the Role of Management Analysis in Government. *The Possibilities and Potentialities of Measuring The Health of Governmental Organizations.* Storrs, Conn.: 1965.

Uotila, J. "Improving Public Administration in Finland," *International Review of Administrative Sciences,* 27(1): 65-70, 1961.

Urwick, L., and Brech, E. F. L. *The Making of Scientific Management.* 3 vols. London: Pitman, 1945.

Van Riper, P., *History of the United States Civil Service.* New York: Row Peterson, 1958.

Vickers, Sir G. *The Art of Judgment.* London: Chapman and Hall, 1965.

———. *Towards a Sociology of Management.* London: Chapman and Hall, 1967.

Viloria, L. A. "The Government Survey and Reorganization Commission: Some Notes on Method," *Philippine Journal of Public Administration,* 5(3): 235-259, 1961.

———. "Reorganization in the Philippine National Government prior to 1954," *Philippine Journal of Public Administraton,* 5(1): 31-51, 1961.

Wadia, M .S. (Ed.) *The Nature and Scope of Management.* Chicago: Scott, Foresman, 1966.

Wagner, D. O. *Social Reformers.* New York: Macmillan, 1959.

Waldo, D. *The Administrative State.* New York: Ronald Press, 1948.

———. *Comparative Public Administration: Prologue, Problems and Promise.* Bloomington, Ind.: Comparative Administration Group, 1964.

———. (Ed.) *Ideas and Issues in Public Administration.* New York: McGraw-Hill, 1953.

Waline, M. "The 1964 Reforms of the Government of Departments and Regions," *International Review of Administrative Sciences,* 31(1): 13-14, 1965.

Wallace, A. F. C. "Revitalization Movements," *American Anthropologist,* 58(2): 264-281, 1956.

Wang, Yun-wu. "Effects of Administrative Reform and Efforts That Should Be Made Hereafter," *Chinese Journal of Public Administration,* 1(2): 5-8, 1964.

Warrell-Bowring, W. F. "The Reorganization of the Administration in Tanganyika," *Journal of Local Administration Overseas,* 2(4): 188-194, 1963.

Wasserman, P. *Measurement and Evaluation of Organizational Reforms.* Ithaca, N.Y.: Cornell University Press, 1959.

Waterston, A. *Development Planning*. Baltimore: Johns Hopkins University Press, 1965.

Weber, M. *From Max Weber, Essays in Sociology*, ed. by H. H. Gerth and C. W. Mills. London: Paul, Trench and Trubner, 1947.

Weidner, E. W. *Technical Assistance in Public Administration Overseas*. Chicago: Public Administration Service, 1964.

Weiner, M. *Modernization: The Dynamics of Growth*. New York: Basic Books, 1966.

Weiss, M. *Main Strategies and Methods for Government Reorganization*. M. A. thesis, Institute of Social Studies, The Hague, 1966.

————. "Towards a Comprehensive Approach to Government Reorganization," *Philippine Journal of Public Administration*, 11(1): 58-71, 1967.

Wells, W. T. "The Law Reform Commission—An Interim Appraisal," *Political Quarterly*, 27(3): 291-299, 1966.

Wengert, E. S. "GSIS: Reflections on Reform and Reorganization," *Philippine Journal of Public Administration*, 1(1): 46-67, 1957.

White, L. D. *Introduction to the Study of Public Administration*. New York: Macmillan, 1955.

Wildavsky, A. "Political Implications of Budgetary Reform," *Public Administration Review*, 21(4): 183-190, 1961.

————. *The Politics of the Budgetary Process*. Boston: Little, Brown, 1964.

Wilkinson, R. *Gentlemanly Power*. London: Oxford University Press, 1964.

Wilson, W. "The Study of Administration," *Political Science Quarterly* (July 1887) pp. 481-504.

Winslow, A. "The Technical Expert," *International Development Review*, 4(3): 17-23, 1962.

Wolins, M. "The Societal Function of Social Welfare," *New Perspectives*, (1) 7-15, 1967.

Wurfel, D. "Foreign Aid and Social Reform in Political Development: A Philippine Case Study," *American Political Science Review*, 53(2): 456-482, 1959.

Young, R. (Ed.) *Approaches to the Study of Politics*. Evanston, Ill.: Northwestern University Press, 1958.

Zaleznik, A., and Moment, D. *The Dynamics of Interpersonal Behavior*. New York: Wiley, 1964.

Znaniecki, F. *The Method of Sociology*. New York: Rinehart, 1934.

————. *Cultural Sciences*. Urbana: University of Illinois Press, 1952.

Zollschan, G. H., and Hirsch, W. (Eds.) *Explorations in Social Change*. Boston: Houghton Mifflin, 1964.

Index